LOKI

AGENT OF ASGARD

KI: AGENT OF ASGARD VOL. 3 — LAST DAYS. Contains material originally published in magazine form as LOKI #12-17. First printing 2015. ISBN# 978-0-7851-9332-6. Published by MARVEL WORLDWIDE, INC., bsidiary of MARVEL ENTERTAINMENT, LLC. OFFICE OF PUBLICATION: 135 West 50th Street, New York, NY 10020. Copyright © 2015 MARVEL. No similarity between any of the names, characters, persons, and/or itutions in this magazine with those of any living or dead person or institution is intended, and any such similarity which may exist is purely coincidental. **Printed in Canada.** ALAN FINE, President, Marvel Entertainment; N BUCKLEY, President, TV, Publishing and Brand Management; JOE QUESADA, Chief Creative Officer; TOM BREVOORT, SVP of Publishing; DAVID BOGART, SVP of Operations & Procurement, Publishing; C.B. CEBULSKI, of International Development & Brand Management; DAVID GABRIEL, SVP Print, Sales & Marketing; JIM O'KEEFE, VP of Operations & Logistics; DAN CARR, Executive Director of Publishing Technology; SUSAN CRESPI, torial Operations Manager; ALEX MORALES, Publishing Operations Manager; STAN LEE, Chairman Emeritus. For information regarding advertising in Marvel Comics or on Marvel.com, please contact Jonathan ingold, VP of Custom Solutions & Ad Sales, at jrheingold@marvel.com. For Marvel subscription inquiries, please call 800-217-9158. **Manufactured between 7/31/2015 and 9/7/2015 by SOLISCO PRINTERS,** TT, QC, CANADA.

9 8 7 6 5 4 3 2 1

LAST DAYS

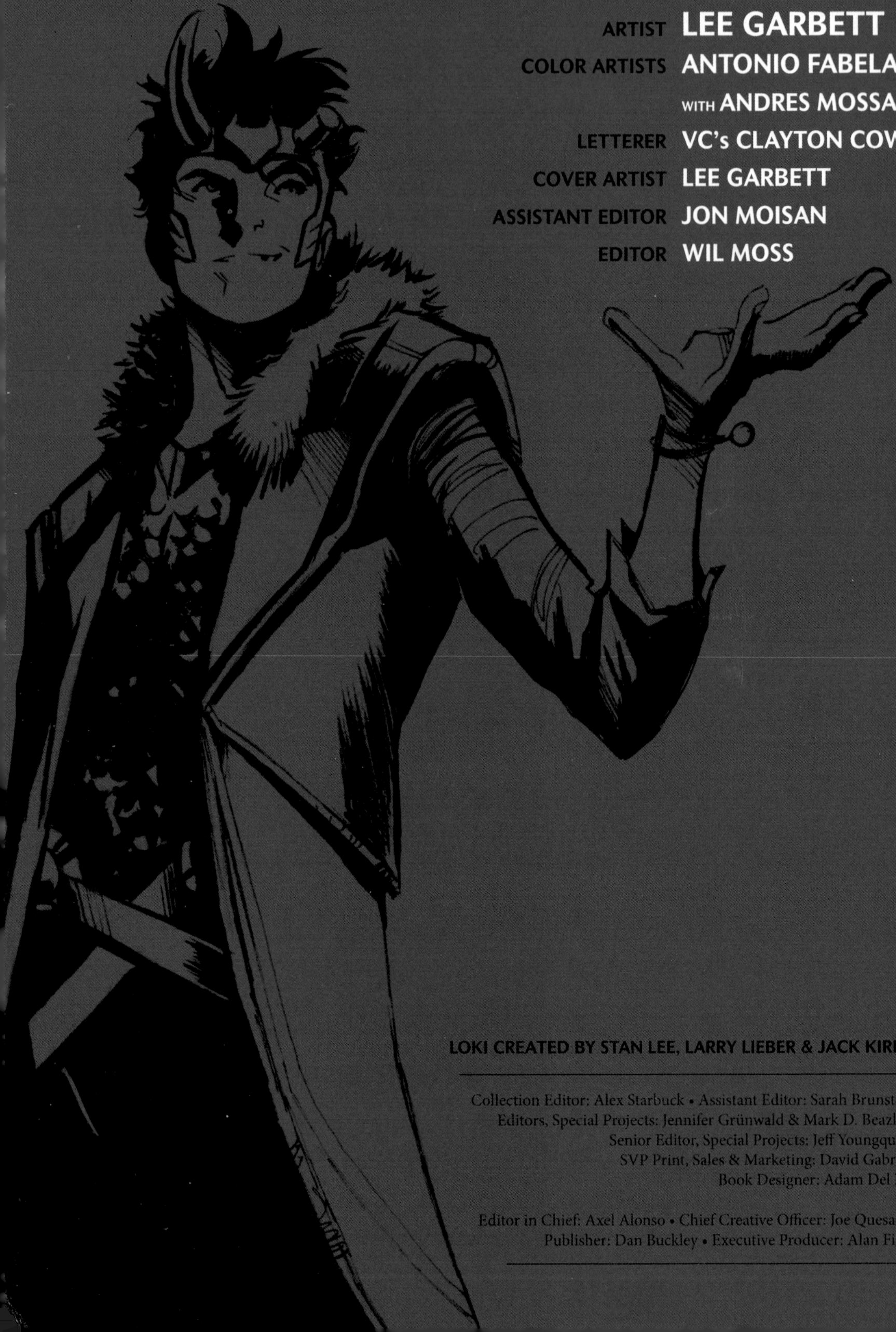

WRITER **AL EWING**
ARTIST **LEE GARBETT**
COLOR ARTISTS **ANTONIO FABELA**
WITH **ANDRES MOSSA** (#14)
LETTERER **VC's CLAYTON COWLES**
COVER ARTIST **LEE GARBETT**
ASSISTANT EDITOR **JON MOISAN**
EDITOR **WIL MOSS**

LOKI CREATED BY STAN LEE, LARRY LIEBER & JACK KIRBY

Collection Editor: Alex Starbuck • Assistant Editor: Sarah Brunstad
Editors, Special Projects: Jennifer Grünwald & Mark D. Beazley
Senior Editor, Special Projects: Jeff Youngquist
SVP Print, Sales & Marketing: David Gabriel
Book Designer: Adam Del Re

Editor in Chief: Axel Alonso • Chief Creative Officer: Joe Quesada
Publisher: Dan Buckley • Executive Producer: Alan Fine

THIS IS THE STORY OF LOKI.

LOKI DIED. LOKI WAS BORN AGAIN.

THE SECOND LOKI WAS YOUNGER AND BETTER—BUT THIS "KID LOKI" TOOK ADVICE FROM AN ECHO OF HIS OLD, WICKED SELF, WHO ENDED UP KILLING HIS SOUL AND STEALING HIS BODY. THAT ECHO BECAME THE THIRD LOKI, WHO FOUND HIMSELF HAUNTED BY THE WICKEDNESS HE'D ONCE FOUND JOY IN. IN AN EFFORT TO CHANGE HIMSELF, HE BEGAN WORKING FOR THE ALL-MOTHER ON BEHALF OF ASGARD, ERASING HIS CENTURIES OF CRIME ONE MISSION AT A TIME.

THOSE MISSIONS, IT TURNED OUT, WERE ENGINEERED BY THE ALL-MOTHER TO BRING ABOUT A PROMISED GOLDEN FUTURE FOR ASGARD. A TOMORROW IN WHICH KING THOR RULED AND "KING LOKI" WAS ETERNALLY BOUND TO PLAY THE VILLAIN—A FUTURE PREDICTED BY NONE OTHER THAN KING LOKI HIMSELF. THIS EMBITTERED FUTURE LOKI HAD TRAVELED BACK TO THE PRESENT TO ENSNARE HIS PAST SELF AND FORCE HIM TO REVEAL WHAT HE HAD DONE TO KID LOKI.

AND IT WORKED. THOR ODINSON, ENRAGED, DRAGGED LOKI—BEATEN, BROKEN AND UNABLE TO LIE—BACK TO ASGARD TO FACE JUDGMENT FOR ALL OF HIS EVILS. HE WAS WEIGHED AND FOUND WANTING, SHUNNED BY HIS PEERS AND BANISHED BY AN ENRAGED ALL-MOTHER. ONLY ODIN, SPEAKING WITH THE STRANGE WISDOM OF THE WORLD-TREE, OFFERED LOKI HOPE BEFORE RETURNING HIM TO HIS HOME IN MIDGARD.

VERITY WILLIS, LOKI'S BEST AND ONLY FRIEND, WAS WAITING FOR HIM—BUT SO WAS KING LOKI, WHO WASTED NO TIME IN LAYING OUT LOKI'S MYRIAD SINS AND ALL THE DAMAGE HE HAD DONE IN HIS SHORT LIFE. VERITY—ABLE TO SEE THROUGH ANY LIE—KNEW THAT KING LOKI WAS TELLING THE TRUTH. SHE WALKED OUT ON THEM BOTH, LEAVING LOKI ALONE.

KING LOKI, VICTORIOUS AT LAST, BOUND HIS YOUNGER SELF AND PREPARED TO SEAL HIS FATE BY TELLING HIS OWN STORY—THE TALE OF HOW ONE LOKI WOULD INEVITABLY BECOME THE OTHER. THE TALE OF THE FINAL FATE AND FINAL FALL OF...

...THE AGENT OF ASGARD.

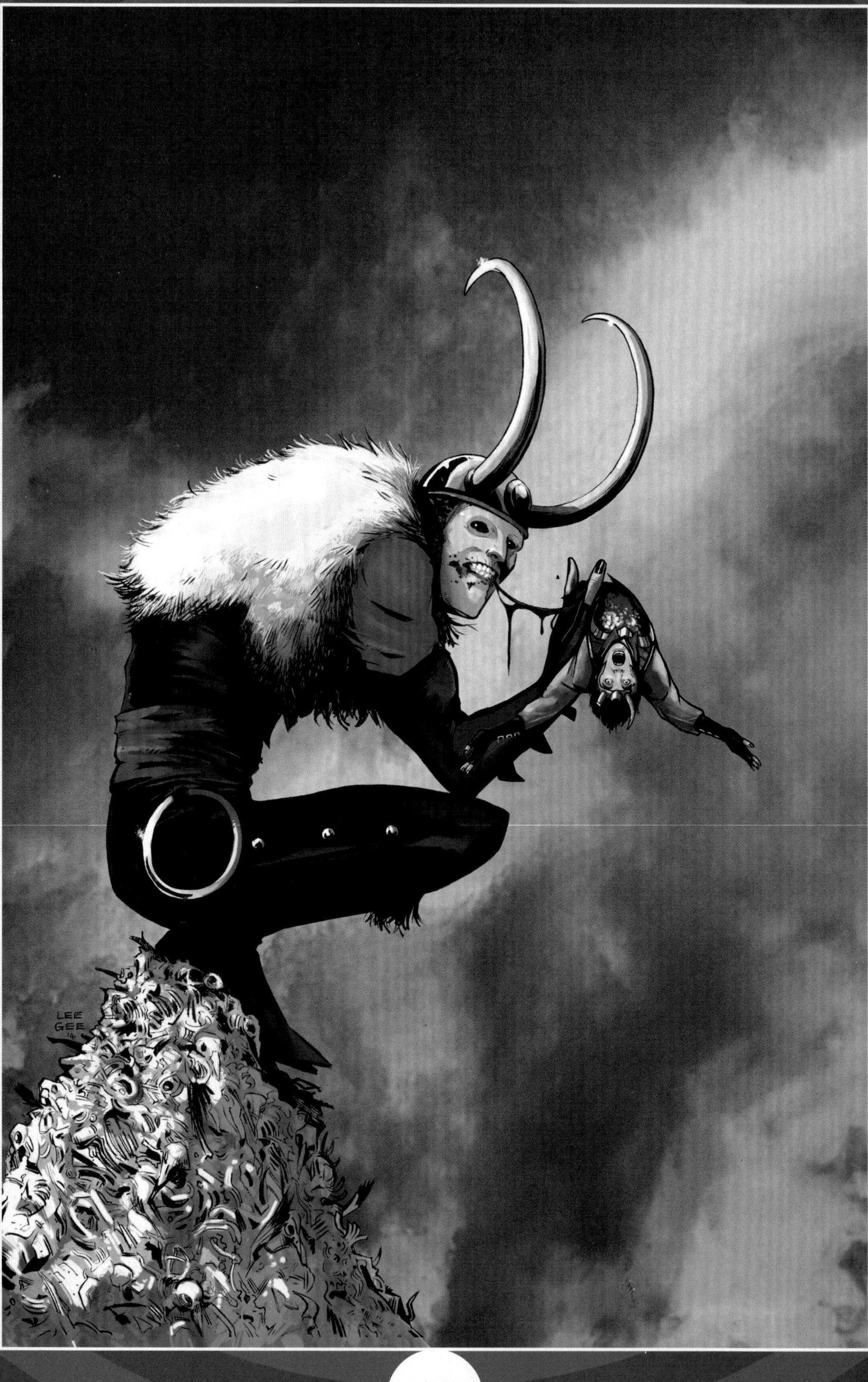
LEE
GEE
'14

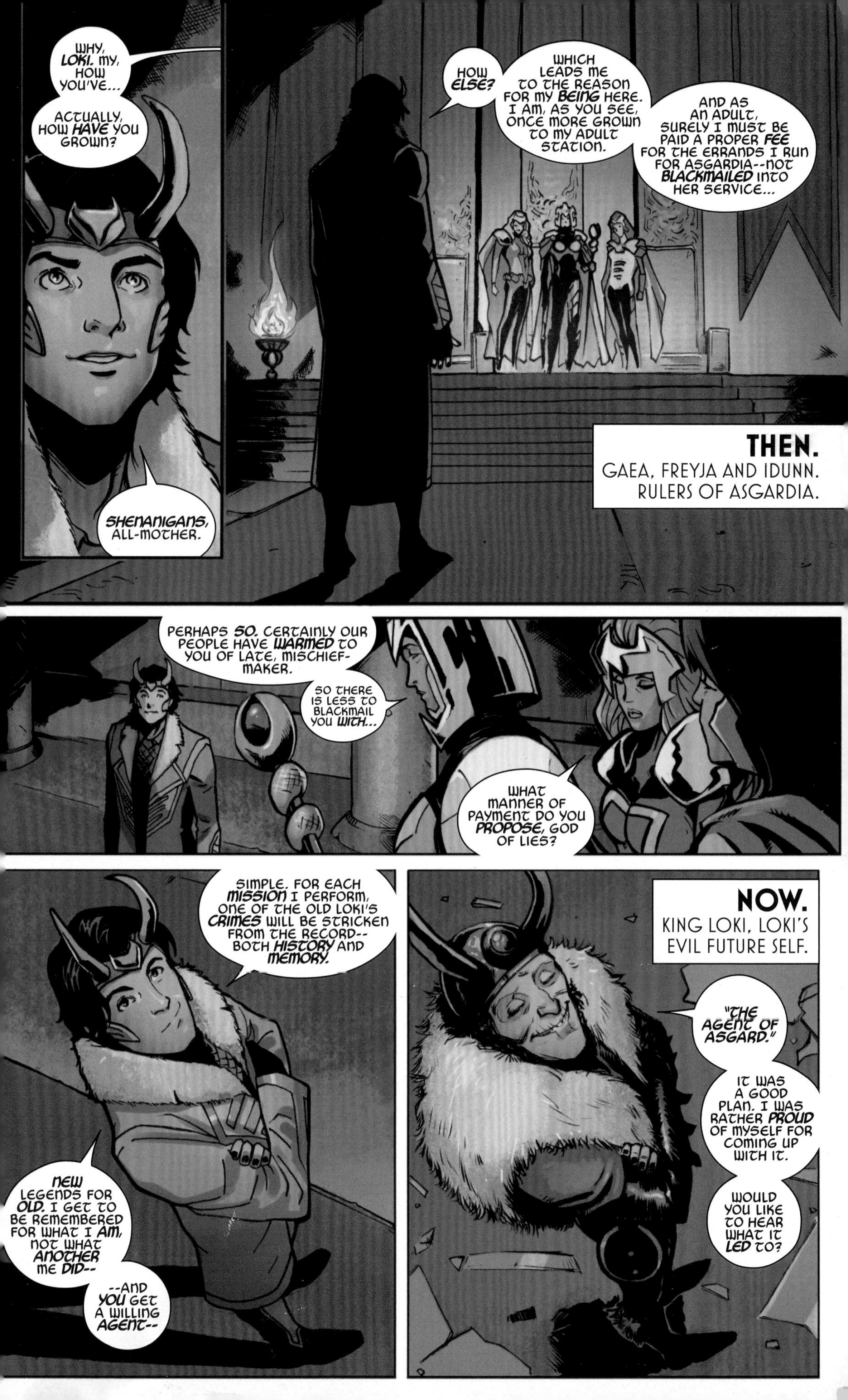

WHY, LOKI. MY, HOW YOU'VE...
ACTUALLY, HOW HAVE YOU GROWN?
SHENANIGANS, ALL-MOTHER.
HOW ELSE?
WHICH LEADS ME TO THE REASON FOR MY BEING HERE. I AM, AS YOU SEE, ONCE MORE GROWN TO MY ADULT STATION.
AND AS AN ADULT, SURELY I MUST BE PAID A PROPER FEE FOR THE ERRANDS I RUN FOR ASGARDIA--NOT BLACKMAILED INTO HER SERVICE...
THEN.
GAEA, FREYJA AND IDUNN. RULERS OF ASGARDIA.
PERHAPS SO. CERTAINLY OUR PEOPLE HAVE WARMED TO YOU OF LATE, MISCHIEF-MAKER.
SO THERE IS LESS TO BLACKMAIL YOU WITH...
WHAT MANNER OF PAYMENT DO YOU PROPOSE, GOD OF LIES?
SIMPLE. FOR EACH MISSION I PERFORM, ONE OF THE OLD LOKI'S CRIMES WILL BE STRICKEN FROM THE RECORD--BOTH HISTORY AND MEMORY.
NEW LEGENDS FOR OLD. I GET TO BE REMEMBERED FOR WHAT I AM, NOT WHAT ANOTHER ME DID--
--AND YOU GET A WILLING AGENT--
NOW.
KING LOKI, LOKI'S EVIL FUTURE SELF.
"THE AGENT OF ASGARD."
IT WAS A GOOD PLAN. I WAS RATHER PROUD OF MYSELF FOR COMING UP WITH IT.
WOULD YOU LIKE TO HEAR WHAT IT LED TO?

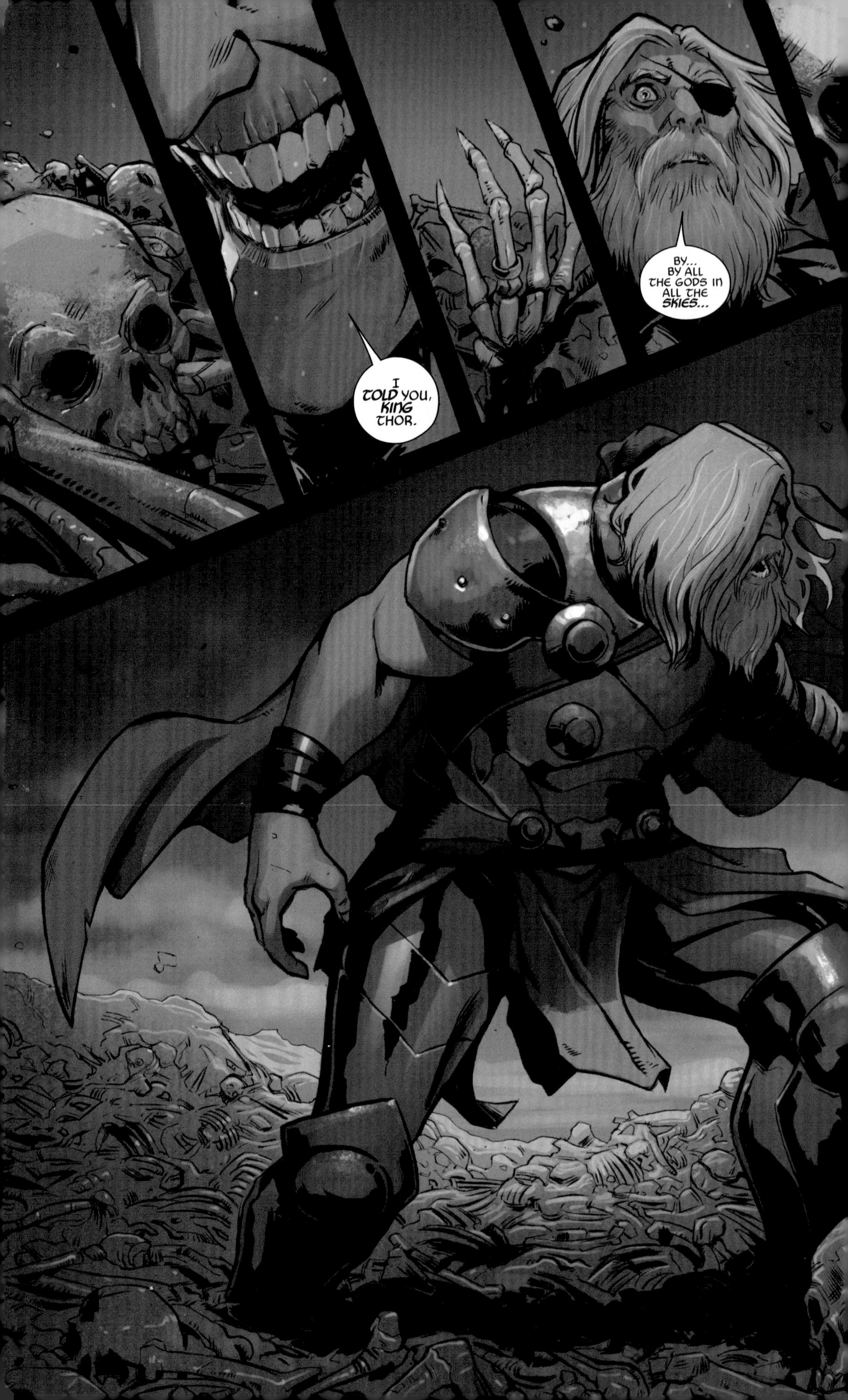
I TOLD YOU, KING THOR.
BY... BY ALL THE GODS IN ALL THE SKIES...

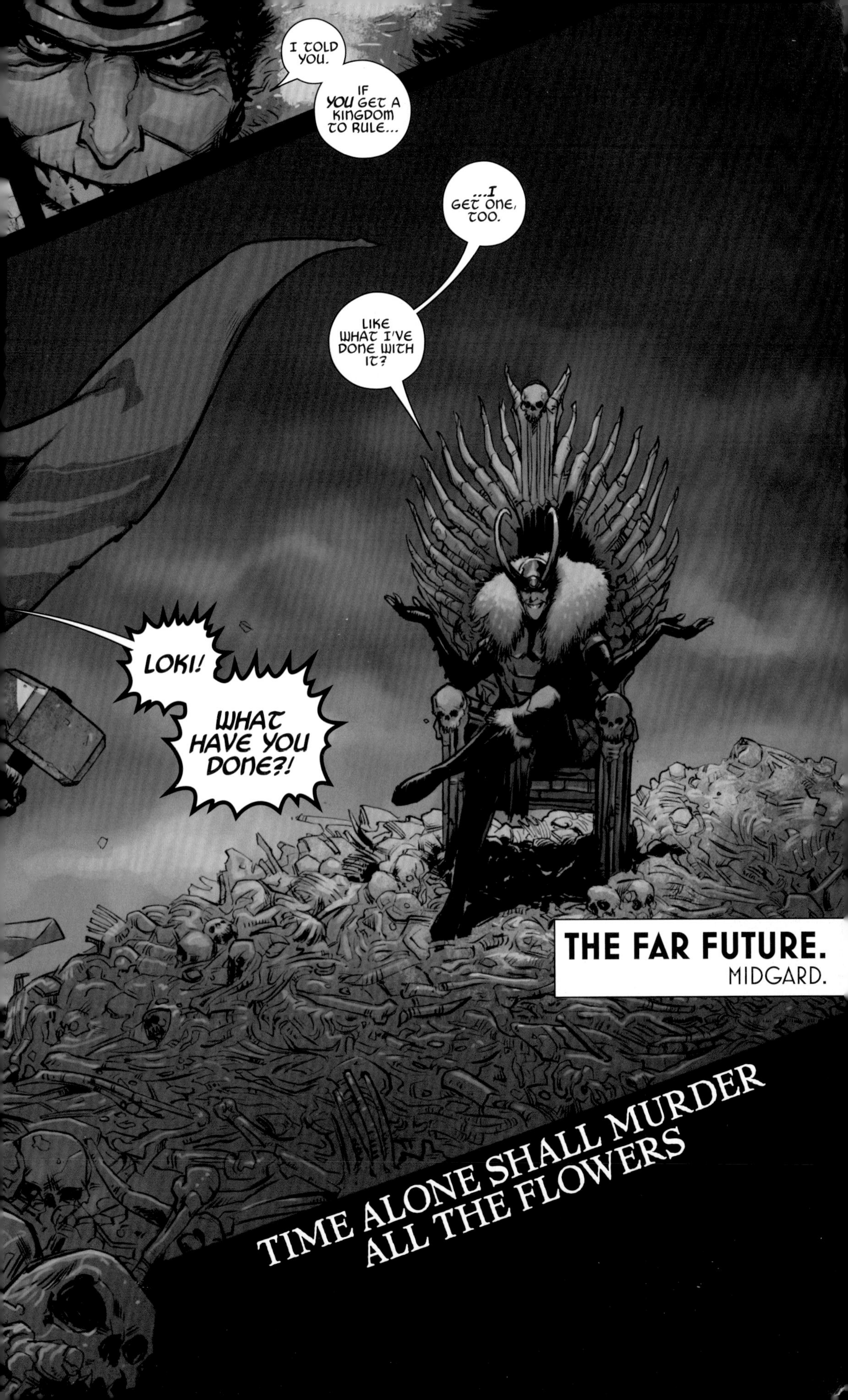

I TOLD YOU.
IF YOU GET A KINGDOM TO RULE...
...I GET ONE, TOO.
LIKE WHAT I'VE DONE WITH IT?
LOKI!
WHAT HAVE YOU DONE?!
THE FAR FUTURE.
MIDGARD.
TIME ALONE SHALL MURDER
ALL THE FLOWERS

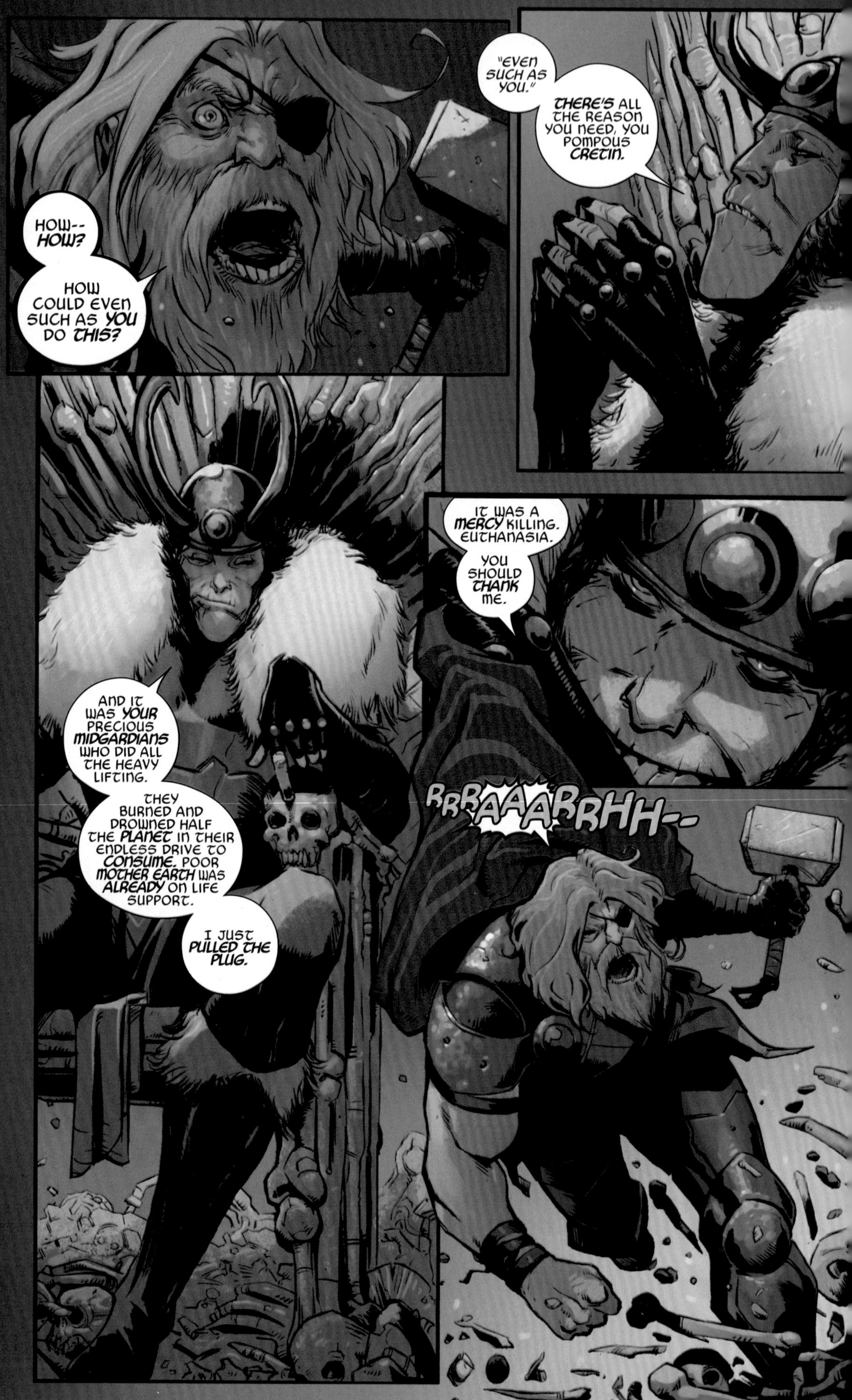
HOW-- HOW?
HOW COULD EVEN SUCH AS YOU DO THIS?
"EVEN SUCH AS YOU."
THERE'S ALL THE REASON YOU NEED, YOU POMPOUS CRETIN.
AND IT WAS YOUR PRECIOUS MIDGARDIANS WHO DID ALL THE HEAVY LIFTING.
THEY BURNED AND DROWNED HALF THE PLANET IN THEIR ENDLESS DRIVE TO CONSUME. POOR MOTHER EARTH WAS ALREADY ON LIFE SUPPORT.
I JUST PULLED THE PLUG.
IT WAS A MERCY KILLING. EUTHANASIA.
YOU SHOULD THANK ME.
RRRAAAARRHH--

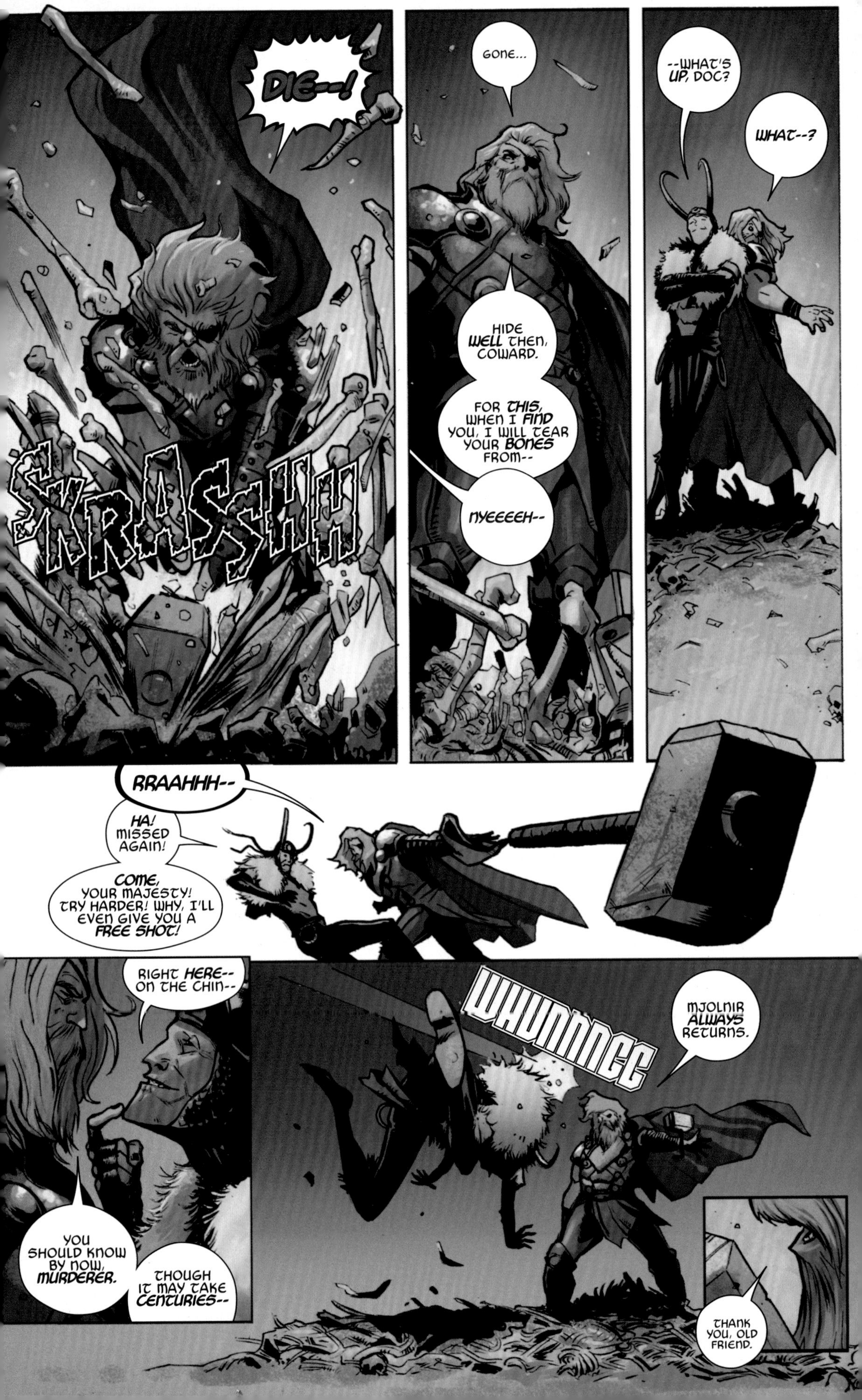
DIE--!
SKRASHH
GONE...
HIDE WELL THEN, COWARD.
FOR THIS, WHEN I FIND YOU, I WILL TEAR YOUR BONES FROM--
NYEEEEH--
--WHAT'S UP, DOC?
WHAT--?
RRAAHHH--
HA! MISSED AGAIN!
COME, YOUR MAJESTY! TRY HARDER! WHY, I'LL EVEN GIVE YOU A FREE SHOT!
RIGHT HERE--ON THE CHIN--
WHUNNNGG
MJOLNIR ALWAYS RETURNS.
YOU SHOULD KNOW BY NOW, MURDERER.
THOUGH IT MAY TAKE CENTURIES--
THANK YOU, OLD FRIEND.

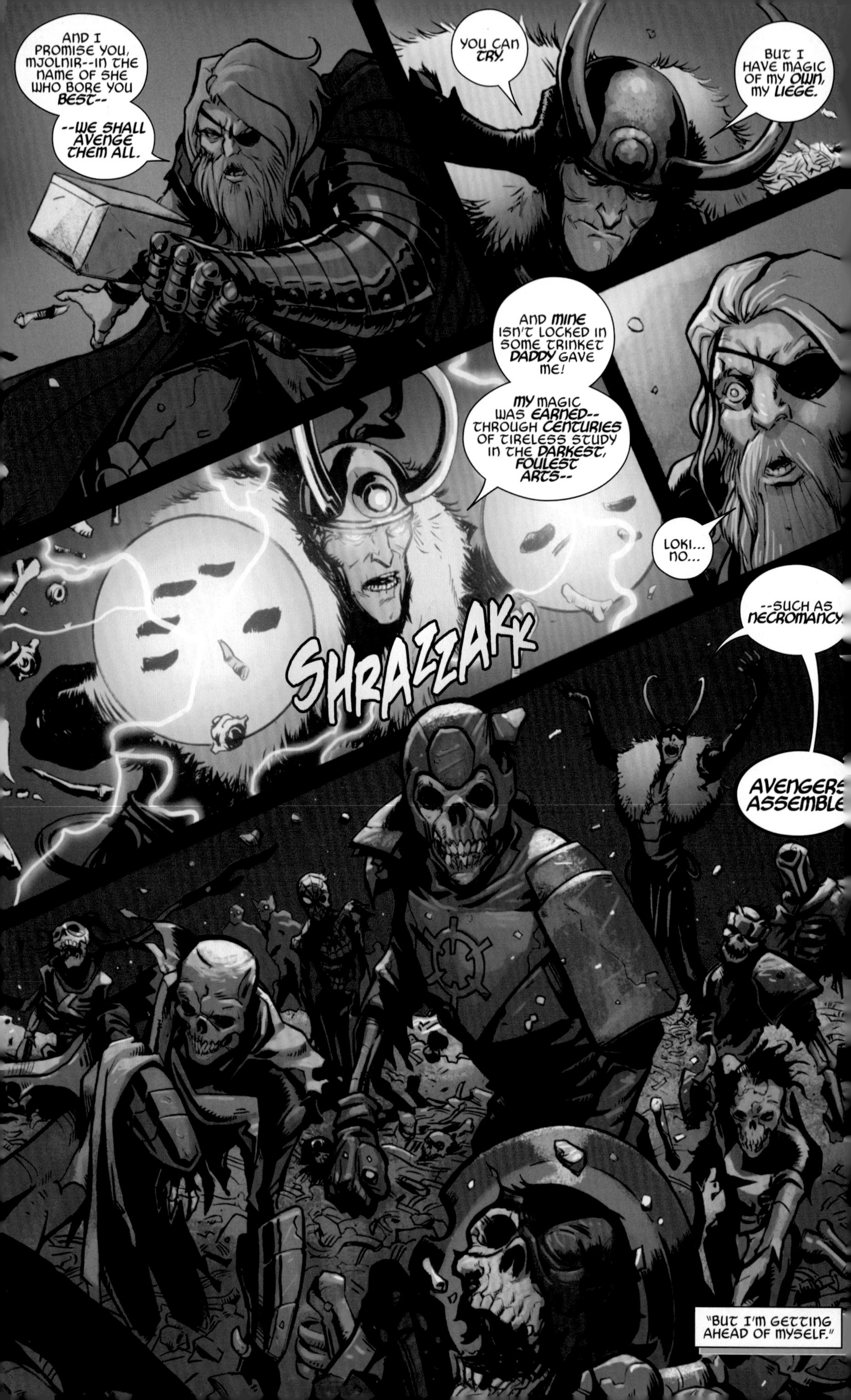
AND I PROMISE YOU, MJOLNIR--IN THE NAME OF SHE WHO BORE YOU BEST--
--WE SHALL AVENGE THEM ALL.
YOU CAN TRY.
BUT I HAVE MAGIC OF MY OWN, MY LIEGE.
AND MINE ISN'T LOCKED IN SOME TRINKET DADDY GAVE ME!
MY MAGIC WAS EARNED--THROUGH CENTURIES OF TIRELESS STUDY IN THE DARKEST, FOULEST ARTS--
LOKI... NO...
SHRAZZAKK
--SUCH AS NECROMANCY!
AVENGERS ASSEMBLE!
"BUT I'M GETTING AHEAD OF MYSELF."

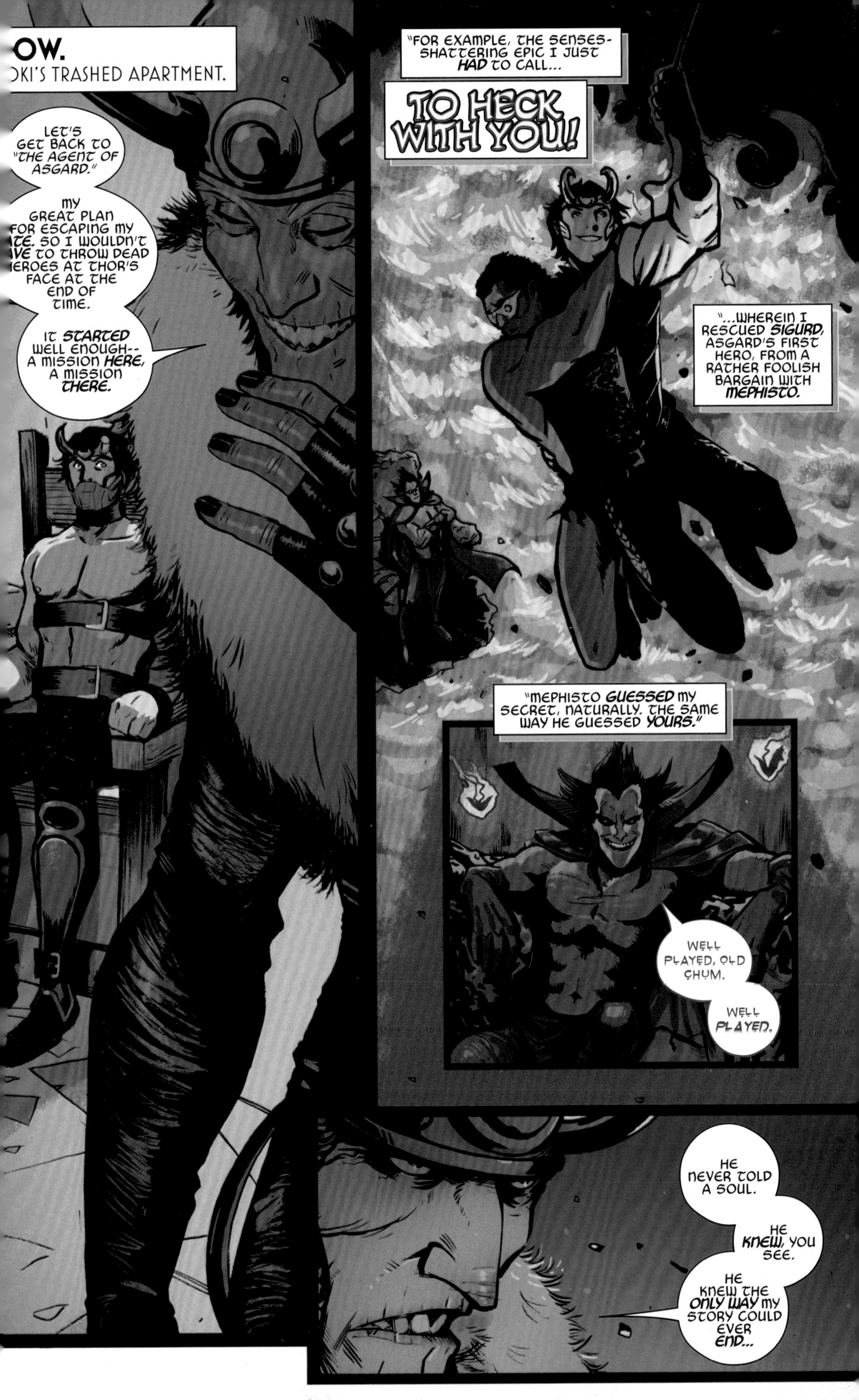
OW.
OKI'S TRASHED APARTMENT.
LET'S GET BACK TO "THE AGENT OF ASGARD."
MY GREAT PLAN FOR ESCAPING MY TE. SO I WOULDN'T VE TO THROW DEAD EROES AT THOR'S FACE AT THE END OF TIME.
IT STARTED WELL ENOUGH-- A MISSION HERE, A MISSION THERE.
"FOR EXAMPLE, THE SENSES-SHATTERING EPIC I JUST HAD TO CALL...
TO HECK WITH YOU!
"...WHEREIN I RESCUED SIGURD, ASGARD'S FIRST HERO, FROM A RATHER FOOLISH BARGAIN WITH MEPHISTO.
"MEPHISTO GUESSED MY SECRET, NATURALLY. THE SAME WAY HE GUESSED YOURS."
WELL PLAYED, OLD CHUM.
WELL PLAYED.
HE NEVER TOLD A SOUL.
HE KNEW, YOU SEE.
HE KNEW THE ONLY WAY MY STORY COULD EVER END...

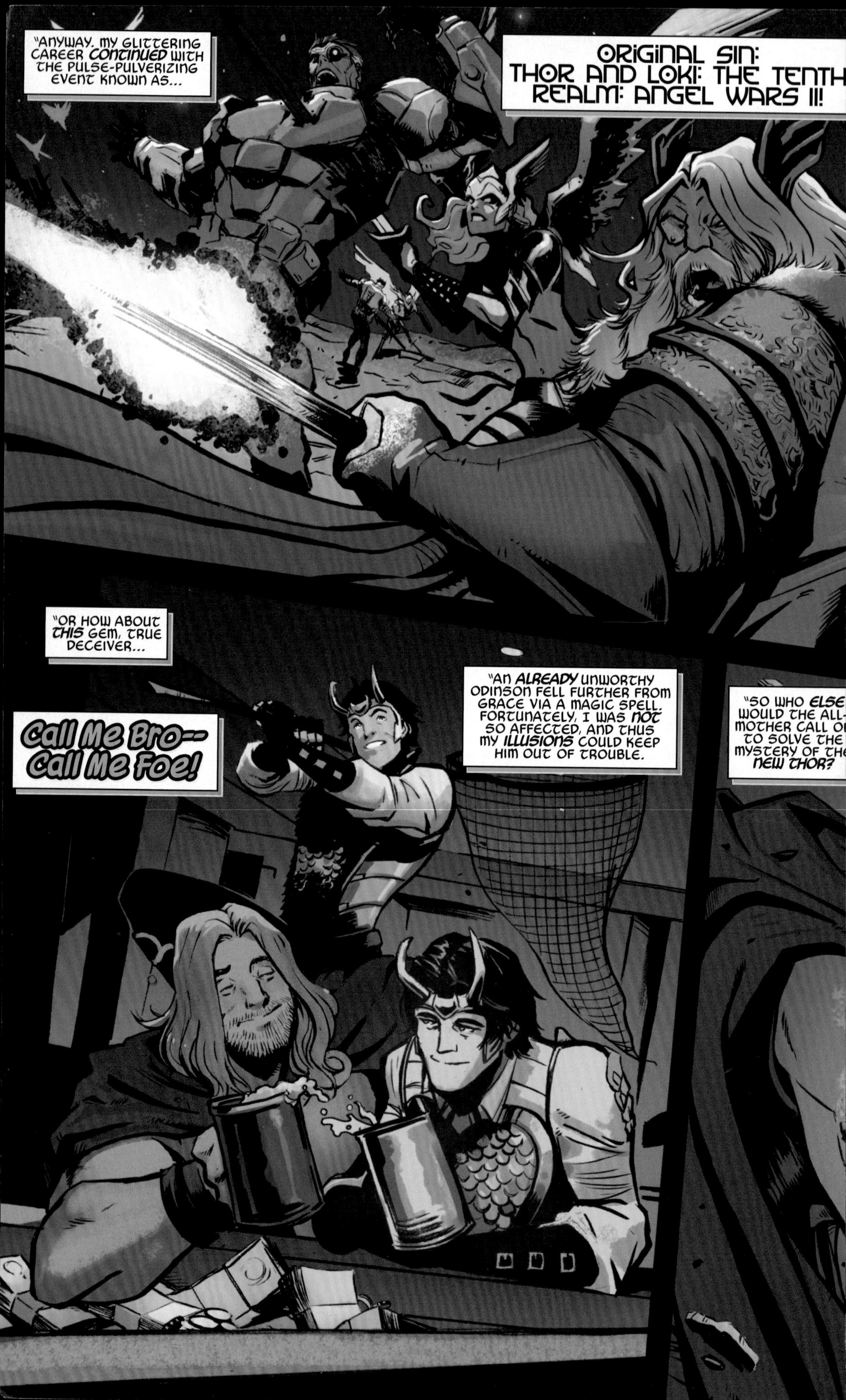

"ANYWAY. MY GLITTERING CAREER CONTINUED WITH THE PULSE-PULVERIZING EVENT KNOWN AS...
ORIGINAL SIN: THOR AND LOKI: THE TENTH REALM: ANGEL WARS II!
"OR HOW ABOUT THIS GEM, TRUE DECEIVER...
Call Me Bro-- Call Me Foe!
"AN ALREADY UNWORTHY ODINSON FELL FURTHER FROM GRACE VIA A MAGIC SPELL. FORTUNATELY, I WAS NOT SO AFFECTED, AND THUS MY ILLUSIONS COULD KEEP HIM OUT OF TROUBLE.
"SO WHO ELSE WOULD THE ALL-MOTHER CALL O TO SOLVE THE MYSTERY OF THE NEW THOR?

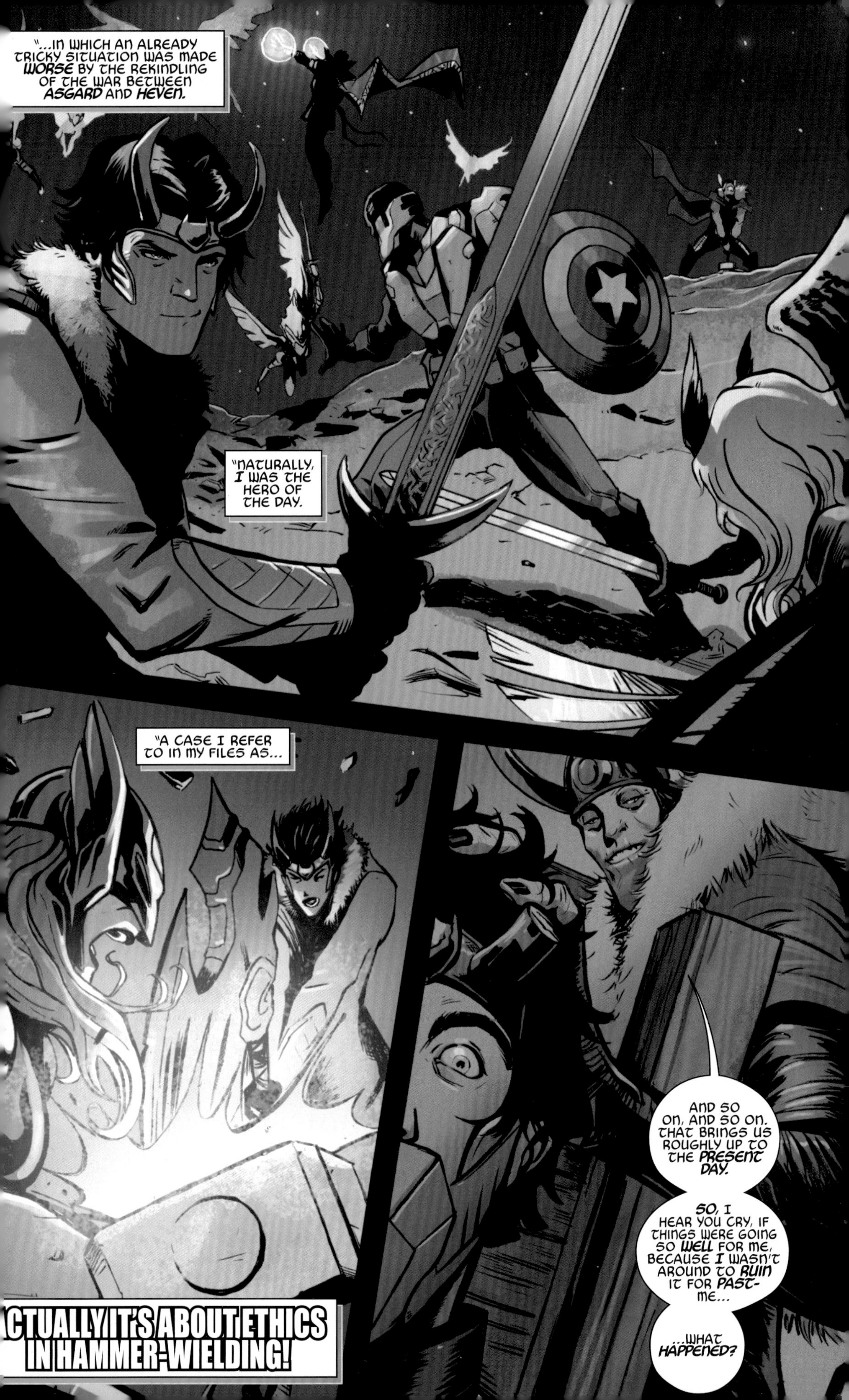
"...IN WHICH AN ALREADY TRICKY SITUATION WAS MADE WORSE BY THE REKINDLING OF THE WAR BETWEEN ASGARD AND HEVEN.
"NATURALLY, I WAS THE HERO OF THE DAY.
"A CASE I REFER TO IN MY FILES AS...
CTUALLY IT'S ABOUT ETHICS IN HAMMER-WIELDING!
AND SO ON, AND SO ON. THAT BRINGS US ROUGHLY UP TO THE PRESENT DAY.
SO, I HEAR YOU CRY, IF THINGS WERE GOING SO WELL FOR ME, BECAUSE I WASN'T AROUND TO RUIN IT FOR PAST-ME...
...WHAT HAPPENED?

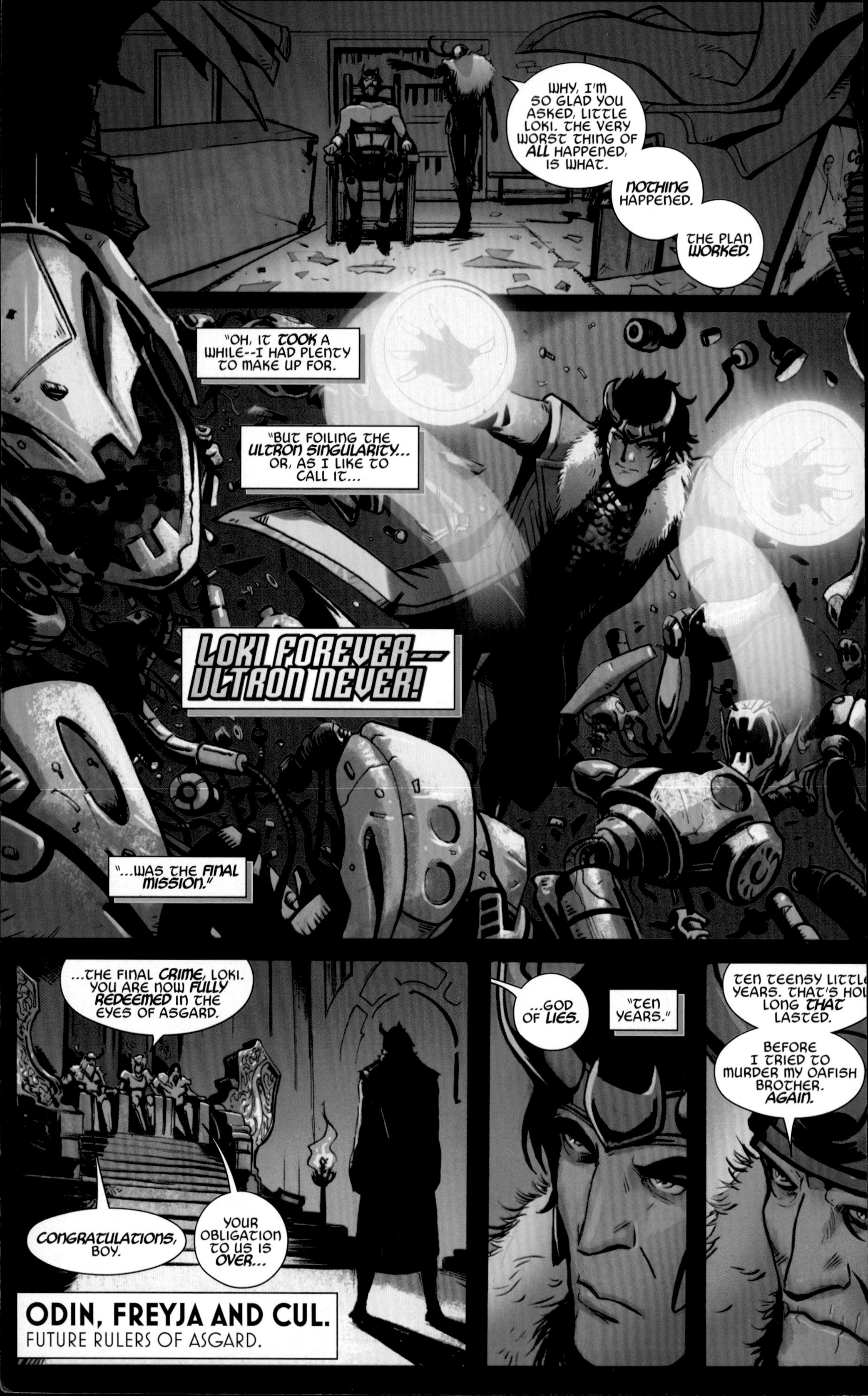
WHY, I'M SO GLAD YOU ASKED, LITTLE LOKI. THE VERY WORST THING OF ALL HAPPENED, IS WHAT.
NOTHING HAPPENED.
THE PLAN WORKED.
"OH, IT TOOK A WHILE--I HAD PLENTY TO MAKE UP FOR.
"BUT FOILING THE ULTRON SINGULARITY... OR, AS I LIKE TO CALL IT...
LOKI FOREVER-- ULTRON NEVER!
"...WAS THE FINAL MISSION."
...THE FINAL CRIME, LOKI. YOU ARE NOW FULLY REDEEMED IN THE EYES OF ASGARD.
CONGRATULATIONS, BOY.
YOUR OBLIGATION TO US IS OVER...
ODIN, FREYJA AND CUL.
FUTURE RULERS OF ASGARD.
...GOD OF LIES.
"TEN YEARS."
TEN TEENSY LITTL YEARS. THAT'S HO LONG THAT LASTED.
BEFORE I TRIED TO MURDER MY OAFISH BROTHER. AGAIN.

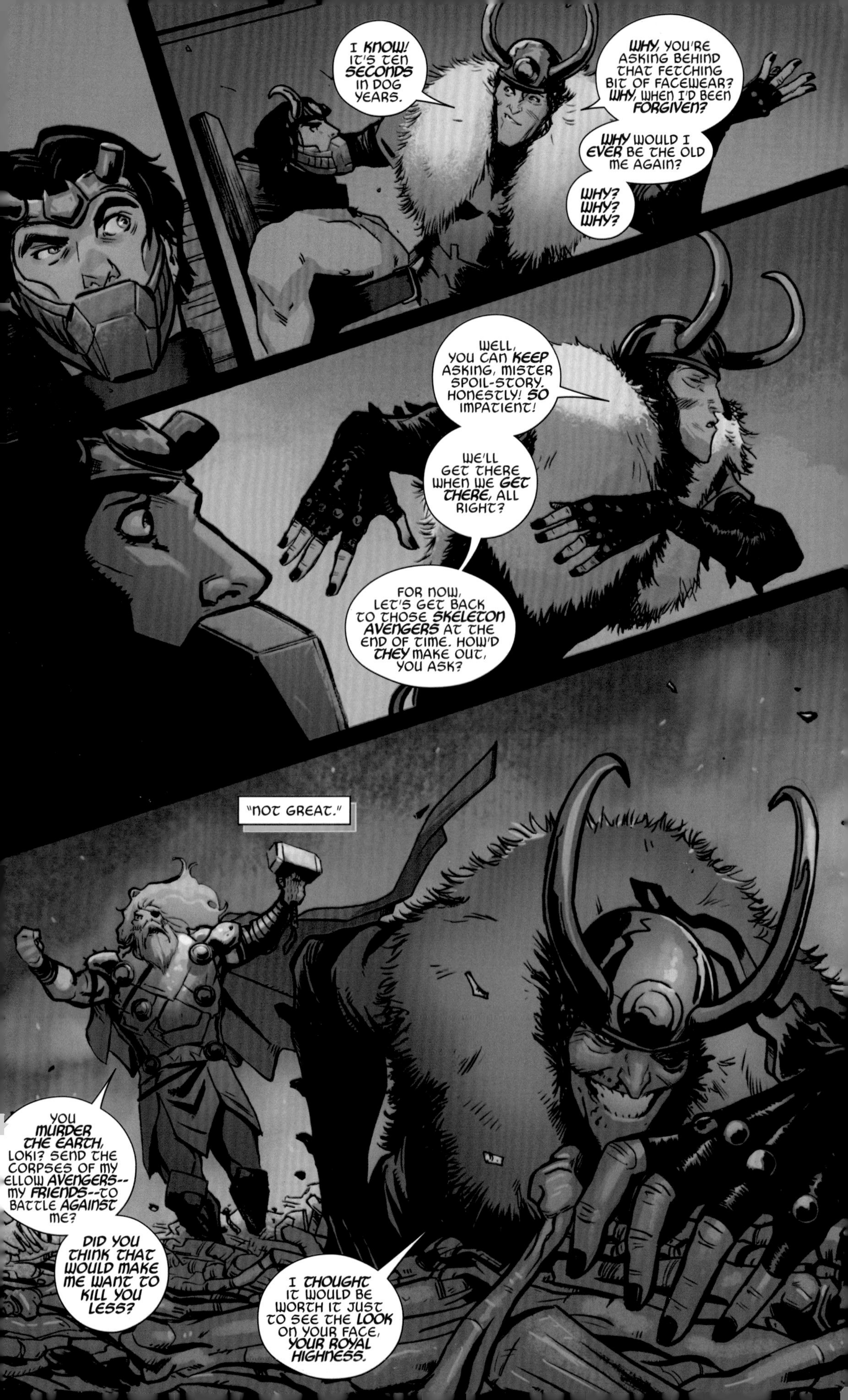
I KNOW! IT'S TEN SECONDS IN DOG YEARS.
WHY, YOU'RE ASKING BEHIND THAT FETCHING BIT OF FACEWEAR? WHY, WHEN I'D BEEN FORGIVEN?
WHY WOULD I EVER BE THE OLD ME AGAIN?
WHY? WHY? WHY?
WELL, YOU CAN KEEP ASKING, MISTER SPOIL-STORY. HONESTLY! SO IMPATIENT!
WE'LL GET THERE WHEN WE GET THERE, ALL RIGHT?
FOR NOW, LET'S GET BACK TO THOSE SKELETON AVENGERS AT THE END OF TIME. HOW'D THEY MAKE OUT, YOU ASK?
"NOT GREAT."
YOU MURDER THE EARTH, LOKI? SEND THE CORPSES OF MY ELLOW AVENGERS--MY FRIENDS--TO BATTLE AGAINST ME?
DID YOU THINK THAT WOULD MAKE ME WANT TO KILL YOU LESS?
I THOUGHT IT WOULD BE WORTH IT JUST TO SEE THE LOOK ON YOUR FACE, YOUR ROYAL HIGHNESS.

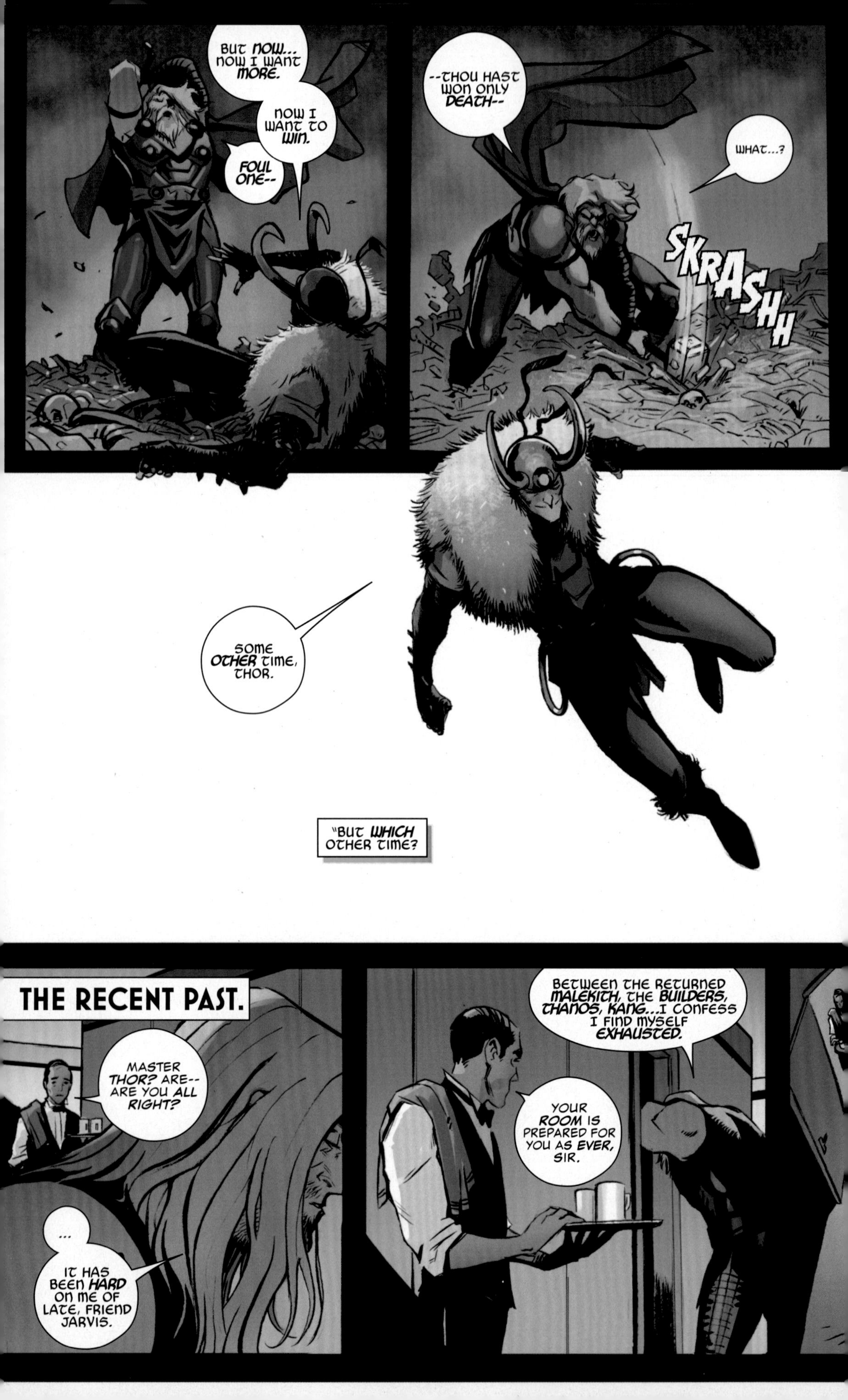
BUT NOW... NOW I WANT MORE.
NOW I WANT TO WIN.
FOUL ONE--
--THOU HAST WON ONLY DEATH--
WHAT...?
SKRASHH
SOME OTHER TIME, THOR.
"BUT WHICH OTHER TIME?
THE RECENT PAST.
MASTER THOR? ARE--ARE YOU ALL RIGHT?
...
IT HAS BEEN HARD ON ME OF LATE, FRIEND JARVIS.
BETWEEN THE RETURNED MALEKITH, THE BUILDERS, THANOS, KANG...I CONFESS I FIND MYSELF EXHAUSTED.
YOUR ROOM IS PREPARED FOR YOU AS EVER, SIR.

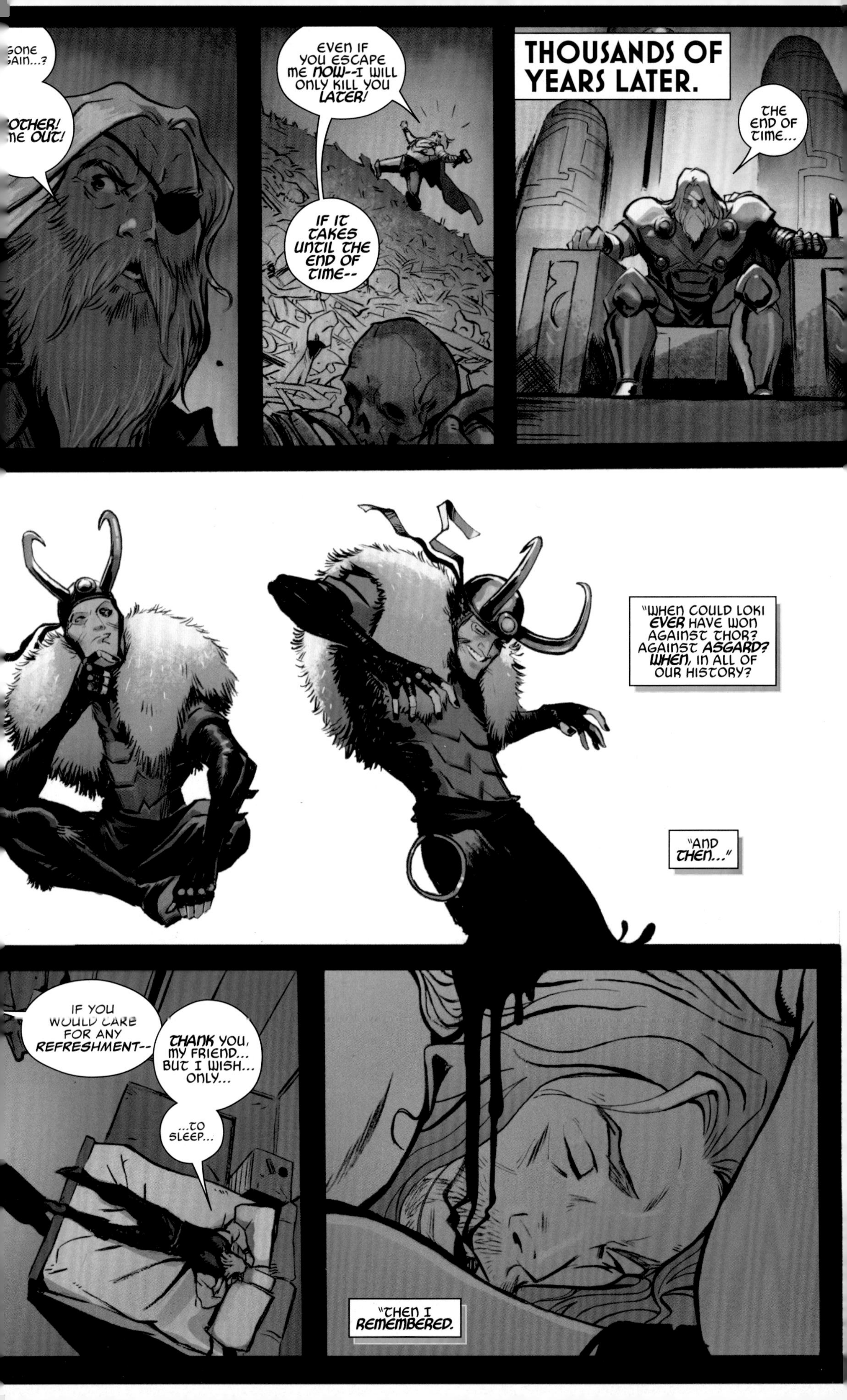
EVEN IF YOU ESCAPE ME NOW--I WILL ONLY KILL YOU LATER!
IF IT TAKES UNTIL THE END OF TIME--
THOUSANDS OF YEARS LATER.
THE END OF TIME...
"WHEN COULD LOKI EVER HAVE WON AGAINST THOR? AGAINST ASGARD? WHEN, IN ALL OF OUR HISTORY?
"AND THEN..."
IF YOU WOULD CARE FOR ANY REFRESHMENT--
THANK YOU, MY FRIEND... BUT I WISH... ONLY...
...TO SLEEP...
"THEN I REMEMBERED.

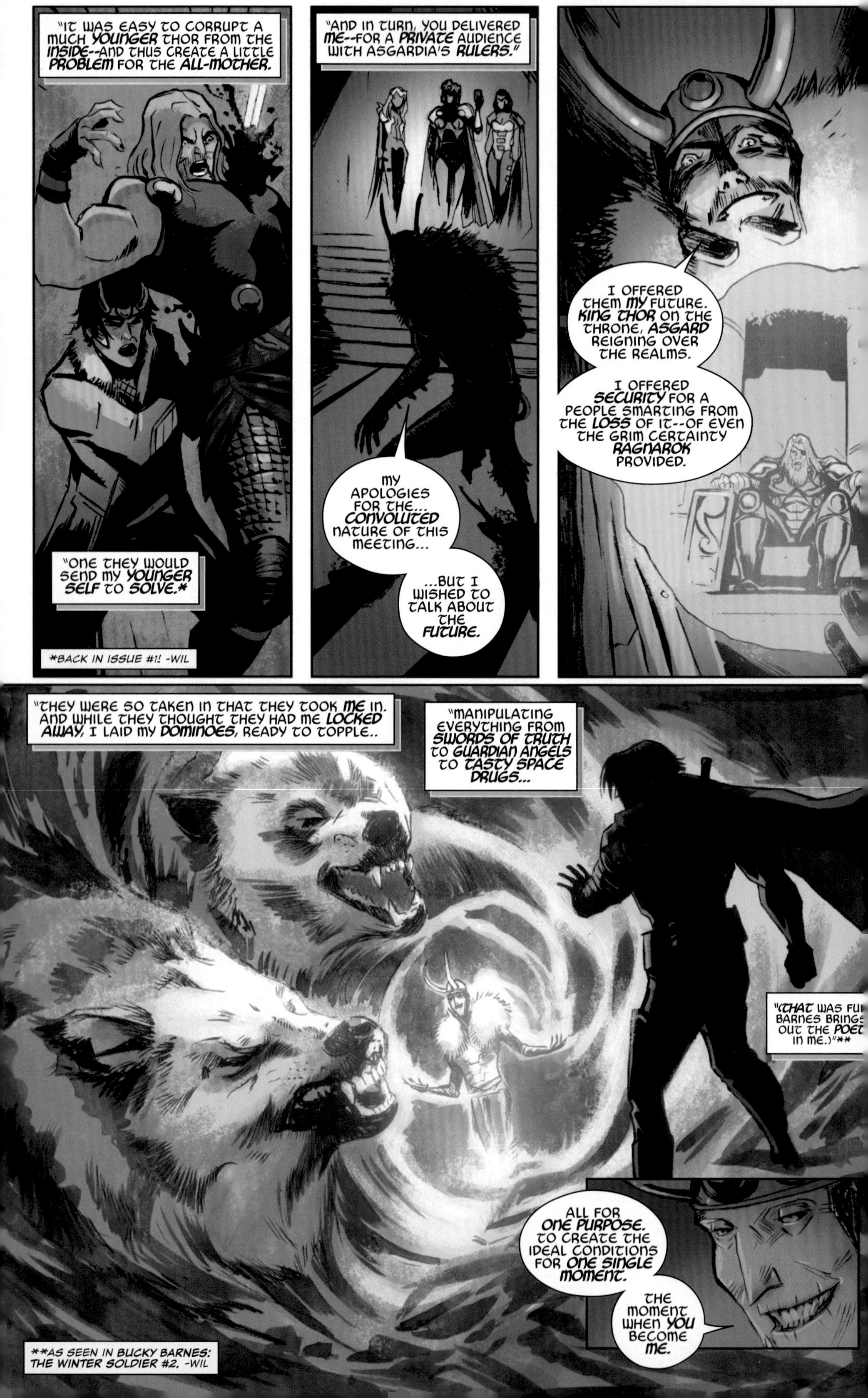
"IT WAS EASY TO CORRUPT A MUCH YOUNGER THOR FROM THE INSIDE--AND THUS CREATE A LITTLE PROBLEM FOR THE ALL-MOTHER.
"ONE THEY WOULD SEND MY YOUNGER SELF TO SOLVE.*
*BACK IN ISSUE #1! -WIL
"AND IN TURN, YOU DELIVERED ME--FOR A PRIVATE AUDIENCE WITH ASGARDIA'S RULERS."
MY APOLOGIES FOR THE... CONVOLUTED NATURE OF THIS MEETING...
...BUT I WISHED TO TALK ABOUT THE FUTURE.
I OFFERED THEM MY FUTURE. KING THOR ON THE THRONE, ASGARD REIGNING OVER THE REALMS.
I OFFERED SECURITY FOR A PEOPLE SMARTING FROM THE LOSS OF IT--OF EVEN THE GRIM CERTAINTY RAGNAROK PROVIDED.
"THEY WERE SO TAKEN IN THAT THEY TOOK ME IN. AND WHILE THEY THOUGHT THEY HAD ME LOCKED AWAY, I LAID MY DOMINOES, READY TO TOPPLE..
"MANIPULATING EVERYTHING FROM SWORDS OF TRUTH TO GUARDIAN ANGELS TO TASTY SPACE DRUGS...
"(THAT WAS FU BARNES BRING OUT THE POET IN ME.)"**
ALL FOR ONE PURPOSE. TO CREATE THE IDEAL CONDITIONS FOR ONE SINGLE MOMENT.
THE MOMENT WHEN YOU BECOME ME.
**AS SEEN IN BUCKY BARNES: THE WINTER SOLDIER #2. -WIL

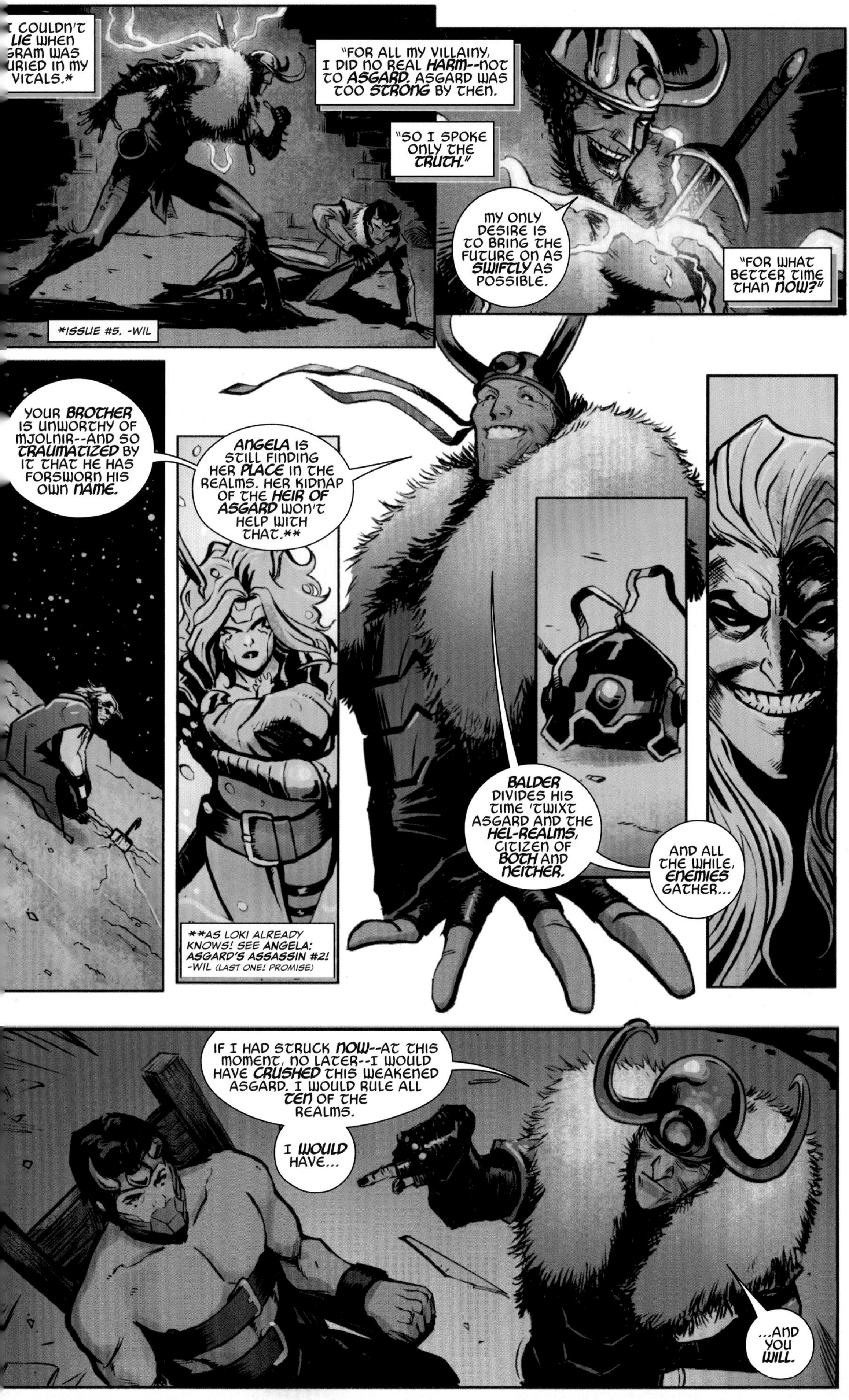

I COULDN'T LIE WHEN GRAM WAS BURIED IN MY VITALS.*
"FOR ALL MY VILLAINY, I DID NO REAL HARM--NOT TO ASGARD. ASGARD WAS TOO STRONG BY THEN.
"SO I SPOKE ONLY THE TRUTH."
MY ONLY DESIRE IS TO BRING THE FUTURE ON AS SWIFTLY AS POSSIBLE.
"FOR WHAT BETTER TIME THAN NOW?"
*ISSUE #5. -WIL
YOUR BROTHER IS UNWORTHY OF MJOLNIR--AND SO TRAUMATIZED BY IT THAT HE HAS FORSWORN HIS OWN NAME.
ANGELA IS STILL FINDING HER PLACE IN THE REALMS. HER KIDNAP OF THE HEIR OF ASGARD WON'T HELP WITH THAT.**
**AS LOKI ALREADY KNOWS! SEE ANGELA: ASGARD'S ASSASSIN #2! -WIL (LAST ONE! PROMISE)
BALDER DIVIDES HIS TIME 'TWIXT ASGARD AND THE HEL-REALMS, CITIZEN OF BOTH AND NEITHER.
AND ALL THE WHILE, ENEMIES GATHER...
IF I HAD STRUCK NOW--AT THIS MOMENT, NO LATER--I WOULD HAVE CRUSHED THIS WEAKENED ASGARD. I WOULD RULE ALL TEN OF THE REALMS.
I WOULD HAVE...
...AND YOU WILL.

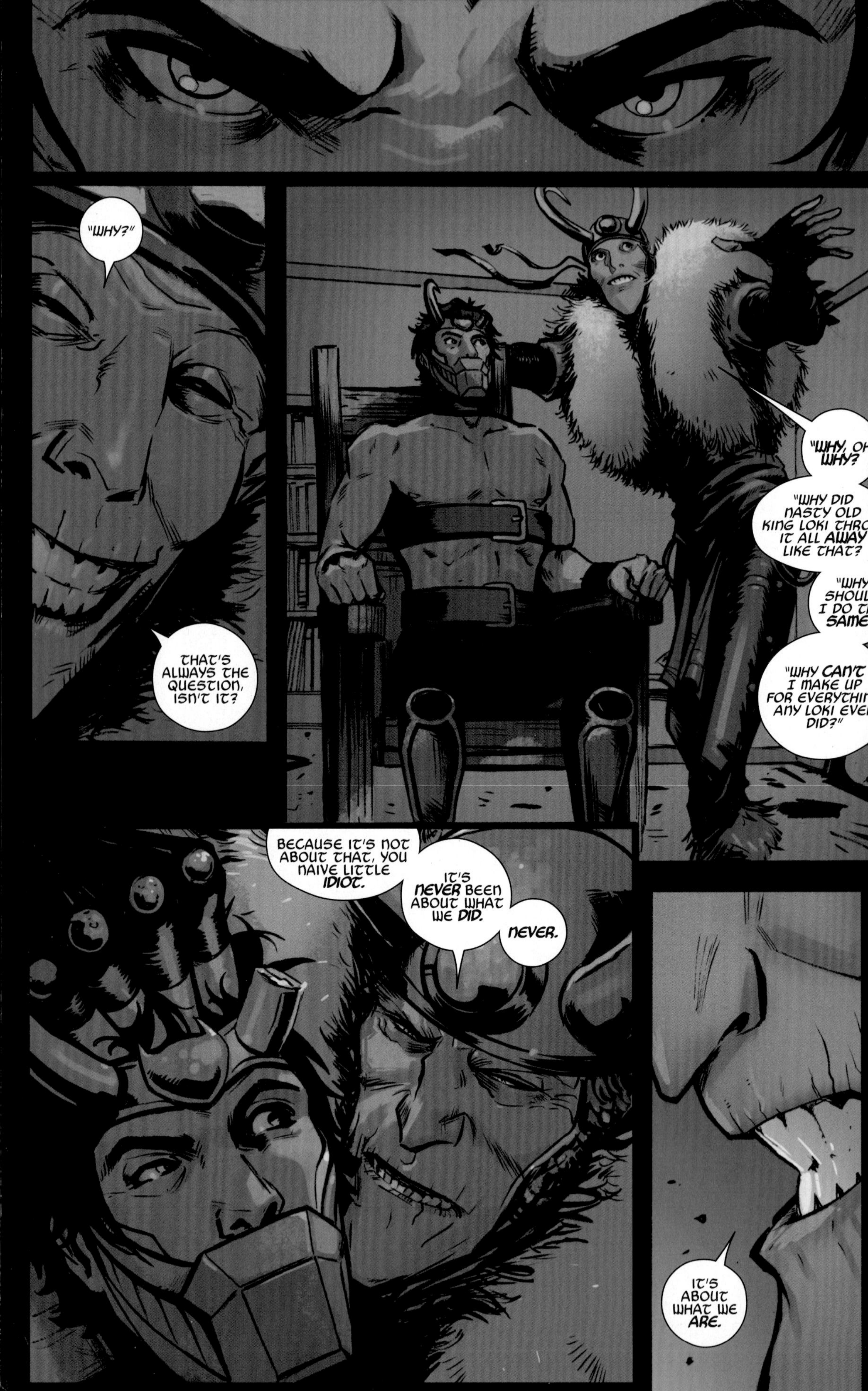
"WHY?"
THAT'S ALWAYS THE QUESTION, ISN'T IT?
"WHY, OH WHY?
"WHY DID NASTY OLD KING LOKI THRO IT ALL AWAY LIKE THAT?
"WHY SHOUL I DO T SAME
"WHY CAN'T I MAKE UP FOR EVERYTHI ANY LOKI EVE DID?"
BECAUSE IT'S NOT ABOUT THAT, YOU NAIVE LITTLE IDIOT.
IT'S NEVER BEEN ABOUT WHAT WE DID.
NEVER.
IT'S ABOUT WHAT WE ARE.

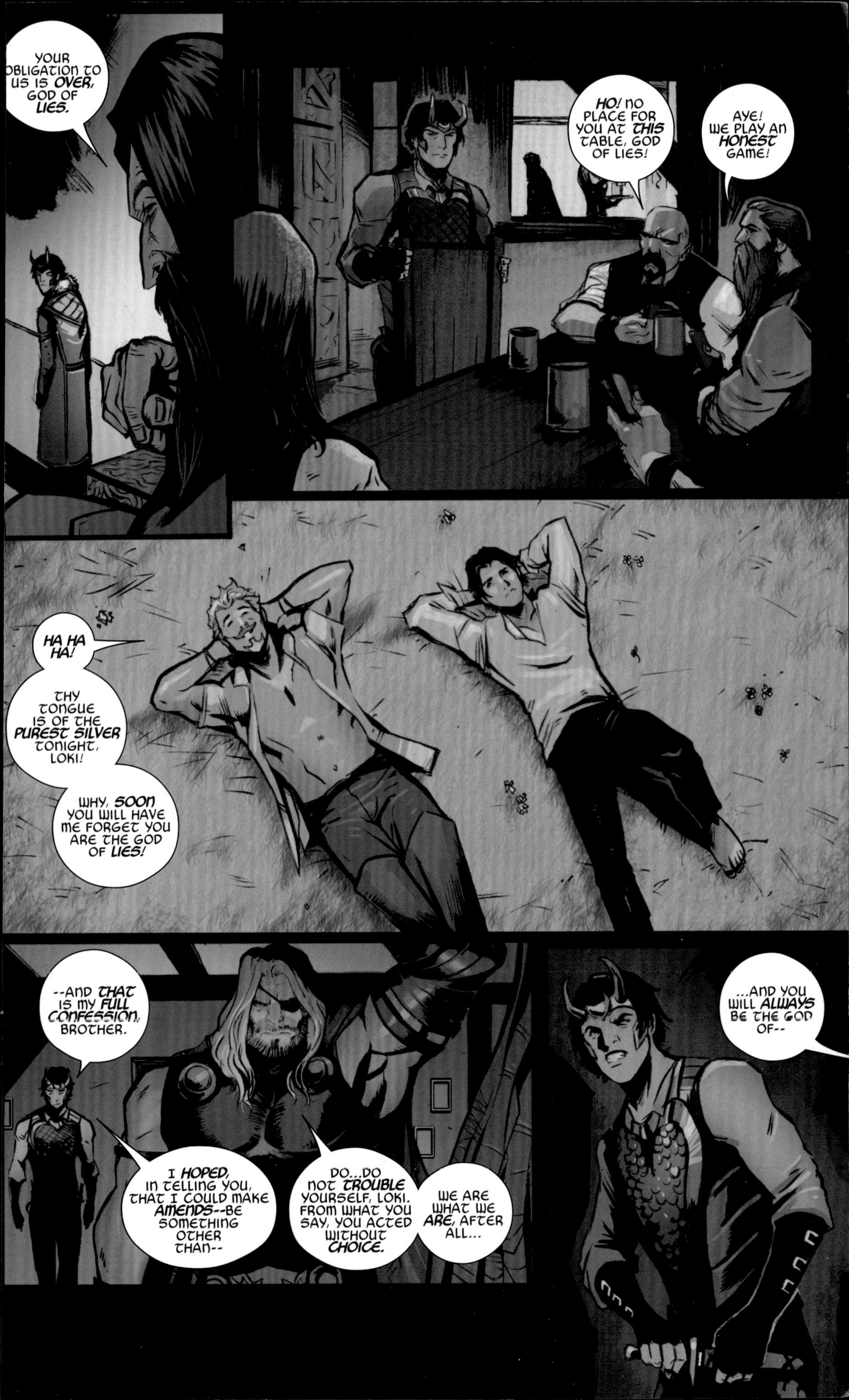
YOUR OBLIGATION TO US IS OVER, GOD OF LIES.
HO! NO PLACE FOR YOU AT THIS TABLE, GOD OF LIES!
AYE! WE PLAY AN HONEST GAME!
HA HA HA!
THY TONGUE IS OF THE PUREST SILVER TONIGHT, LOKI!
WHY, SOON YOU WILL HAVE ME FORGET YOU ARE THE GOD OF LIES!
--AND THAT IS MY FULL CONFESSION, BROTHER.
I HOPED, IN TELLING YOU, THAT I COULD MAKE AMENDS--BE SOMETHING OTHER THAN--
DO...DO NOT TROUBLE YOURSELF, LOKI. FROM WHAT YOU SAY, YOU ACTED WITHOUT CHOICE.
WE ARE WHAT WE ARE, AFTER ALL...
...AND YOU WILL ALWAYS BE THE GOD OF--

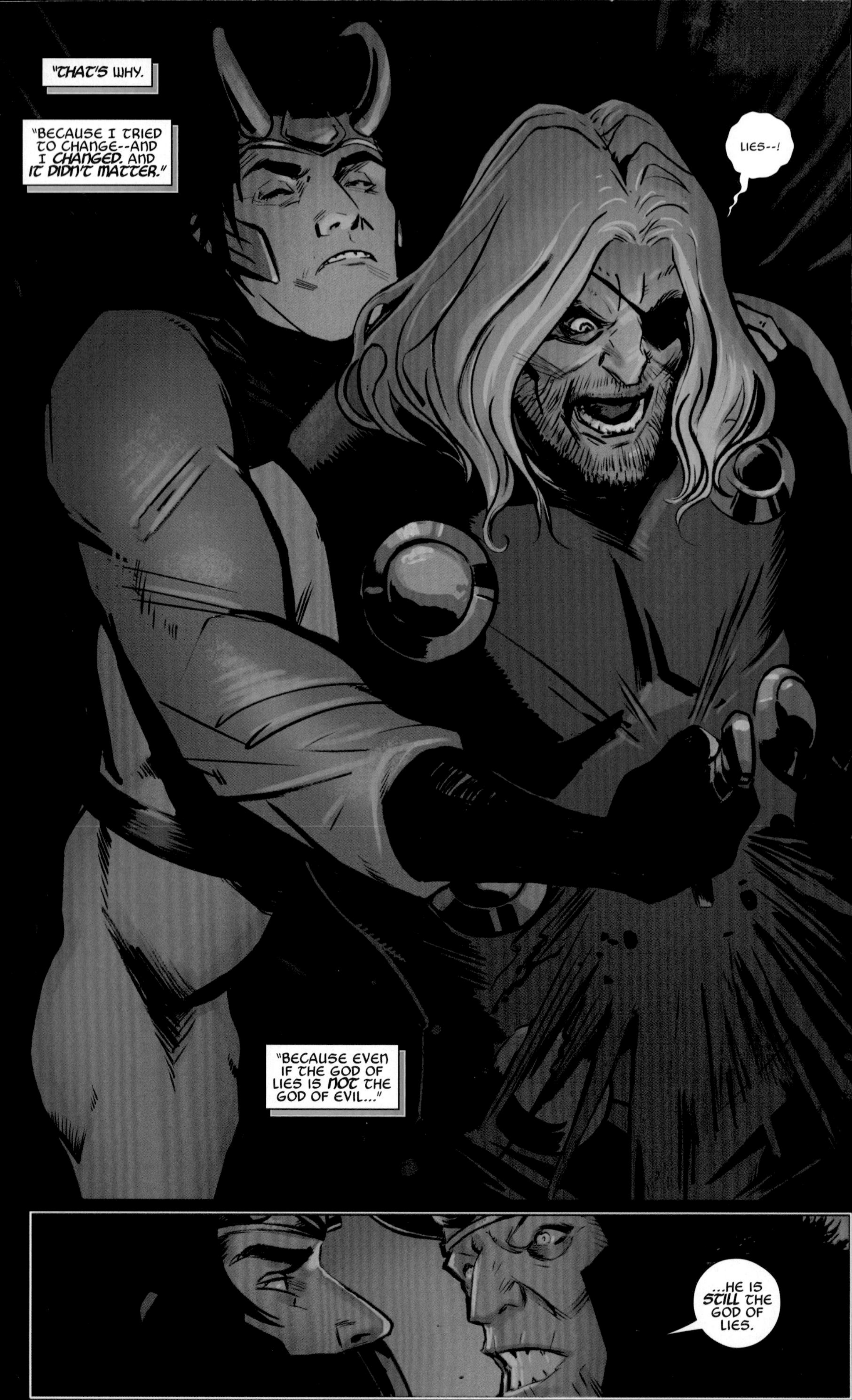
"THAT'S WHY.
"BECAUSE I TRIED TO CHANGE--AND I CHANGED. AND IT DIDN'T MATTER."
LIES--!
"BECAUSE EVEN IF THE GOD OF LIES IS NOT THE GOD OF EVIL..."
...HE IS STILL THE GOD OF LIES.

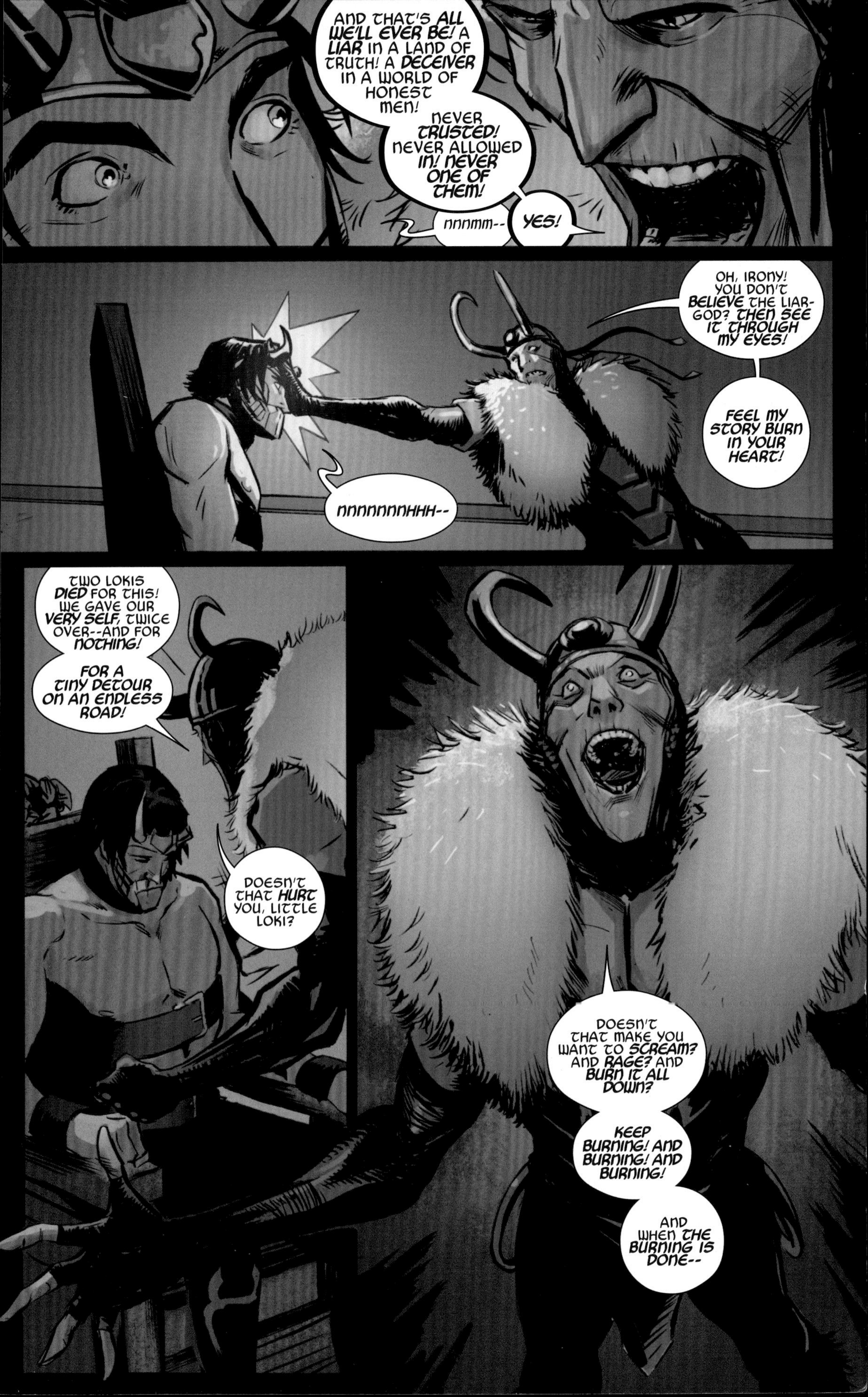
AND THAT'S ALL WE'LL EVER BE! A LIAR IN A LAND OF TRUTH! A DECEIVER IN A WORLD OF HONEST MEN!
NEVER TRUSTED! NEVER ALLOWED IN! NEVER ONE OF THEM!
NNNMM--
YES!
OH, IRONY! YOU DON'T BELIEVE THE LIAR-GOD? THEN SEE IT THROUGH MY EYES!
FEEL MY STORY BURN IN YOUR HEART!
NNNNNNNHHH--
TWO LOKIS DIED FOR THIS! WE GAVE OUR VERY SELF, TWICE OVER--AND FOR NOTHING!
FOR A TINY DETOUR ON AN ENDLESS ROAD!
DOESN'T THAT HURT YOU, LITTLE LOKI?
DOESN'T THAT MAKE YOU WANT TO SCREAM? AND RAGE? AND BURN IT ALL DOWN?
KEEP BURNING! AND BURNING! AND BURNING!
AND WHEN THE BURNING IS DONE--

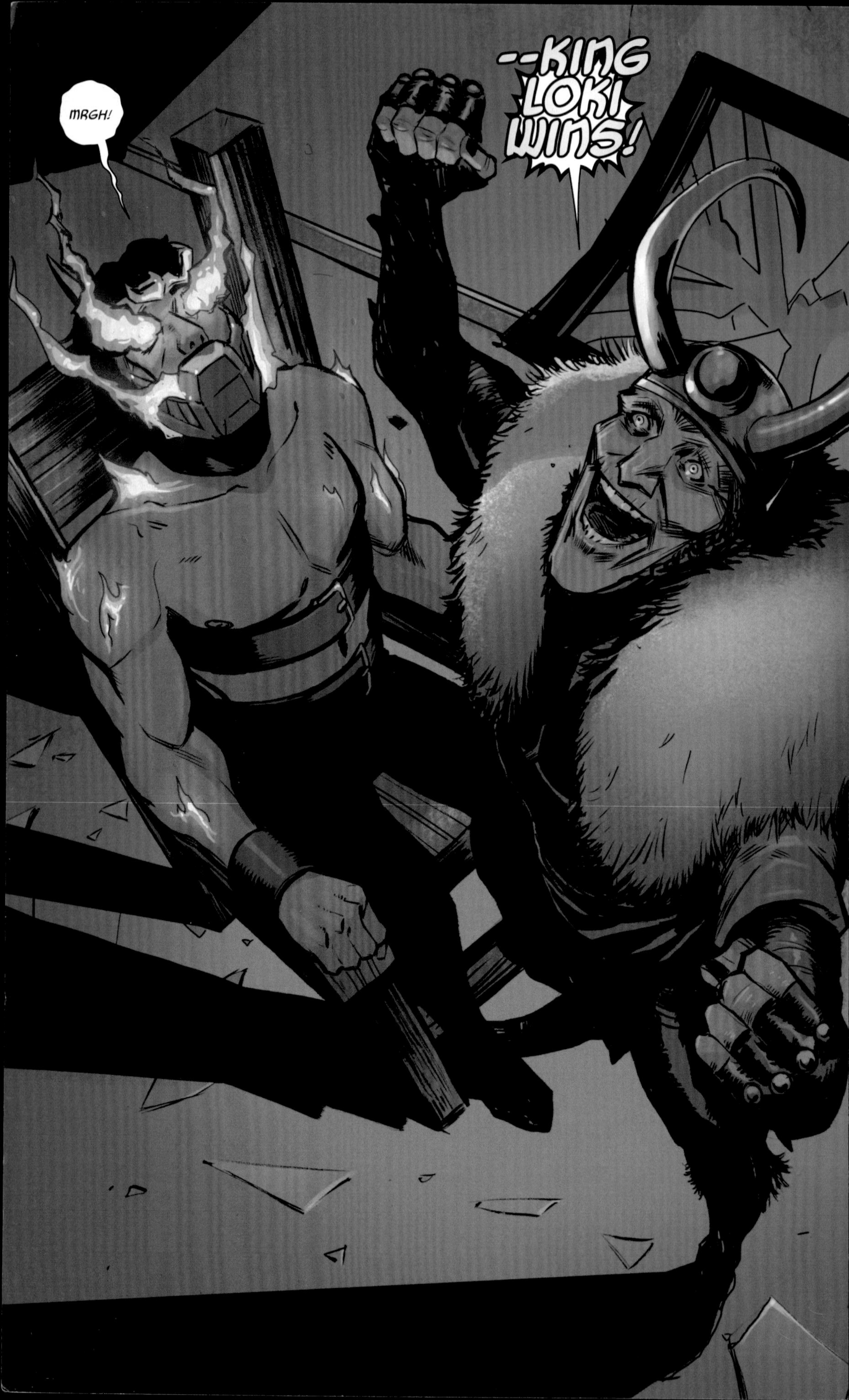
MRGH!
--KING LOKI WINS!

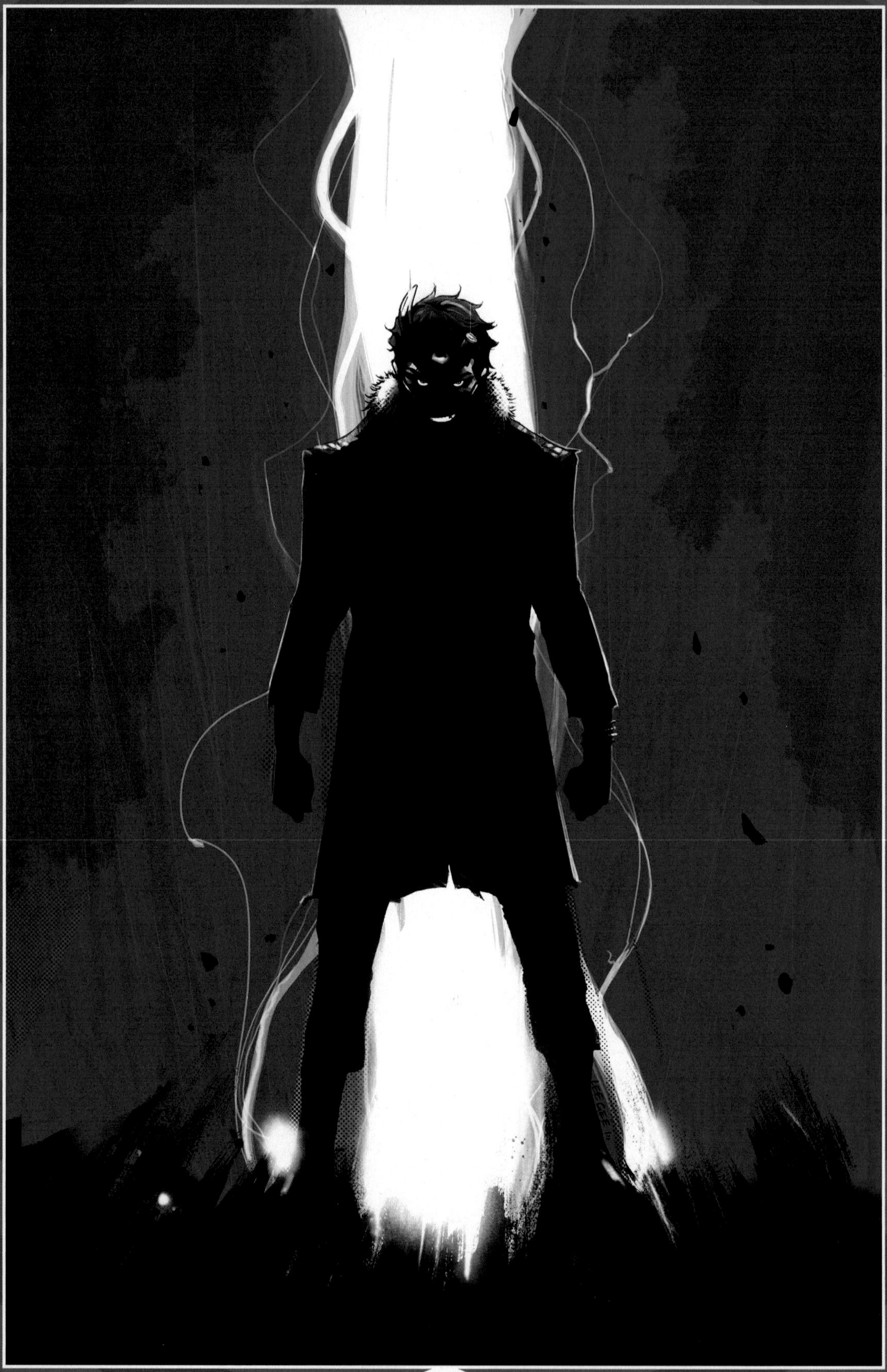

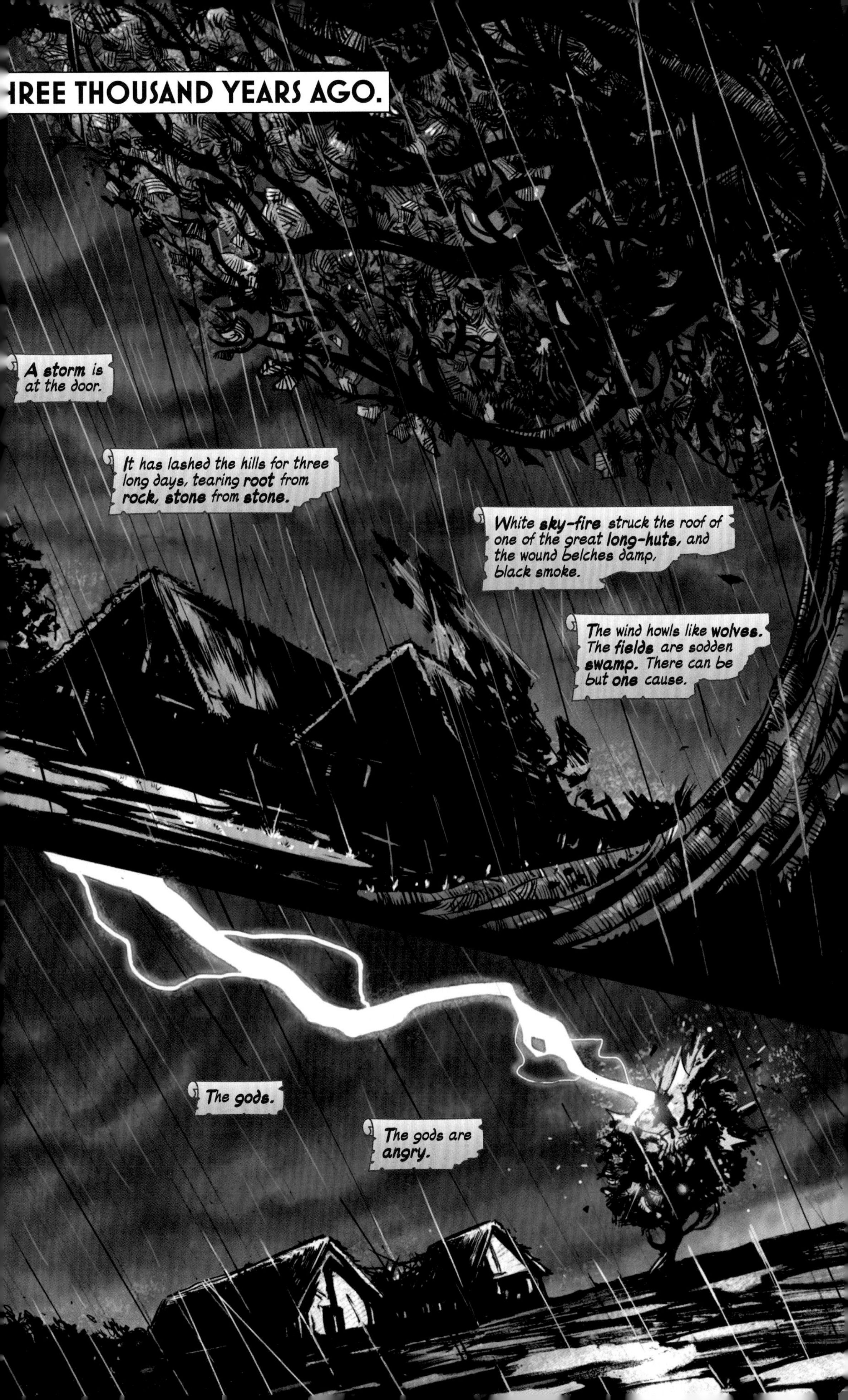

HREE THOUSAND YEARS AGO.
A storm is at the door.
It has lashed the hills for three long days, tearing root from rock, stone from stone.
White sky-fire struck the roof of one of the great long-huts, and the wound belches damp, black smoke.
The wind howls like wolves. The fields are sodden swamp. There can be but one cause.
The gods.
The gods are angry.

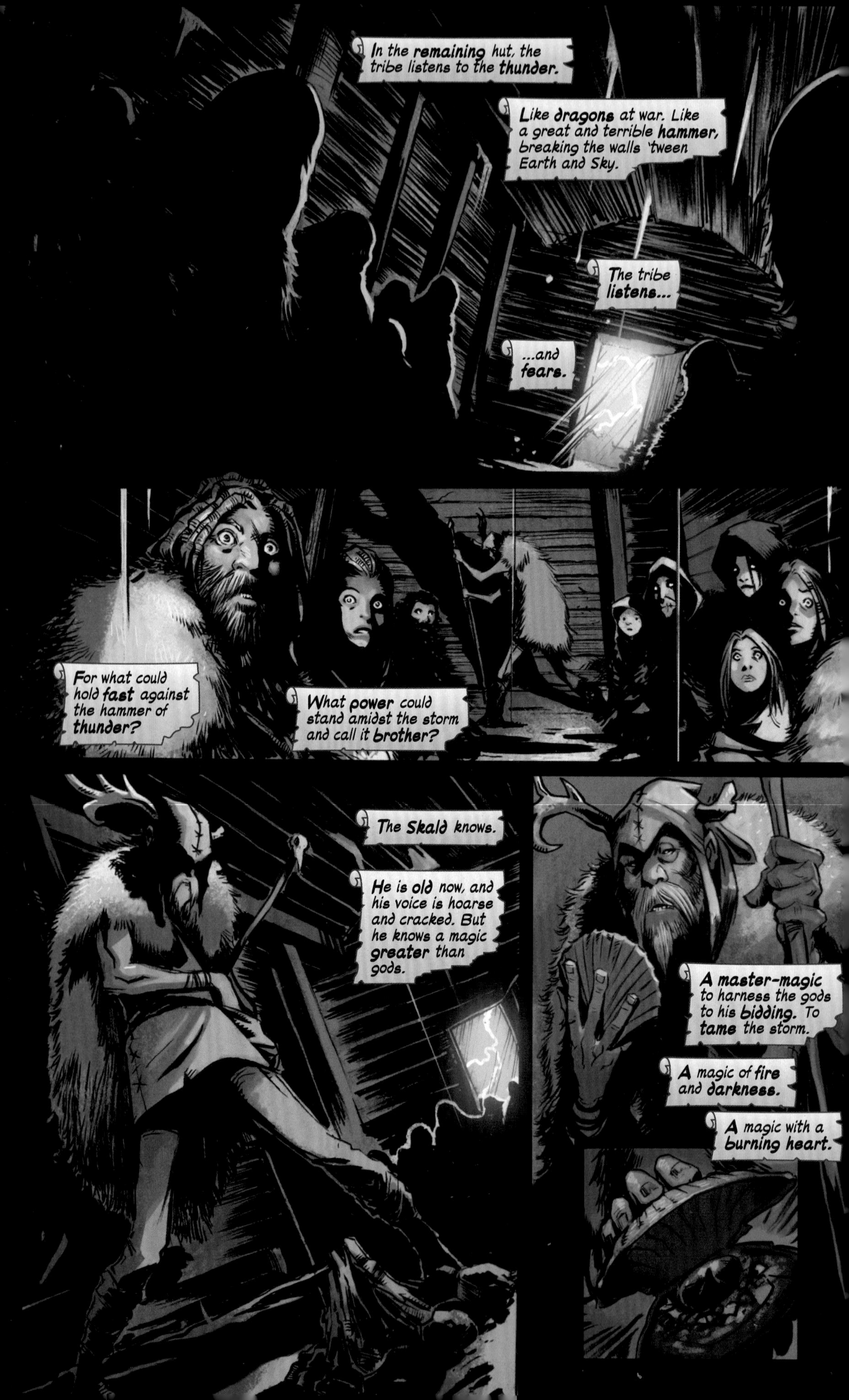
In the remaining hut, the tribe listens to the thunder.
Like dragons at war. Like a great and terrible hammer, breaking the walls 'tween Earth and Sky.
The tribe listens...
...and fears.
For what could hold fast against the hammer of thunder?
What power could stand amidst the storm and call it brother?
The Skald knows.
He is old now, and his voice is hoarse and cracked. But he knows a magic greater than gods.
A master-magic to harness the gods to his bidding. To tame the storm.
A magic of fire and darkness.
A magic with a burning heart.

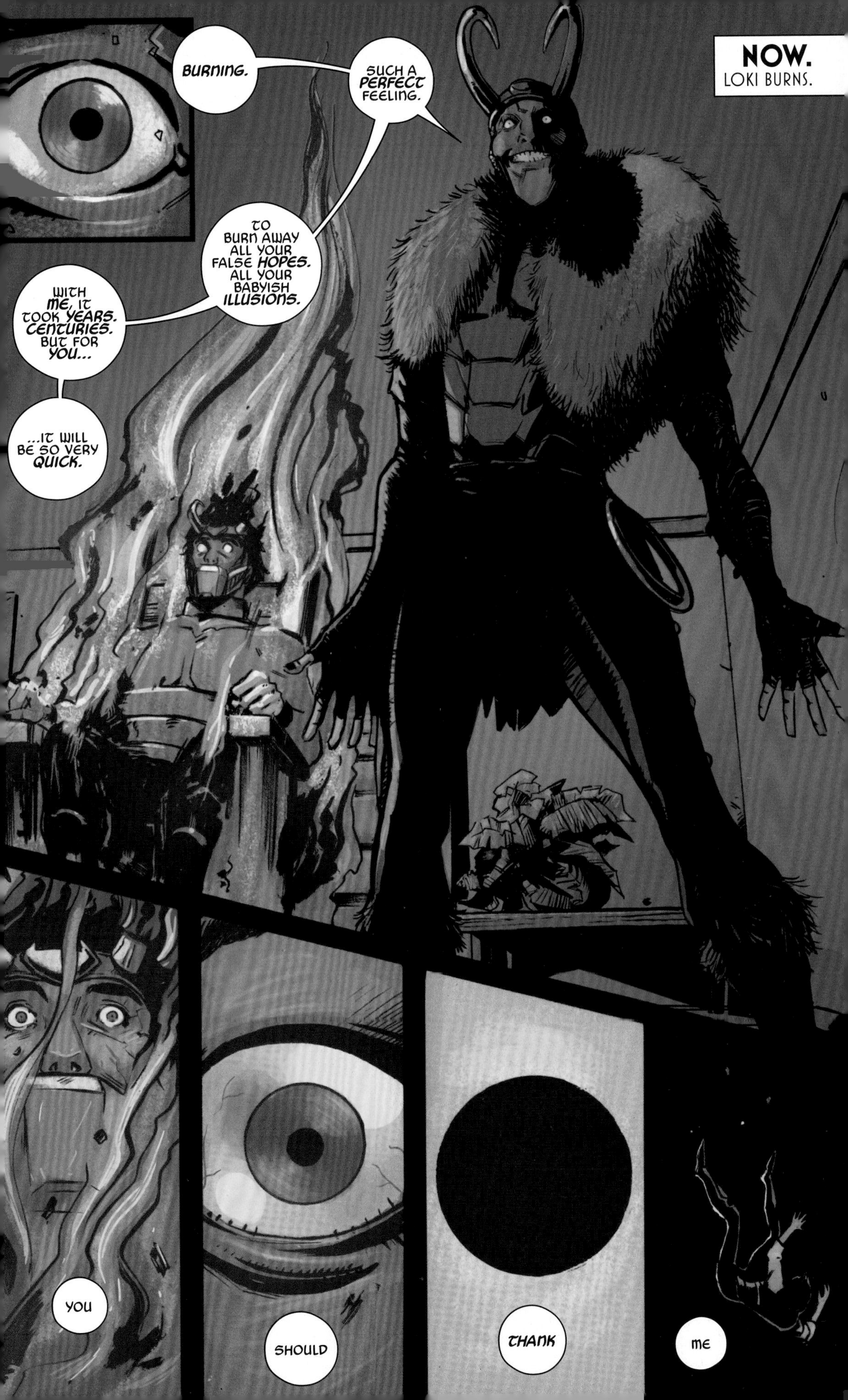
NOW.
LOKI BURNS.
BURNING.
SUCH A PERFECT FEELING.
TO BURN AWAY ALL YOUR FALSE HOPES. ALL YOUR BABYISH ILLUSIONS.
WITH ME, IT TOOK YEARS. CENTURIES. BUT FOR YOU...
...IT WILL BE SO VERY QUICK.
YOU
SHOULD
THANK
ME

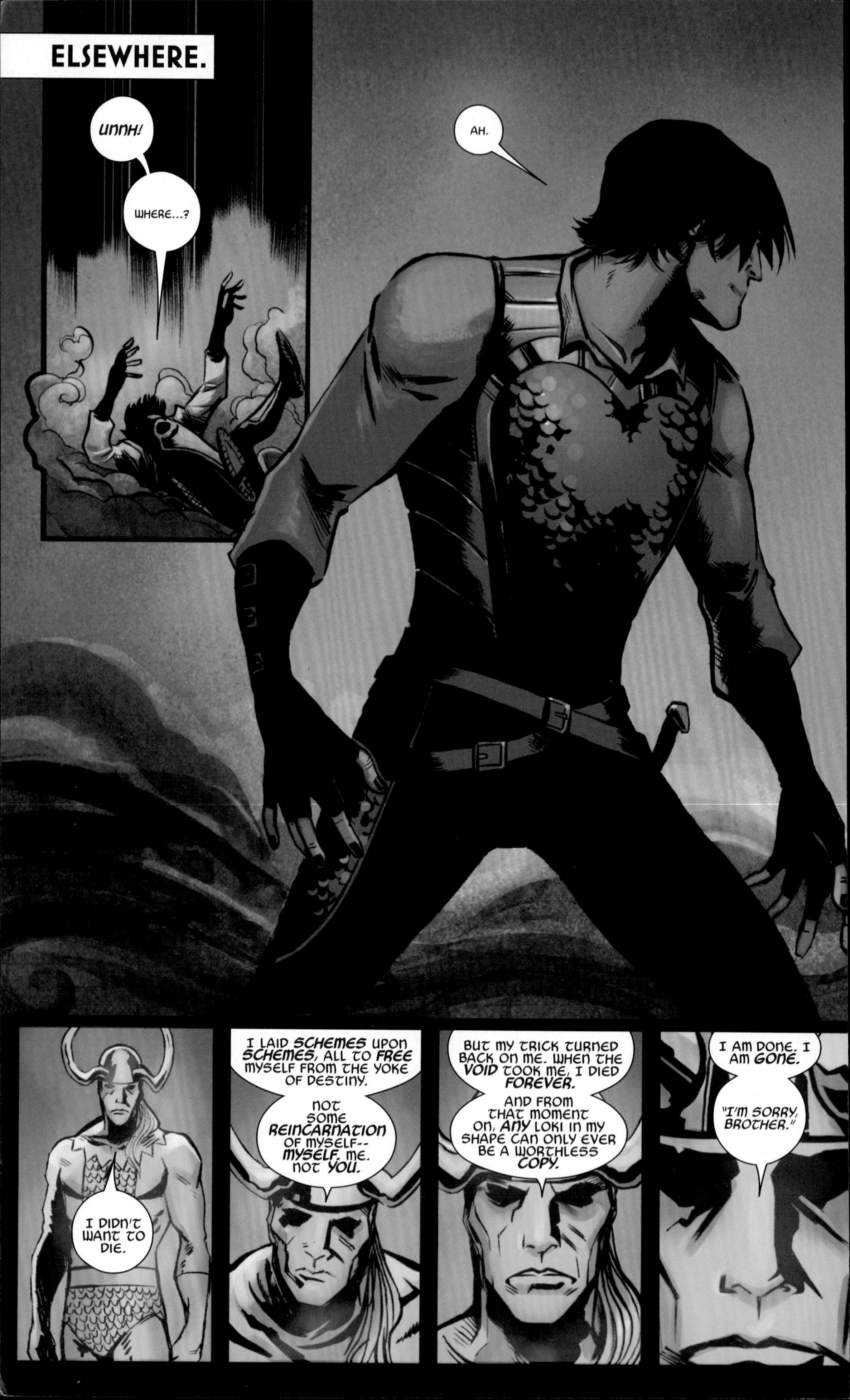
ELSEWHERE.
UNNH!
WHERE...?
AH.
I DIDN'T WANT TO DIE.
I LAID SCHEMES UPON SCHEMES, ALL TO FREE MYSELF FROM THE YOKE OF DESTINY.
NOT SOME REINCARNATION OF MYSELF-- MYSELF. ME. NOT YOU.
BUT MY TRICK TURNED BACK ON ME. WHEN THE VOID TOOK ME, I DIED FOREVER.
AND FROM THAT MOMENT ON, ANY LOKI IN MY SHAPE CAN ONLY EVER BE A WORTHLESS COPY.
I AM DONE. I AM GONE.
"I'M SORRY, BROTHER."

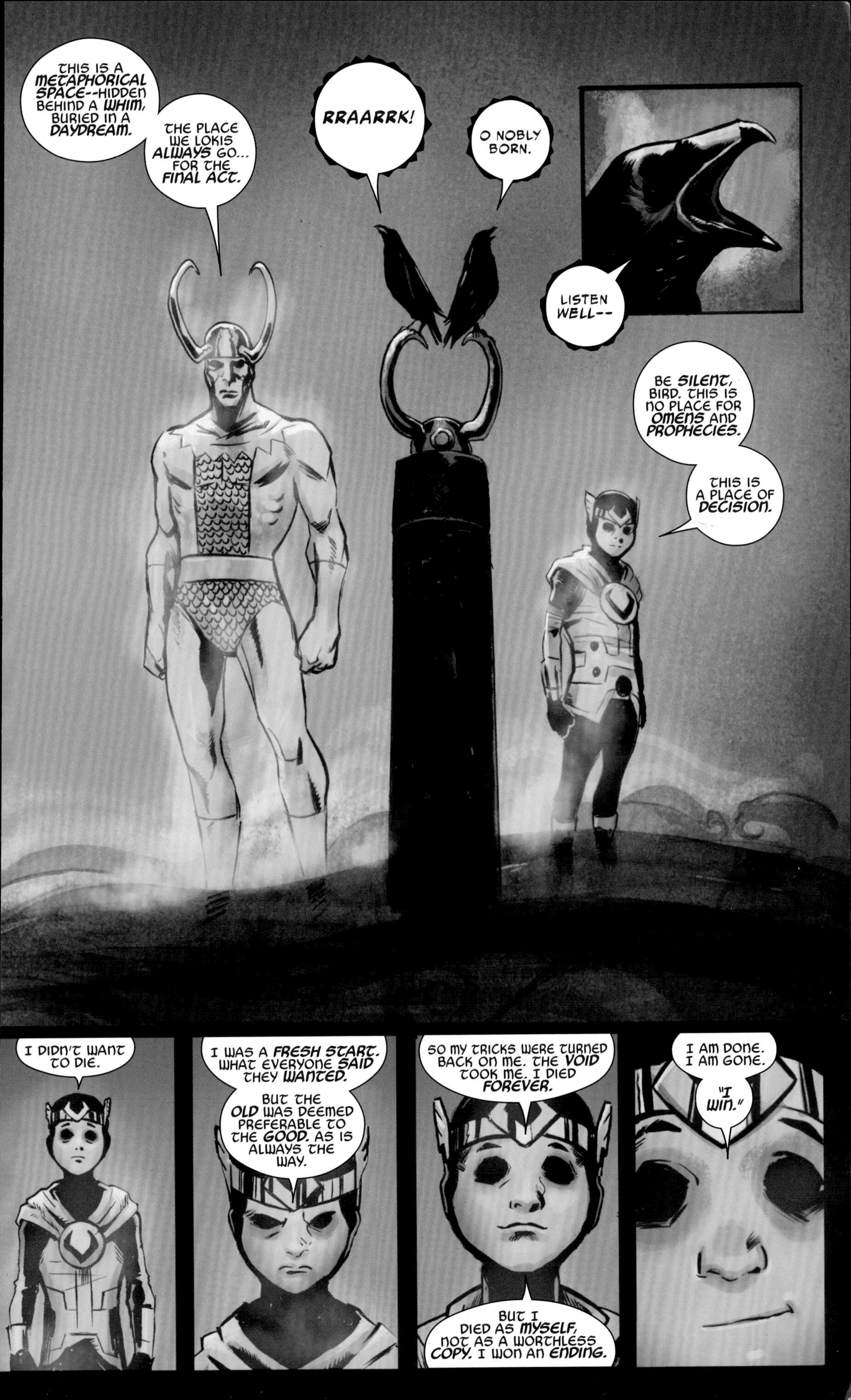
THIS IS A METAPHORICAL SPACE--HIDDEN BEHIND A WHIM, BURIED IN A DAYDREAM.
THE PLACE WE LOKIS ALWAYS GO... FOR THE FINAL ACT.
RRAARRK!
O NOBLY BORN.
LISTEN WELL--
BE SILENT, BIRD. THIS IS NO PLACE FOR OMENS AND PROPHECIES.
THIS IS A PLACE OF DECISION.
I DIDN'T WANT TO DIE.
I WAS A FRESH START. WHAT EVERYONE SAID THEY WANTED.
BUT THE OLD WAS DEEMED PREFERABLE TO THE GOOD. AS IS ALWAYS THE WAY.
SO MY TRICKS WERE TURNED BACK ON ME. THE VOID TOOK ME. I DIED FOREVER.
BUT I DIED AS MYSELF, NOT AS A WORTHLESS COPY. I WON AN ENDING.
I AM DONE. I AM GONE.
"I WIN."

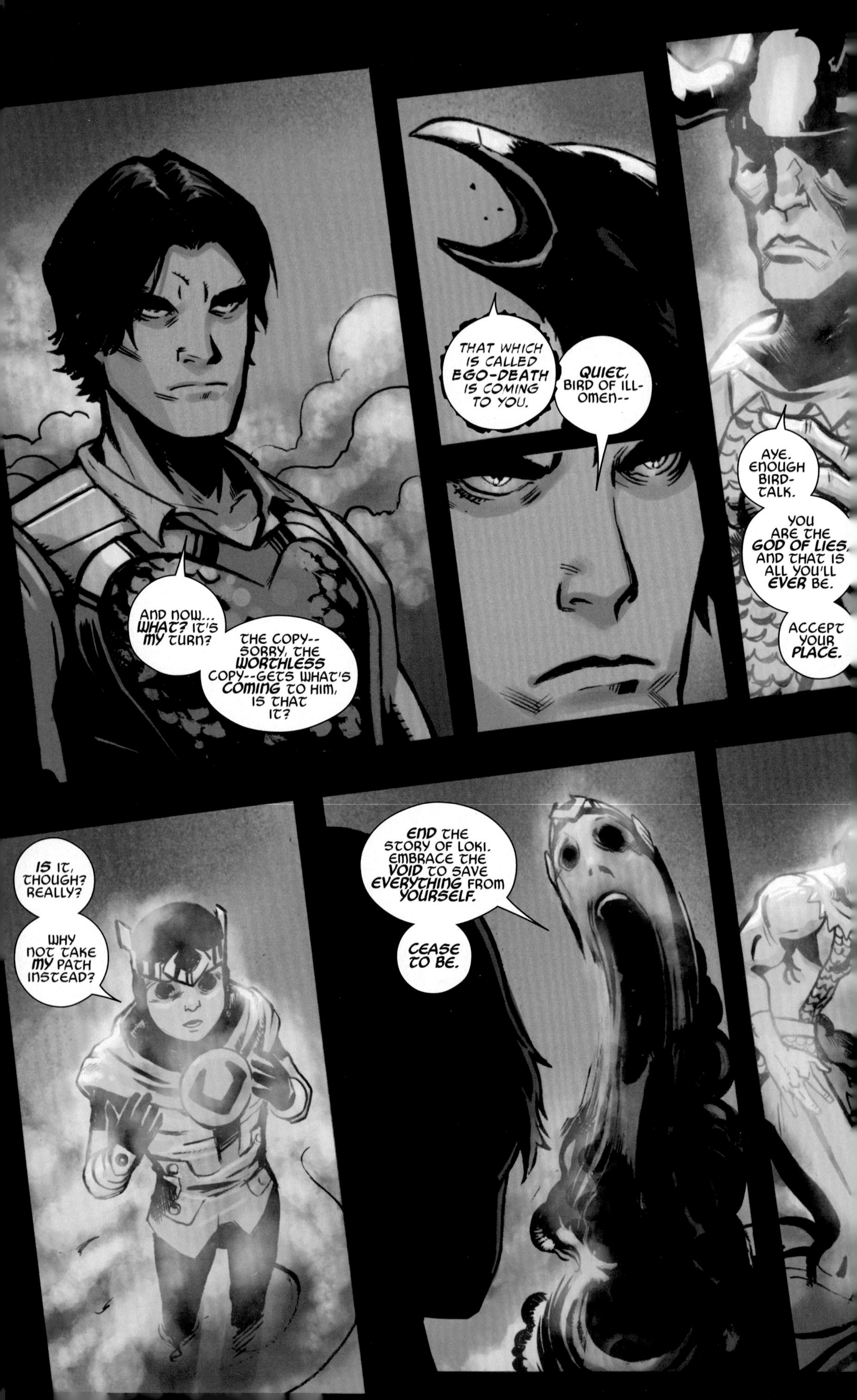
AND NOW... WHAT? IT'S MY TURN?
THE COPY-- SORRY, THE WORTHLESS COPY--GETS WHAT'S COMING TO HIM, IS THAT IT?
THAT WHICH IS CALLED EGO-DEATH IS COMING TO YOU.
QUIET, BIRD OF ILL-OMEN--
AYE. ENOUGH BIRD-TALK.
YOU ARE THE GOD OF LIES, AND THAT IS ALL YOU'LL EVER BE.
ACCEPT YOUR PLACE.
IS IT, THOUGH? REALLY?
WHY NOT TAKE MY PATH INSTEAD?
END THE STORY OF LOKI. EMBRACE THE VOID TO SAVE EVERYTHING FROM YOURSELF.
CEASE TO BE.

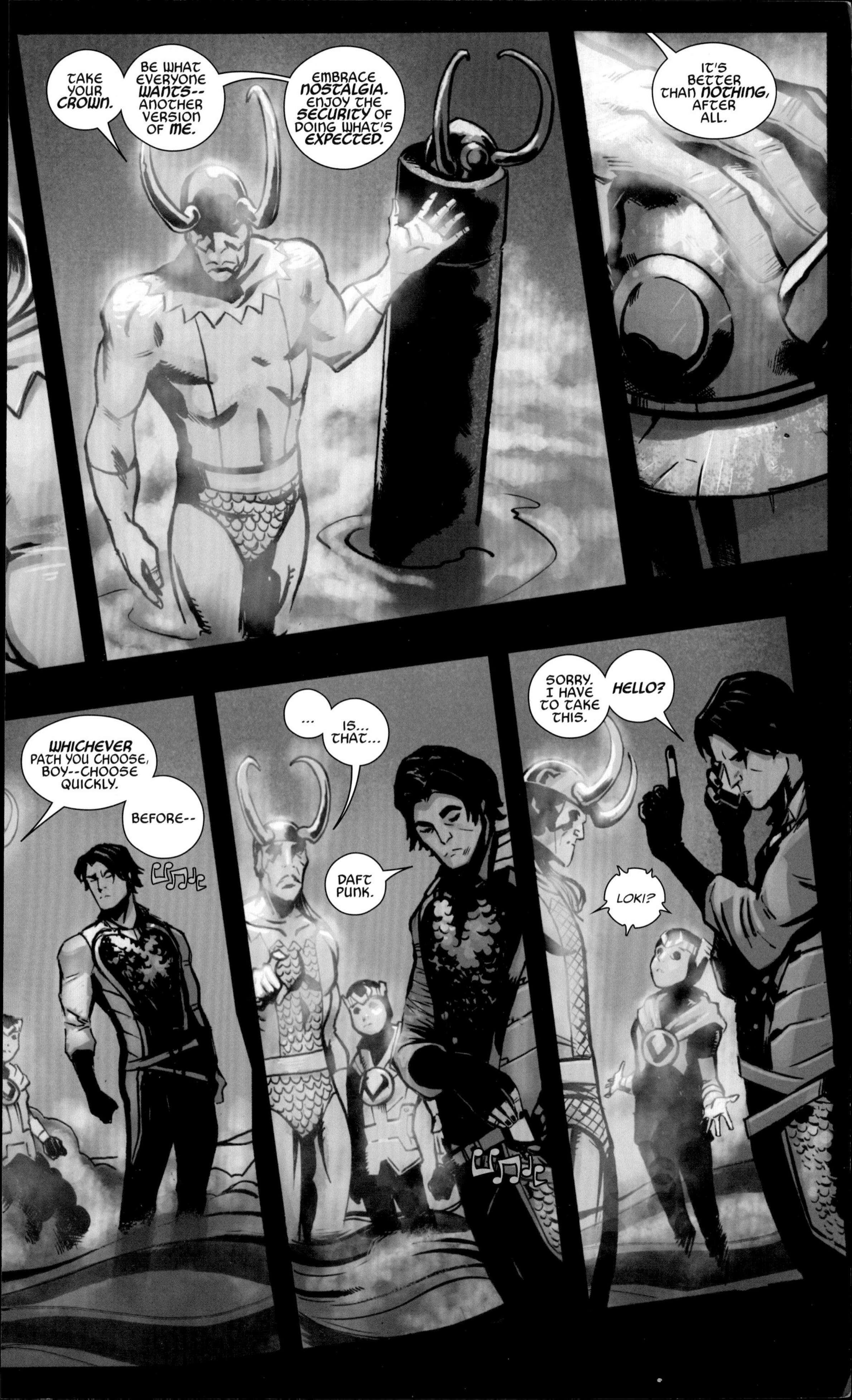
TAKE YOUR CROWN.
BE WHAT EVERYONE WANTS-- ANOTHER VERSION OF ME.
EMBRACE NOSTALGIA. ENJOY THE SECURITY OF DOING WHAT'S EXPECTED.
IT'S BETTER THAN NOTHING, AFTER ALL.
WHICHEVER PATH YOU CHOOSE, BOY--CHOOSE QUICKLY.
BEFORE--
... IS... THAT...
DAFT PUNK.
SORRY. I HAVE TO TAKE THIS.
HELLO?
LOKI?

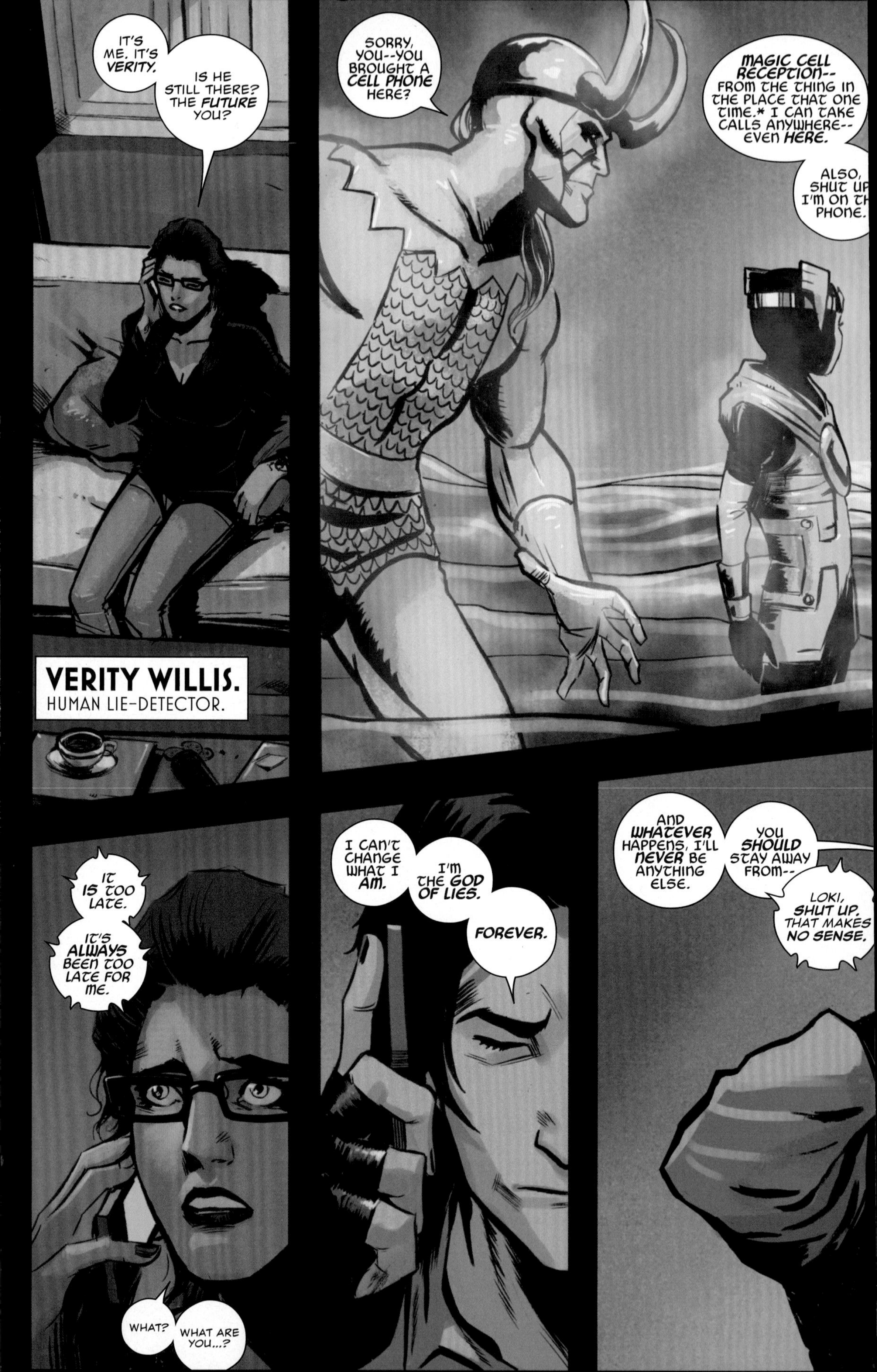

IT'S ME. IT'S VERITY.
IS HE STILL THERE? THE FUTURE YOU?
VERITY WILLIS. HUMAN LIE-DETECTOR.
SORRY, YOU--YOU BROUGHT A CELL PHONE HERE?
MAGIC CELL RECEPTION-- FROM THE THING IN THE PLACE THAT ONE TIME.* I CAN TAKE CALLS ANYWHERE-- EVEN HERE.
ALSO, SHUT UP I'M ON TH PHONE.
IT IS TOO LATE.
IT'S ALWAYS BEEN TOO LATE FOR ME.
WHAT?
WHAT ARE YOU...?
I CAN'T CHANGE WHAT I AM.
I'M THE GOD OF LIES.
FOREVER.
AND WHATEVER HAPPENS, I'LL NEVER BE ANYTHING ELSE.
YOU SHOULD STAY AWAY FROM--
LOKI, SHUT UP. THAT MAKES NO SENSE.

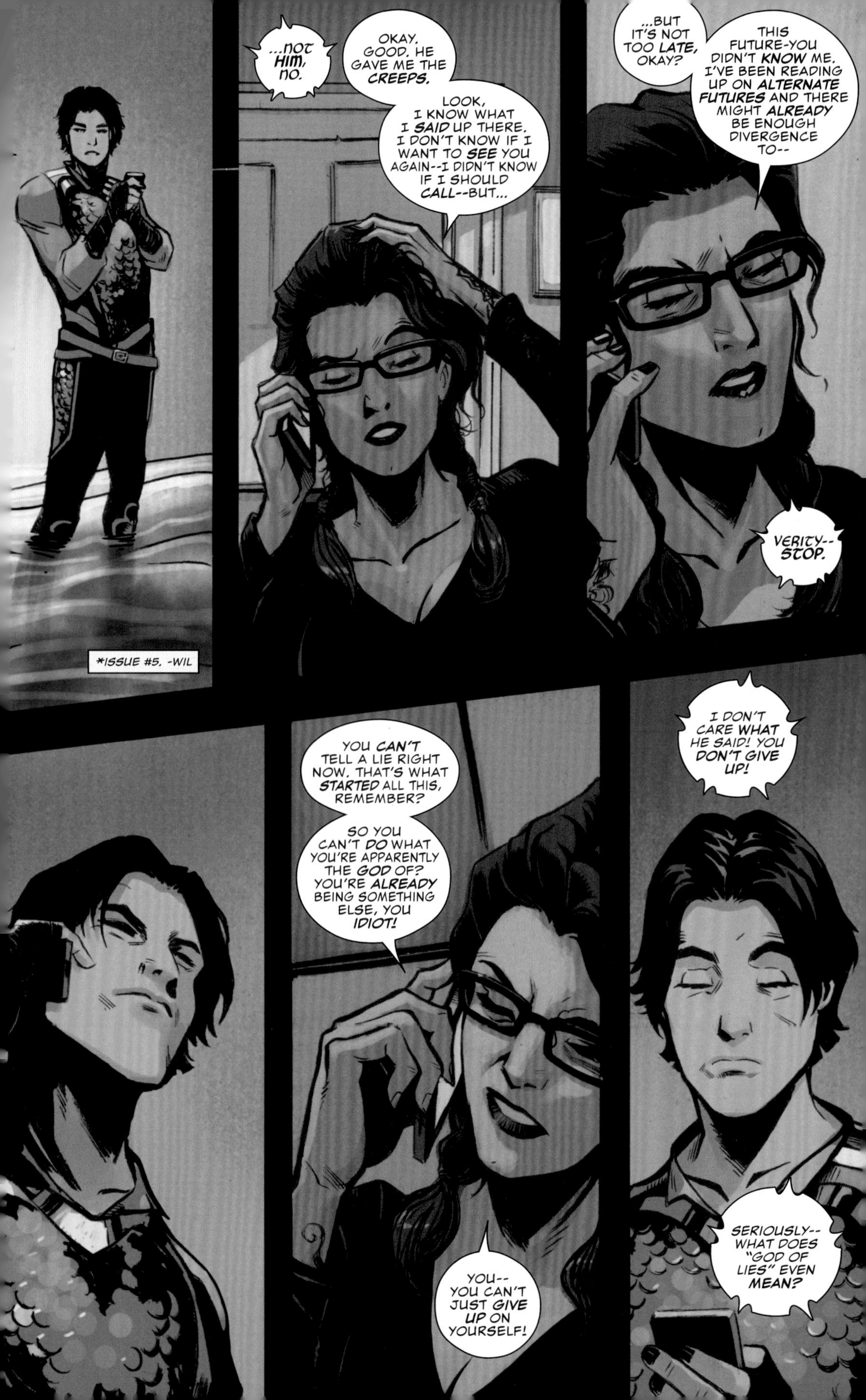

...not HIM, no.
*ISSUE #5. -WIL
OKAY. GOOD. HE GAVE ME THE CREEPS.
LOOK, I KNOW WHAT I SAID UP THERE. I DON'T KNOW IF I WANT TO SEE YOU AGAIN--I DIDN'T KNOW IF I SHOULD CALL--BUT...
...BUT IT'S NOT TOO LATE, OKAY?
THIS FUTURE-YOU DIDN'T KNOW ME. I'VE BEEN READING UP ON ALTERNATE FUTURES AND THERE MIGHT ALREADY BE ENOUGH DIVERGENCE TO--
VERITY-- STOP.
YOU CAN'T TELL A LIE RIGHT NOW. THAT'S WHAT STARTED ALL THIS, REMEMBER?
SO YOU CAN'T DO WHAT YOU'RE APPARENTLY THE GOD OF? YOU'RE ALREADY BEING SOMETHING ELSE, YOU IDIOT!
YOU-- YOU CAN'T JUST GIVE UP ON YOURSELF!
I DON'T CARE WHAT HE SAID! YOU DON'T GIVE UP!
SERIOUSLY-- WHAT DOES "GOD OF LIES" EVEN MEAN?

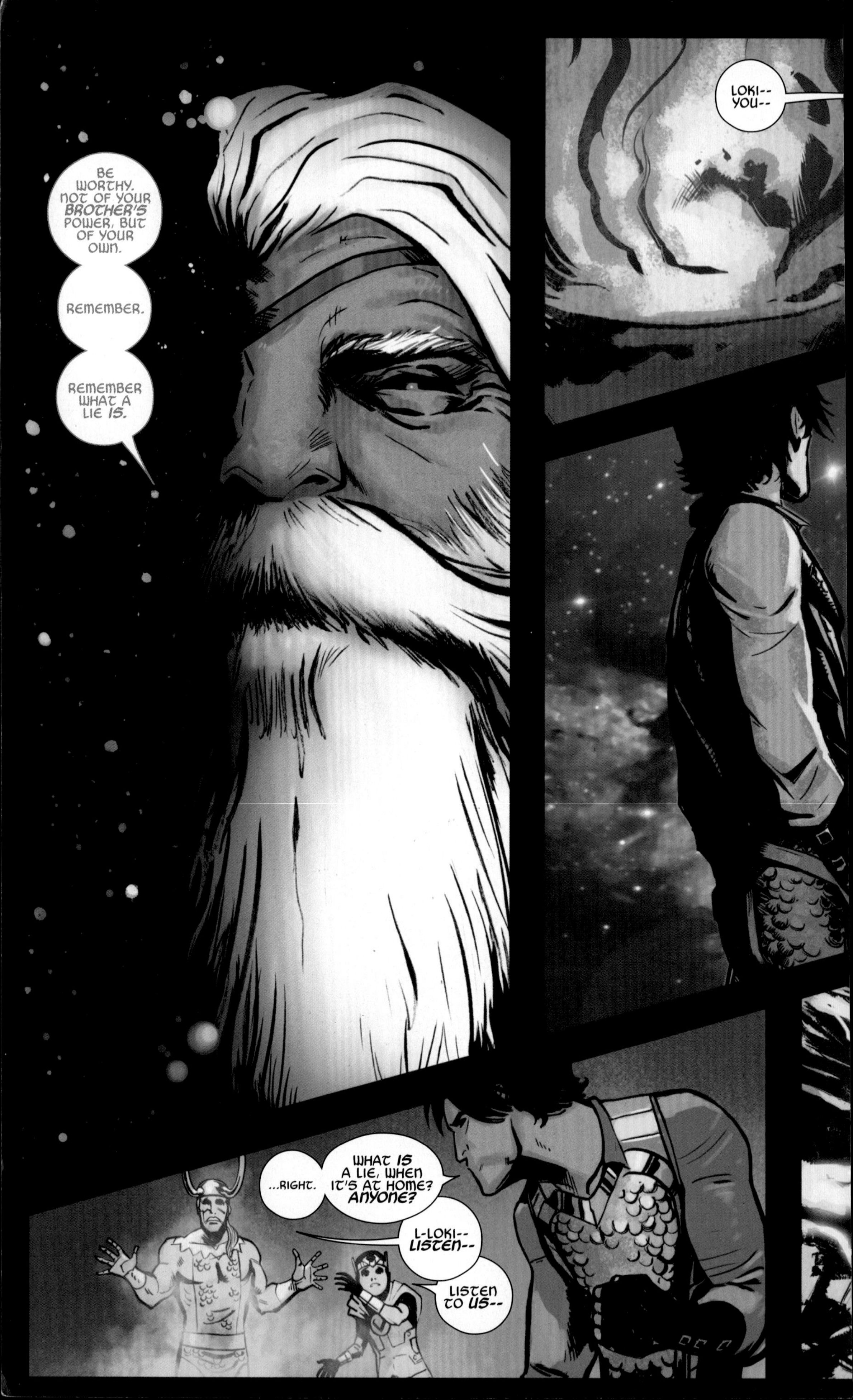
BE WORTHY. NOT OF YOUR BROTHER'S POWER, BUT OF YOUR OWN.
REMEMBER.
REMEMBER WHAT A LIE IS.
LOKI-- YOU--
...RIGHT.
WHAT IS A LIE, WHEN IT'S AT HOME? ANYONE?
L-LOKI-- LISTEN--
LISTEN TO US--

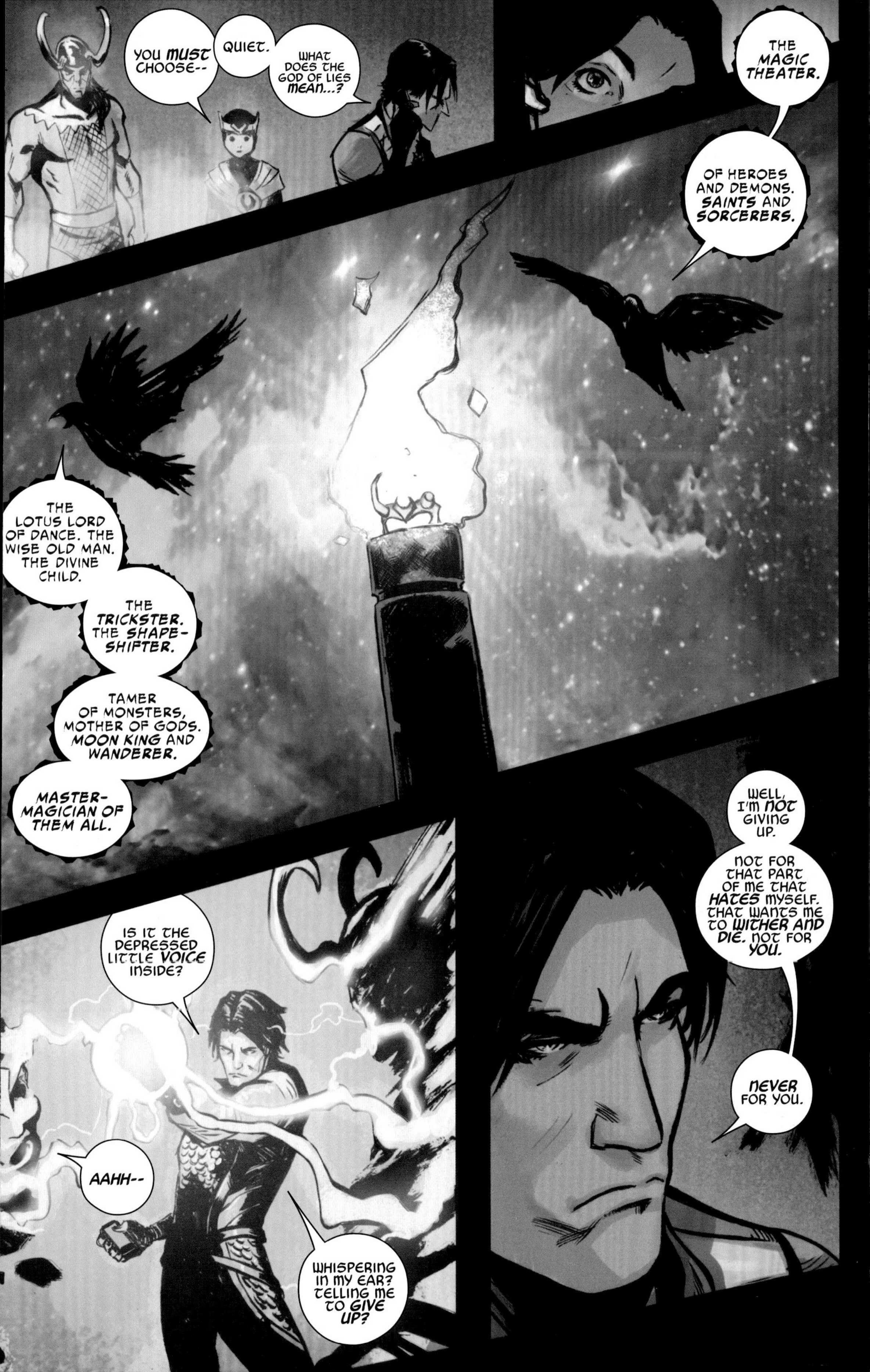

YOU MUST CHOOSE--
QUIET.
WHAT DOES THE GOD OF LIES MEAN...?
THE MAGIC THEATER.
OF HEROES AND DEMONS. SAINTS AND SORCERERS.
THE LOTUS LORD OF DANCE. THE WISE OLD MAN. THE DIVINE CHILD.
THE TRICKSTER. THE SHAPE-SHIFTER.
TAMER OF MONSTERS, MOTHER OF GODS. MOON KING AND WANDERER.
MASTER-MAGICIAN OF THEM ALL.
IS IT THE DEPRESSED LITTLE VOICE INSIDE?
AAHH--
WHISPERING IN MY EAR? TELLING ME TO GIVE UP?
WELL, I'M NOT GIVING UP.
NOT FOR THAT PART OF ME THAT HATES MYSELF. THAT WANTS ME TO WITHER AND DIE. NOT FOR YOU.
NEVER FOR YOU.

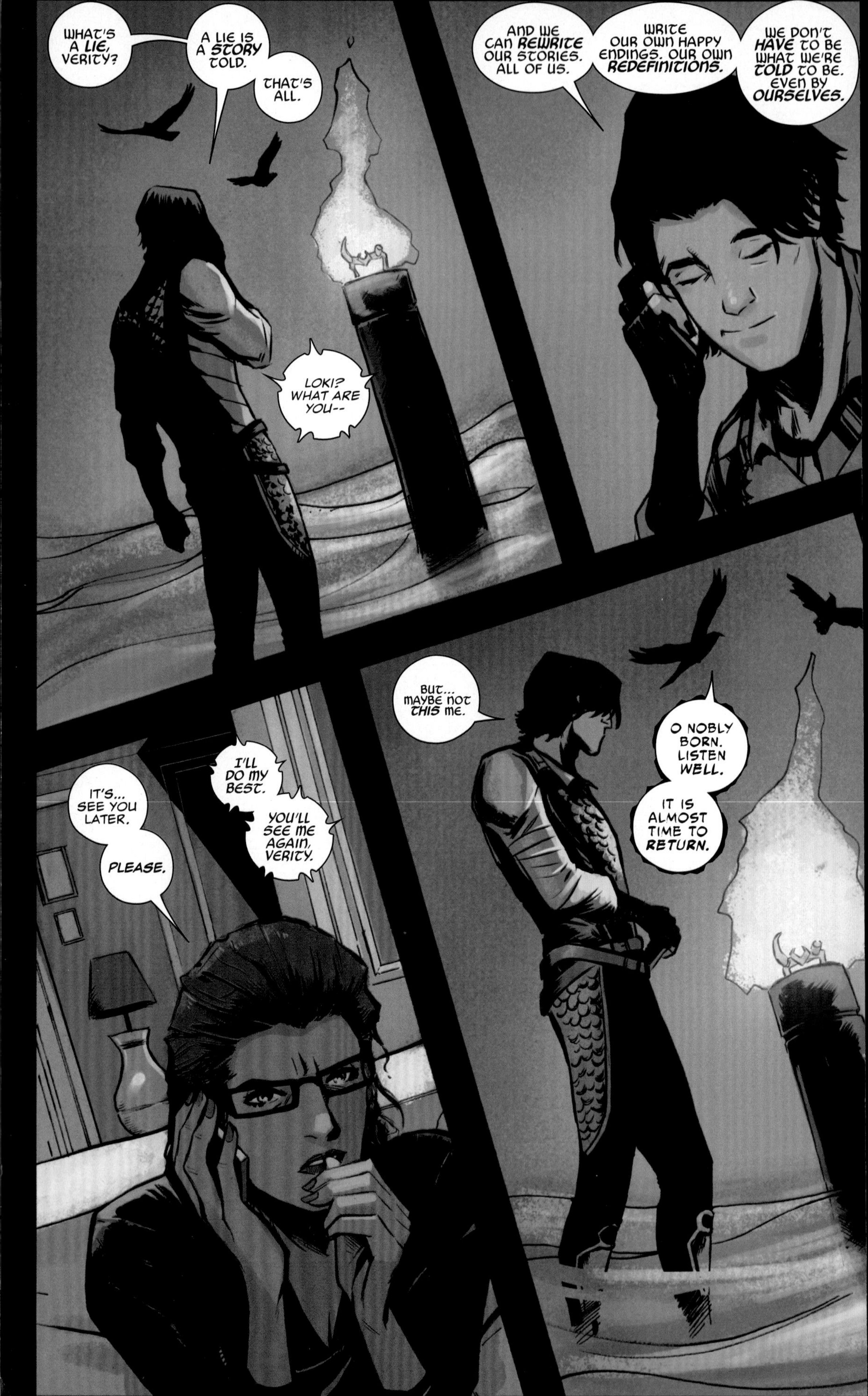
WHAT'S A LIE, VERITY?
A LIE IS A STORY TOLD.
THAT'S ALL.
LOKI? WHAT ARE YOU--
AND WE CAN REWRITE OUR STORIES. ALL OF US.
WRITE OUR OWN HAPPY ENDINGS. OUR OWN REDEFINITIONS.
WE DON'T HAVE TO BE WHAT WE'RE TOLD TO BE. EVEN BY OURSELVES.
IT'S... SEE YOU LATER.
PLEASE.
I'LL DO MY BEST.
YOU'LL SEE ME AGAIN, VERITY.
BUT... MAYBE NOT THIS ME.
O NOBLY BORN. LISTEN WELL.
IT IS ALMOST TIME TO RETURN.

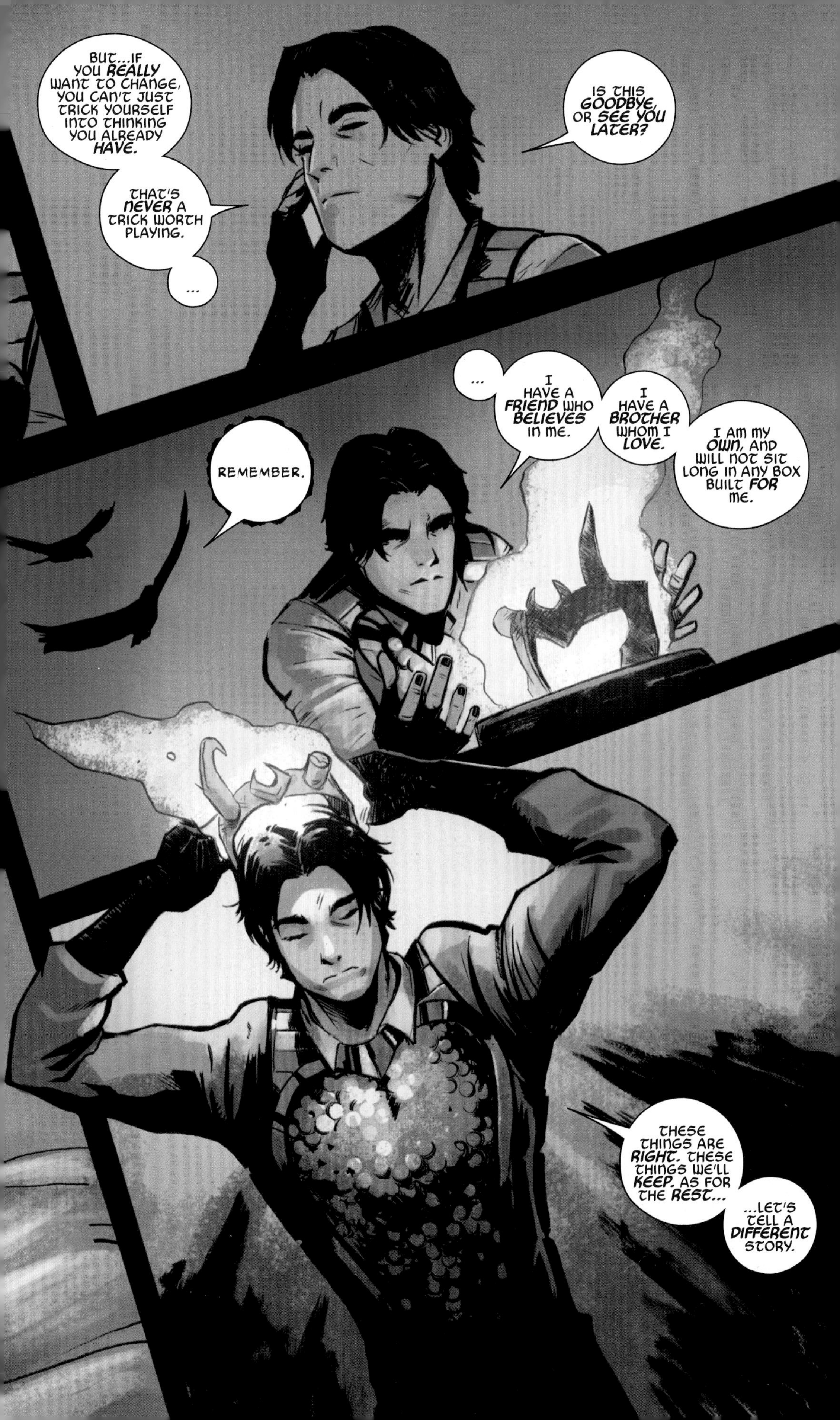
BUT...IF YOU REALLY WANT TO CHANGE, YOU CAN'T JUST TRICK YOURSELF INTO THINKING YOU ALREADY HAVE.
THAT'S NEVER A TRICK WORTH PLAYING.
...
IS THIS GOODBYE, OR SEE YOU LATER?
REMEMBER.
...
I HAVE A FRIEND WHO BELIEVES IN ME.
I HAVE A BROTHER WHOM I LOVE.
I AM MY OWN, AND WILL NOT SIT LONG IN ANY BOX BUILT FOR ME.
THESE THINGS ARE RIGHT. THESE THINGS WE'LL KEEP. AS FOR THE REST...
...LET'S TELL A DIFFERENT STORY.

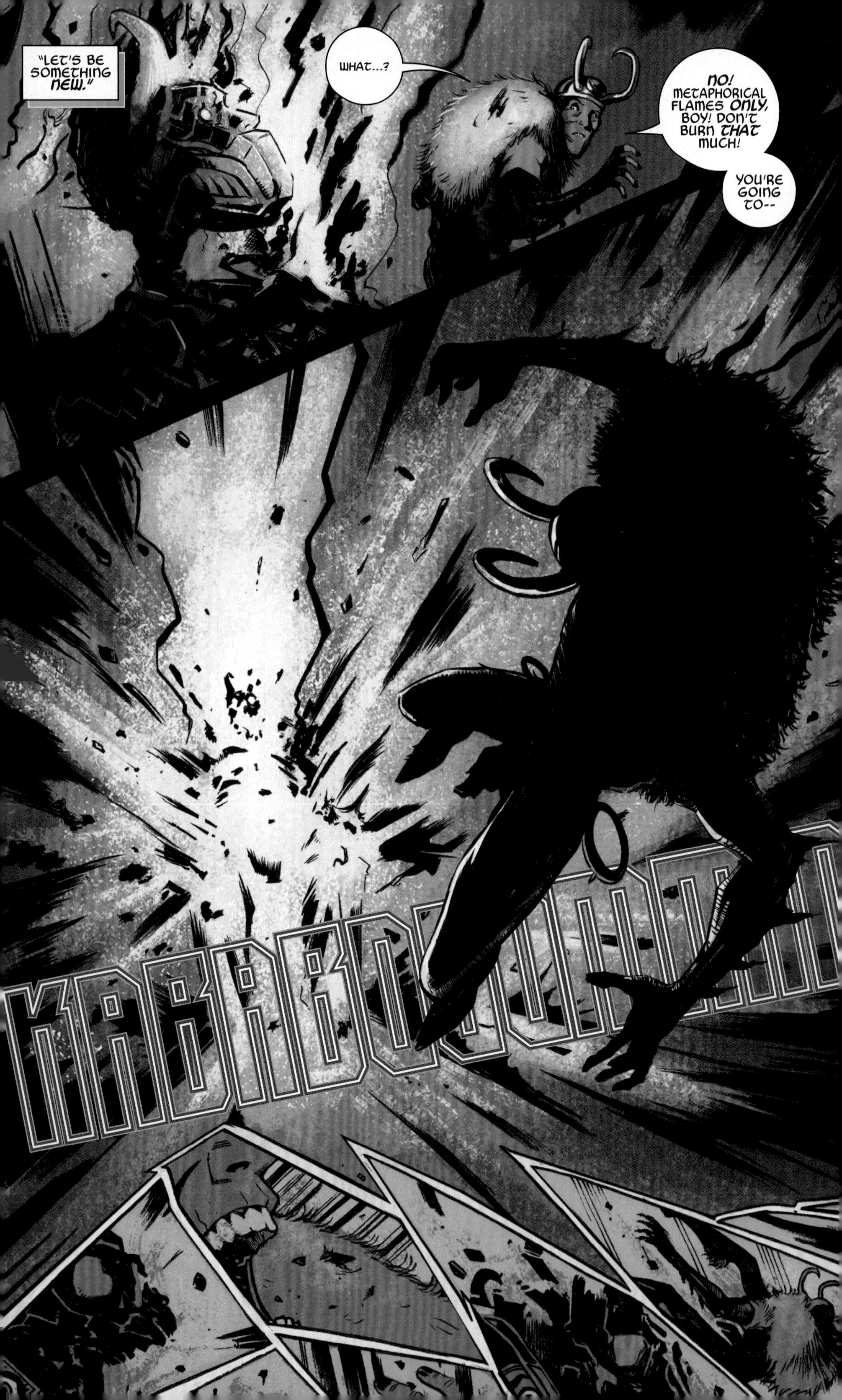

"LET'S BE SOMETHING NEW."
WHAT...?
NO! METAPHORICAL FLAMES ONLY, BOY! DON'T BURN THAT MUCH!
YOU'RE GOING TO--
KRABOOOOM

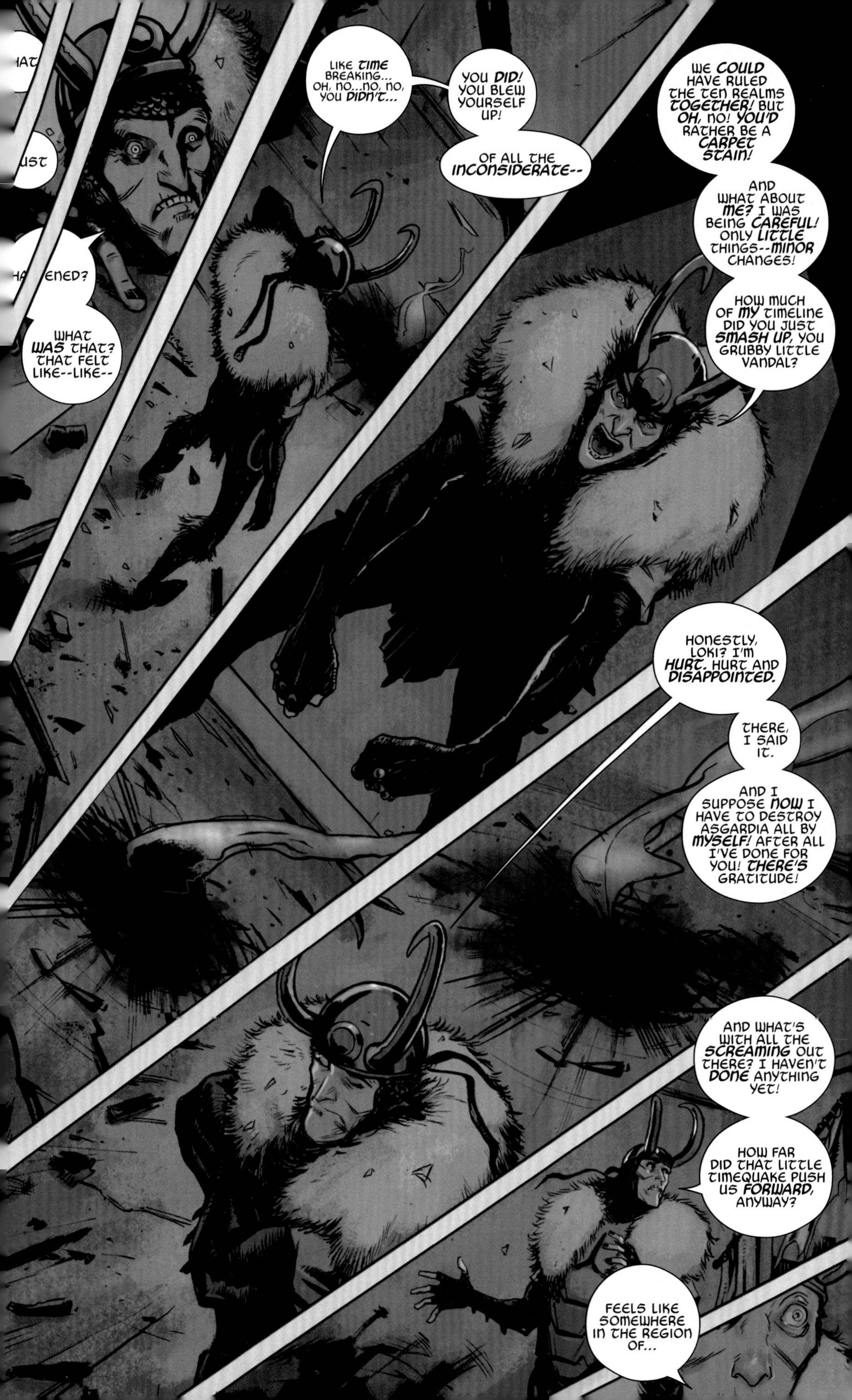
WHAT WAS THAT? THAT FELT LIKE--LIKE--
LIKE TIME BREAKING... OH, NO...NO, NO, YOU DIDN'T...
YOU DID! YOU BLEW YOURSELF UP!
OF ALL THE INCONSIDERATE--
WE COULD HAVE RULED THE TEN REALMS TOGETHER! BUT OH, NO! YOU'D RATHER BE A CARPET STAIN!
AND WHAT ABOUT ME? I WAS BEING CAREFUL! ONLY LITTLE THINGS--MINOR CHANGES!
HOW MUCH OF MY TIMELINE DID YOU JUST SMASH UP, YOU GRUBBY LITTLE VANDAL?
HONESTLY, LOKI? I'M HURT. HURT AND DISAPPOINTED.
THERE, I SAID IT.
AND I SUPPOSE NOW I HAVE TO DESTROY ASGARDIA ALL BY MYSELF! AFTER ALL I'VE DONE FOR YOU! THERE'S GRATITUDE!
AND WHAT'S WITH ALL THE SCREAMING OUT THERE? I HAVEN'T DONE ANYTHING YET!
HOW FAR DID THAT LITTLE TIMEQUAKE PUSH US FORWARD, ANYWAY?
FEELS LIKE SOMEWHERE IN THE REGION OF...

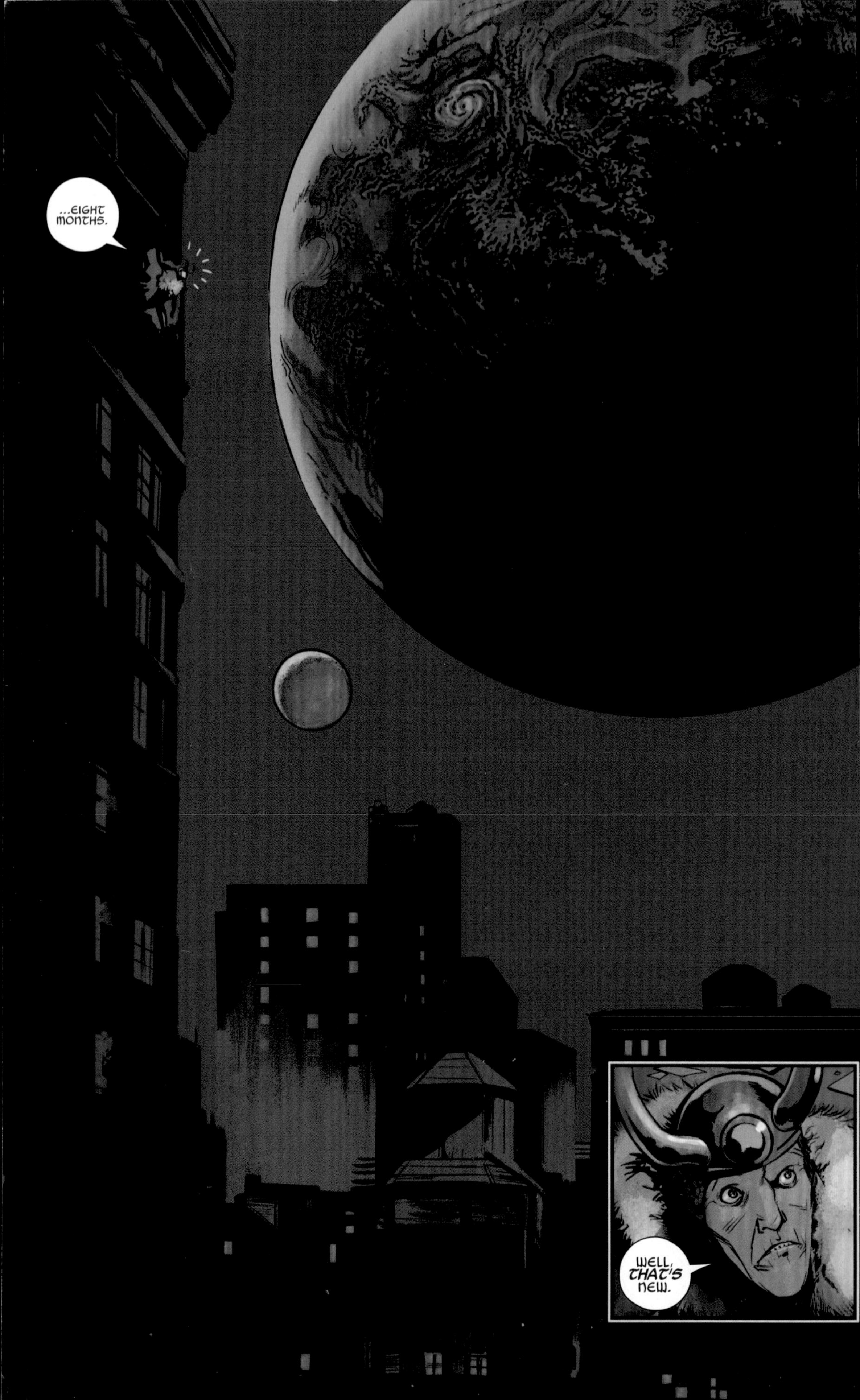
...EIGHT MONTHS.
WELL, THAT'S NEW.

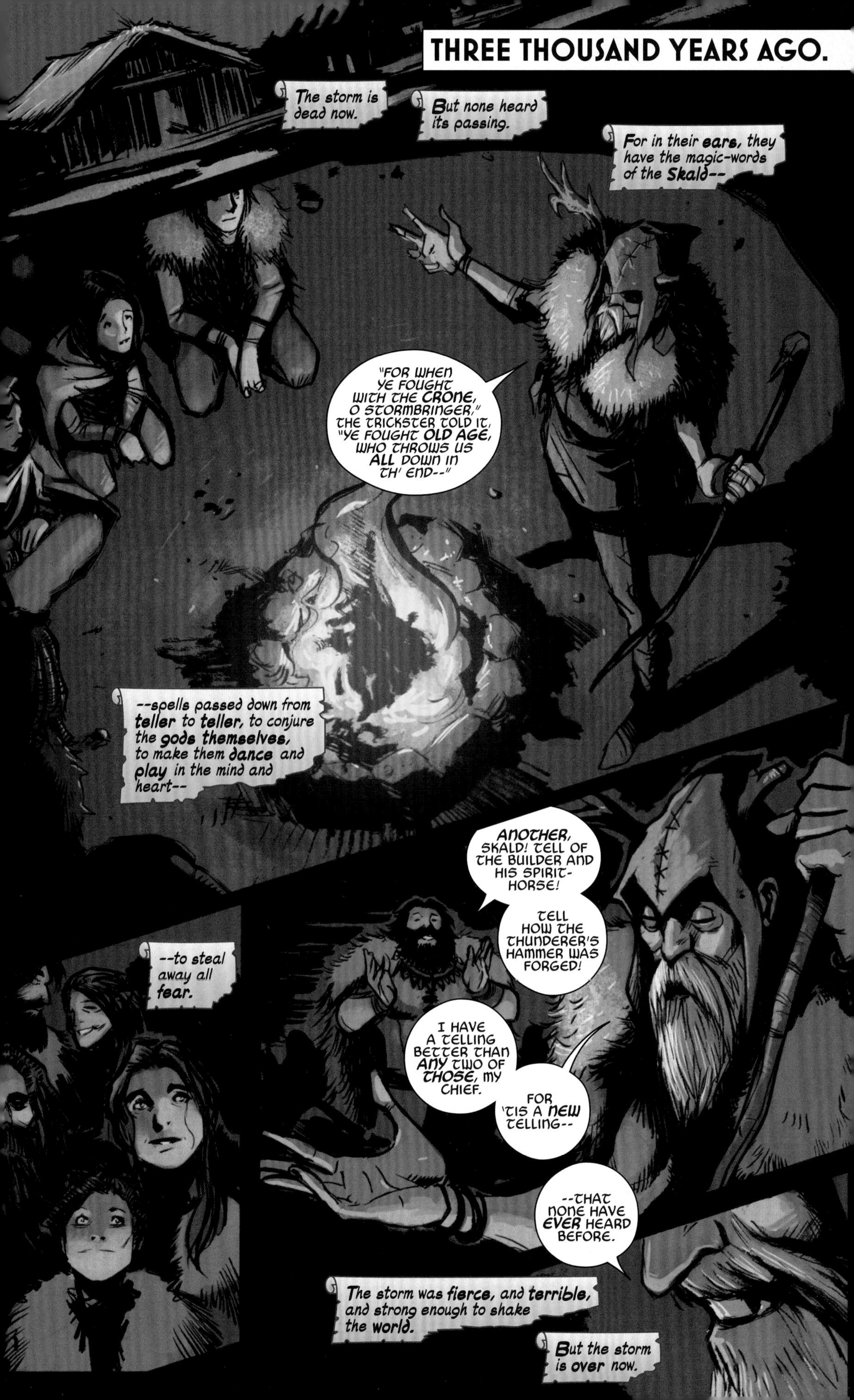
THREE THOUSAND YEARS AGO.
The storm is dead now.
But none heard its passing.
For in their ears, they have the magic-words of the Skald--
"FOR WHEN YE FOUGHT WITH THE CRONE, O STORMBRINGER," THE TRICKSTER TOLD IT, "YE FOUGHT OLD AGE, WHO THROWS US ALL DOWN IN TH' END--"
--spells passed down from teller to teller, to conjure the gods themselves, to make them dance and play in the mind and heart--
--to steal away all fear.
ANOTHER, SKALD! TELL OF THE BUILDER AND HIS SPIRIT-HORSE!
TELL HOW THE THUNDERER'S HAMMER WAS FORGED!
I HAVE A TELLING BETTER THAN ANY TWO OF THOSE, MY CHIEF.
FOR 'TIS A NEW TELLING--
--THAT NONE HAVE EVER HEARD BEFORE.
The storm was fierce, and terrible, and strong enough to shake the world.
But the storm is over now.

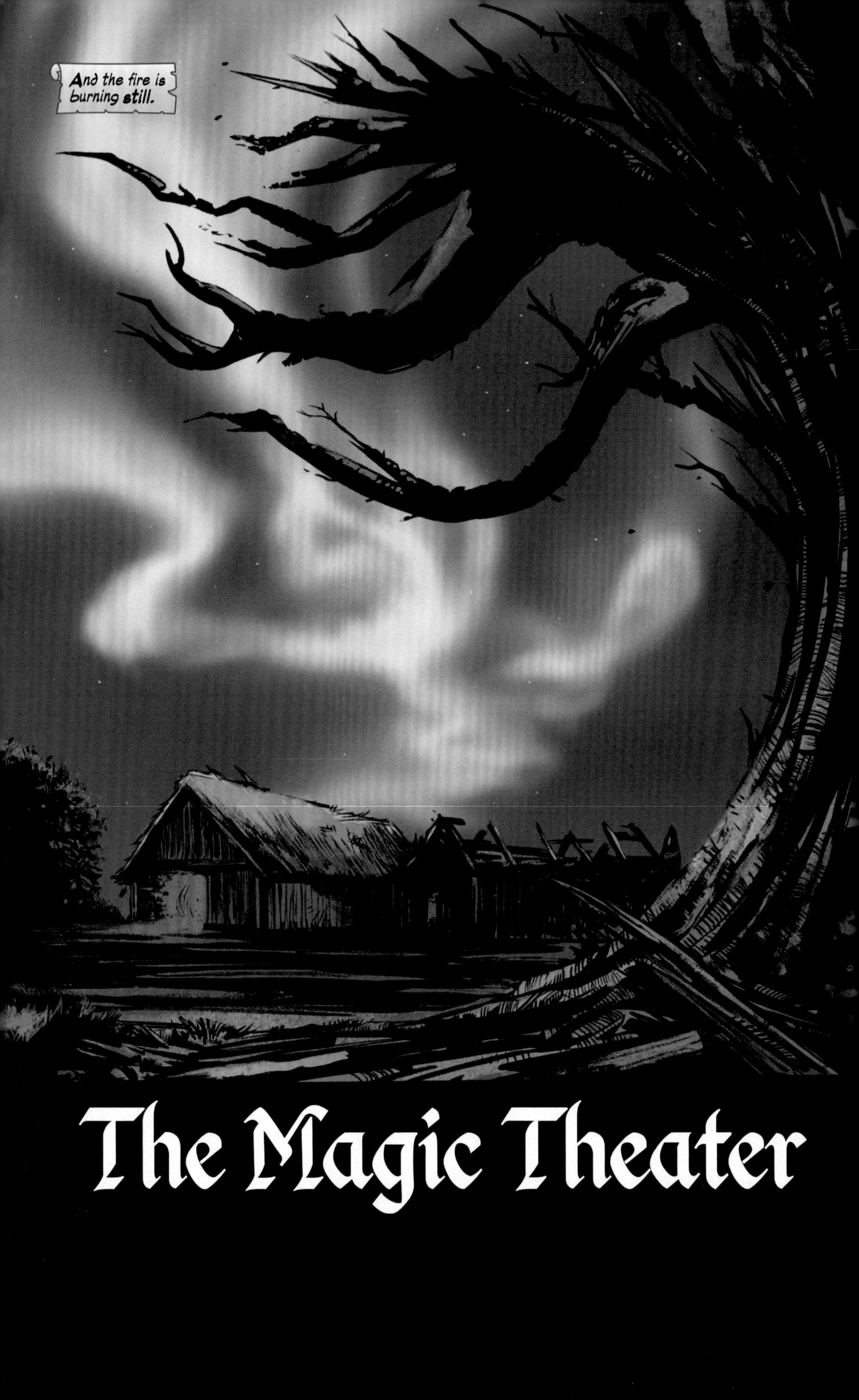
And the fire is burning still.

The Magic Theater

EPILOGUE.

EIGHT MONTHS PASSED.

Verity tried visiting Loki at his apartment, but it was gone--as if it had never been. Which, according to the building ans, it never had. She tried calling around, but Lorelei and Sigurd were imprisoned in the realms of gods, and Thor--or the dinson--didn't have a phone.

So she scoured the news, checking for super-battles and green-gold costumes. Looking for some sign that her friend as alive and okay.

And as she searched, and waited, and worried, she found herself reading.

Reading fiction. Fantasy. Myths and legends. It was painful at first, but over the long months she learned how to tune ıt the constant, nagging whine in the base of her skull that the books were lying to her. Because now, after everything--after oki--she knew that even if the writer thought they were just telling a story…the story could still be true.

It wasn't the same. But it was something. It was a happy ending…

…but it wasn't *the* ending.

Outside, the sky turned red.

There was a knock at the door.

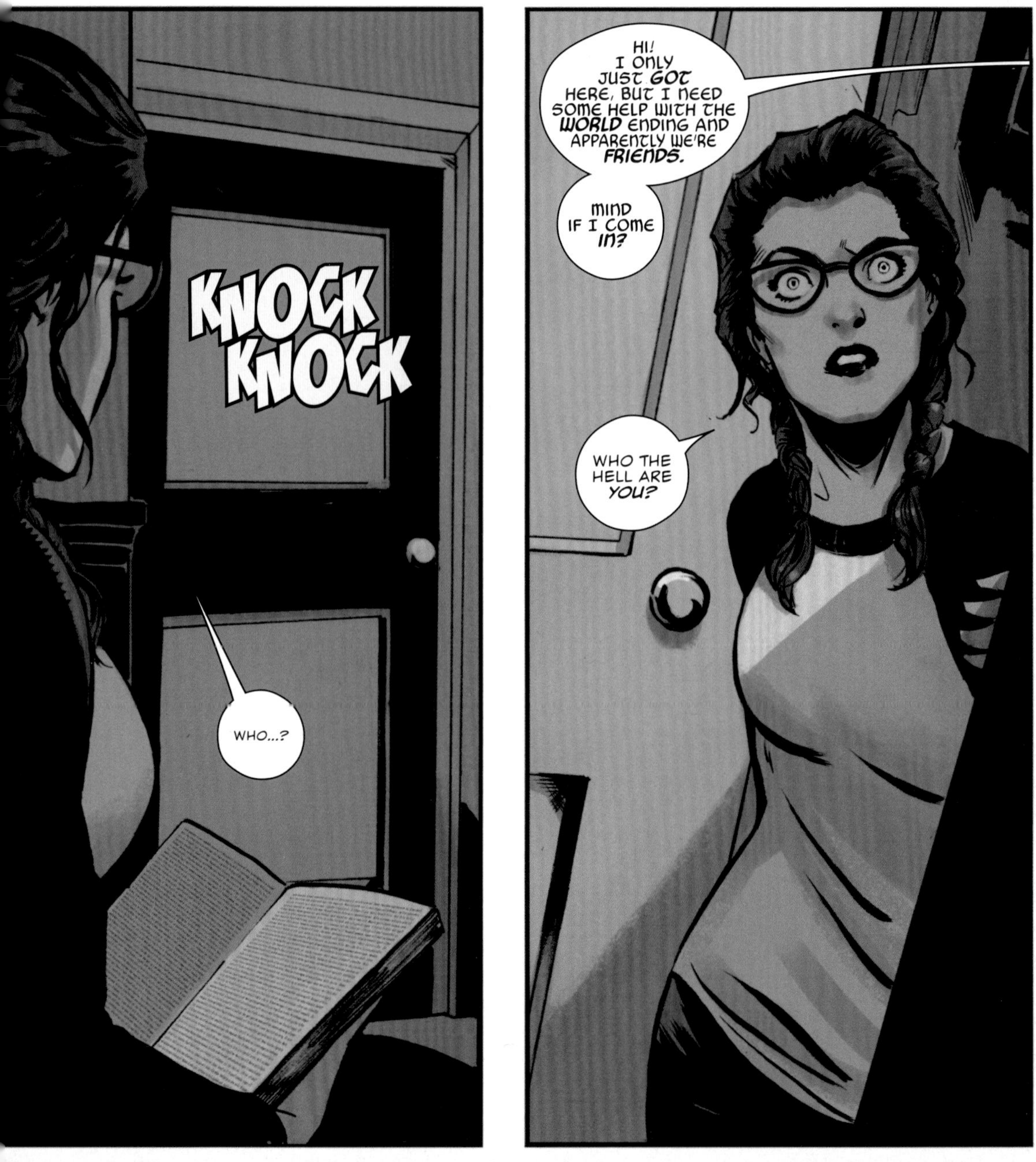
KNOCK KNOCK
WHO...?
HI! I ONLY JUST GOT HERE, BUT I NEED SOME HELP WITH THE WORLD ENDING AND APPARENTLY WE'RE FRIENDS.
MIND IF I COME IN?
WHO THE HELL ARE YOU?

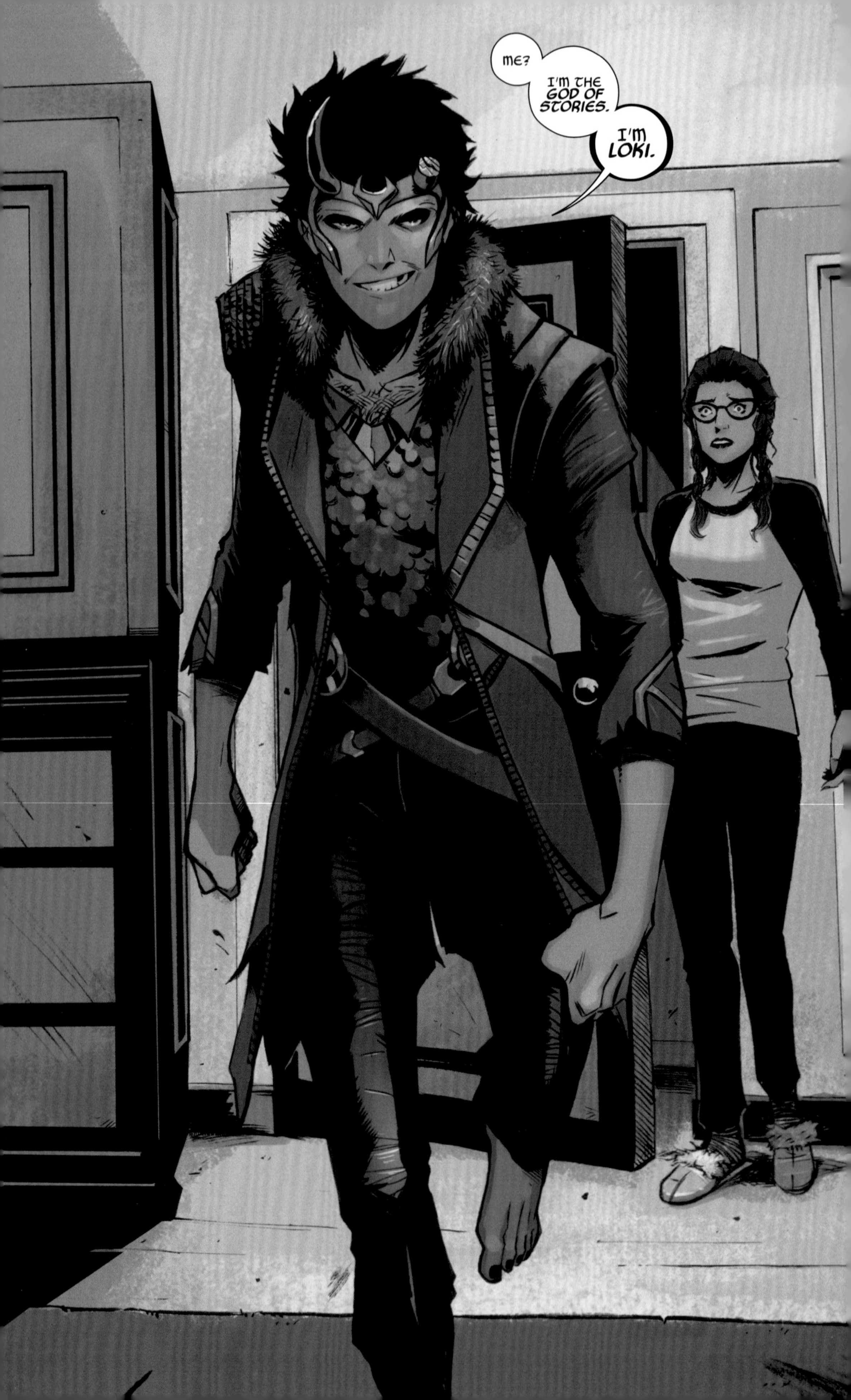
ME?
I'M THE GOD OF STORIES.
I'M LOKI.

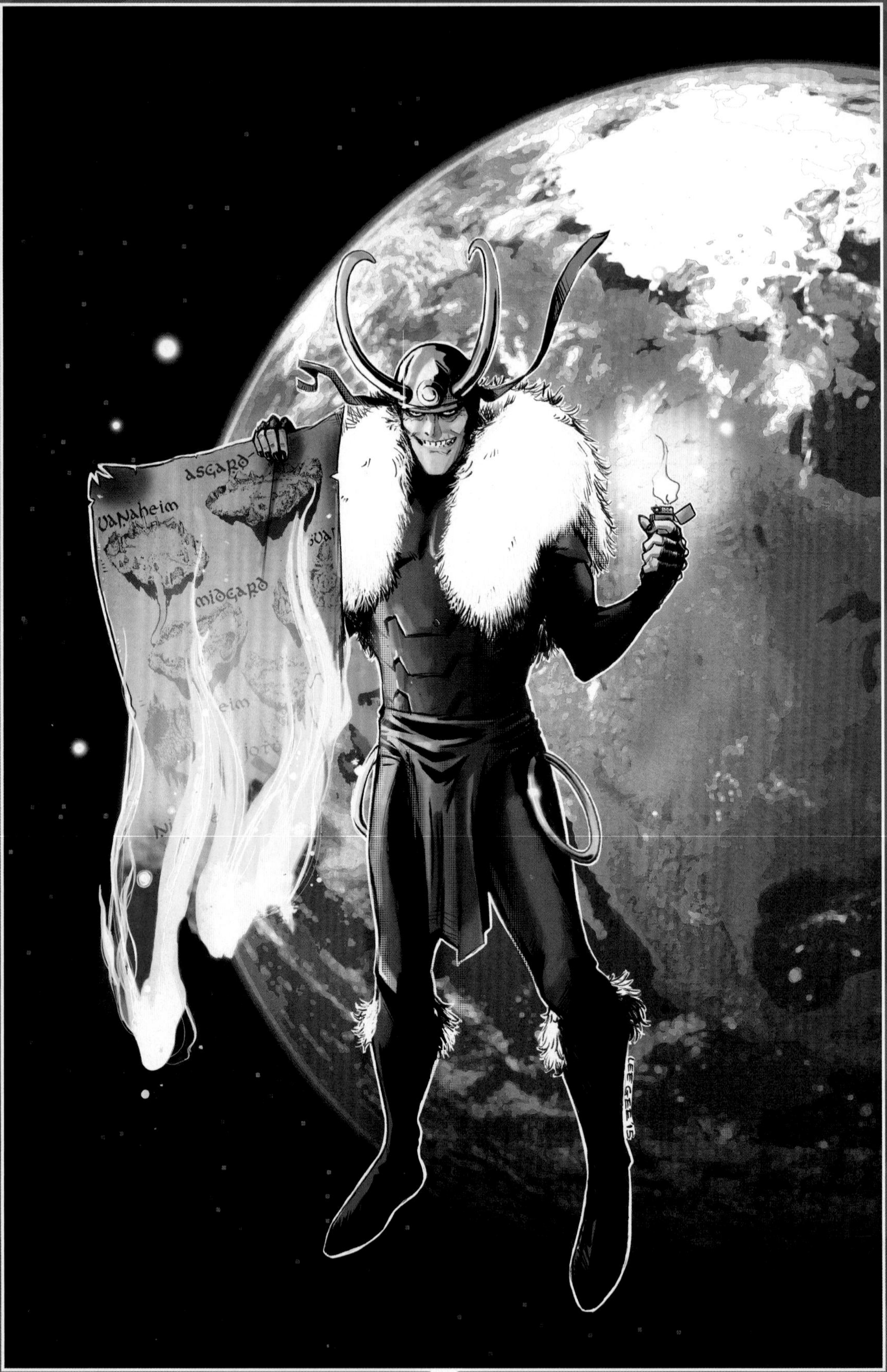
ASGARD
VANAHEIM
MIDGARD

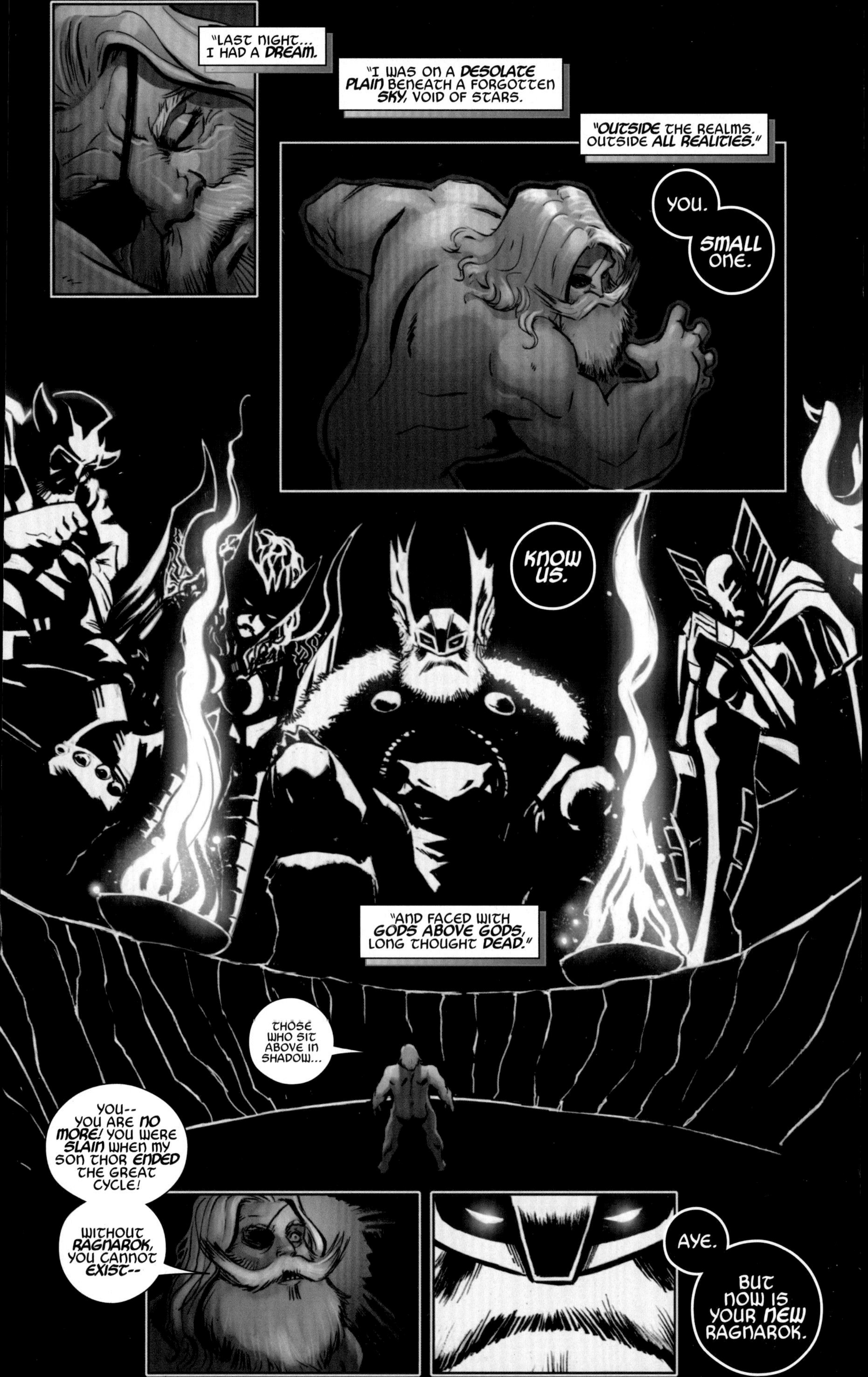
"LAST NIGHT... I HAD A DREAM.
"I WAS ON A DESOLATE PLAIN BENEATH A FORGOTTEN SKY, VOID OF STARS.
"OUTSIDE THE REALMS. OUTSIDE ALL REALITIES."
YOU.
SMALL ONE.
KNOW US.
"AND FACED WITH GODS ABOVE GODS, LONG THOUGHT DEAD."
THOSE WHO SIT ABOVE IN SHADOW...
YOU-- YOU ARE NO MORE! YOU WERE SLAIN WHEN MY SON THOR ENDED THE GREAT CYCLE!
WITHOUT RAGNAROK, YOU CANNOT EXIST--
AYE.
BUT NOW IS YOUR NEW RAGNAROK.

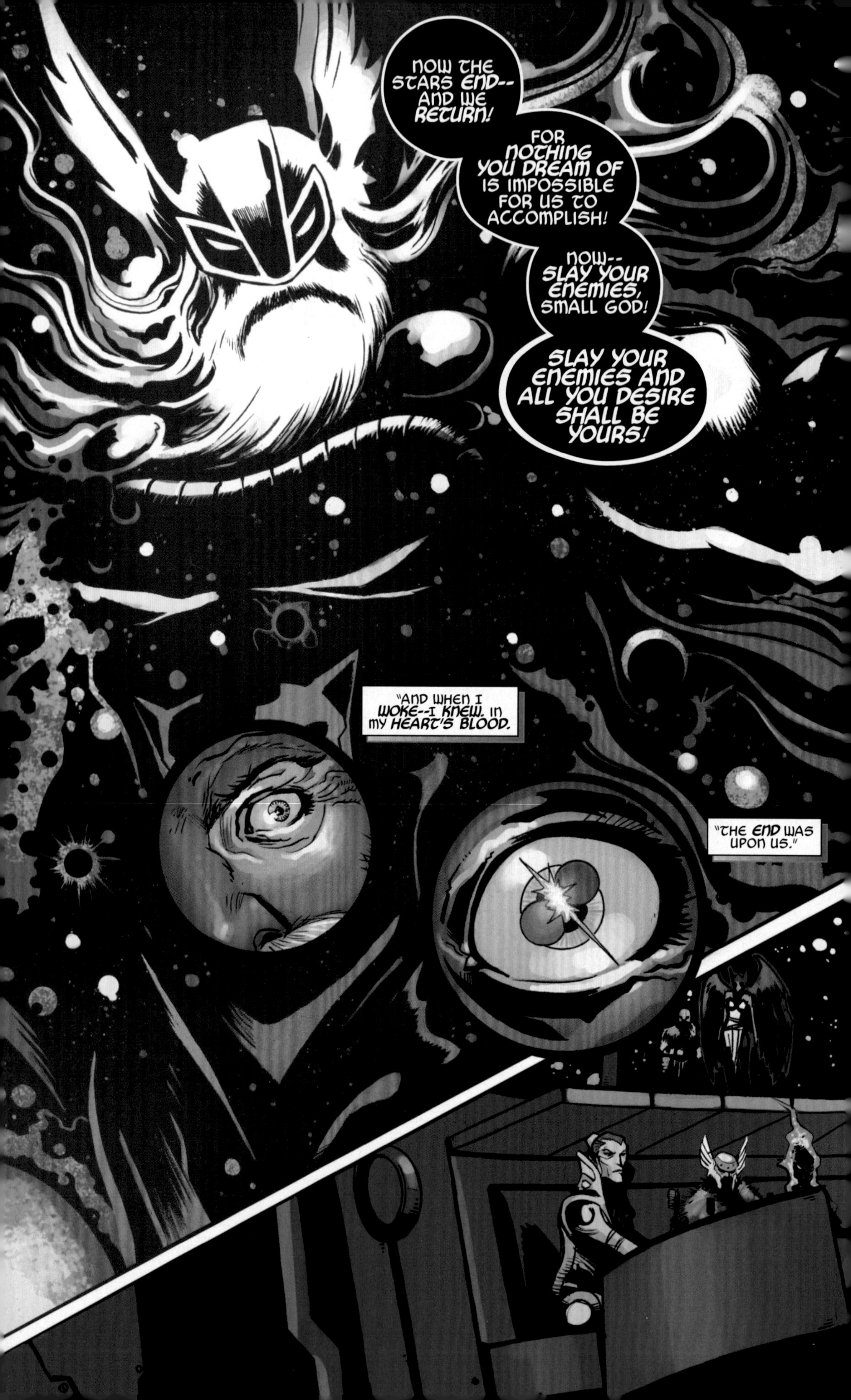
NOW THE STARS END--AND WE RETURN!
FOR NOTHING YOU DREAM OF IS IMPOSSIBLE FOR US TO ACCOMPLISH!
NOW--SLAY YOUR ENEMIES, SMALL GOD!
SLAY YOUR ENEMIES AND ALL YOU DESIRE SHALL BE YOURS!
"AND WHEN I WOKE--I KNEW. IN MY HEART'S BLOOD.
"THE END WAS UPON US."

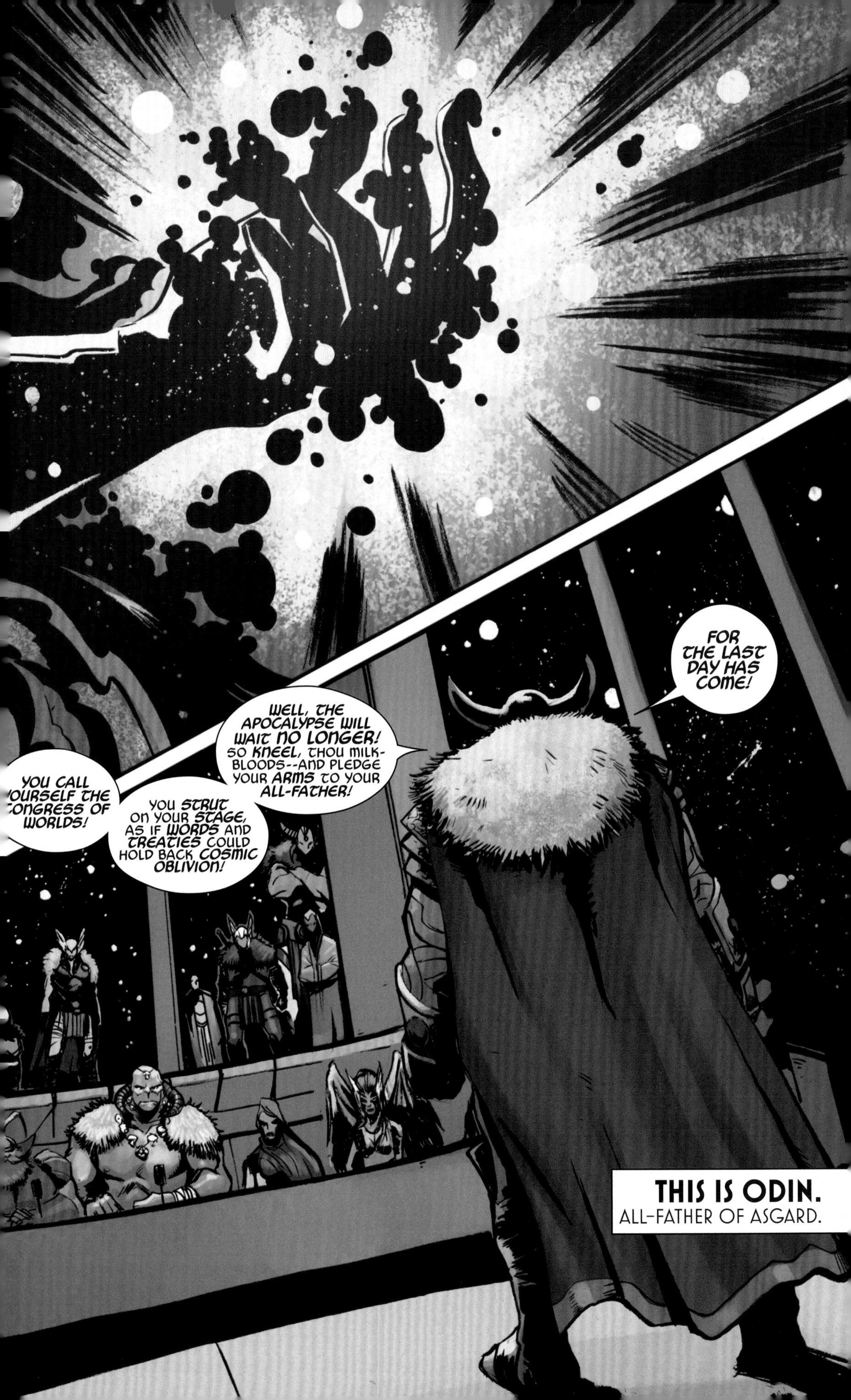
YOU CALL YOURSELF THE CONGRESS OF WORLDS!
YOU STRUT ON YOUR STAGE, AS IF WORDS AND TREATIES COULD HOLD BACK COSMIC OBLIVION!
WELL, THE APOCALYPSE WILL WAIT NO LONGER! SO KNEEL, THOU MILK-BLOODS--AND PLEDGE YOUR ARMS TO YOUR ALL-FATHER!
FOR THE LAST DAY HAS COME!
THIS IS ODIN.
ALL-FATHER OF ASGARD.

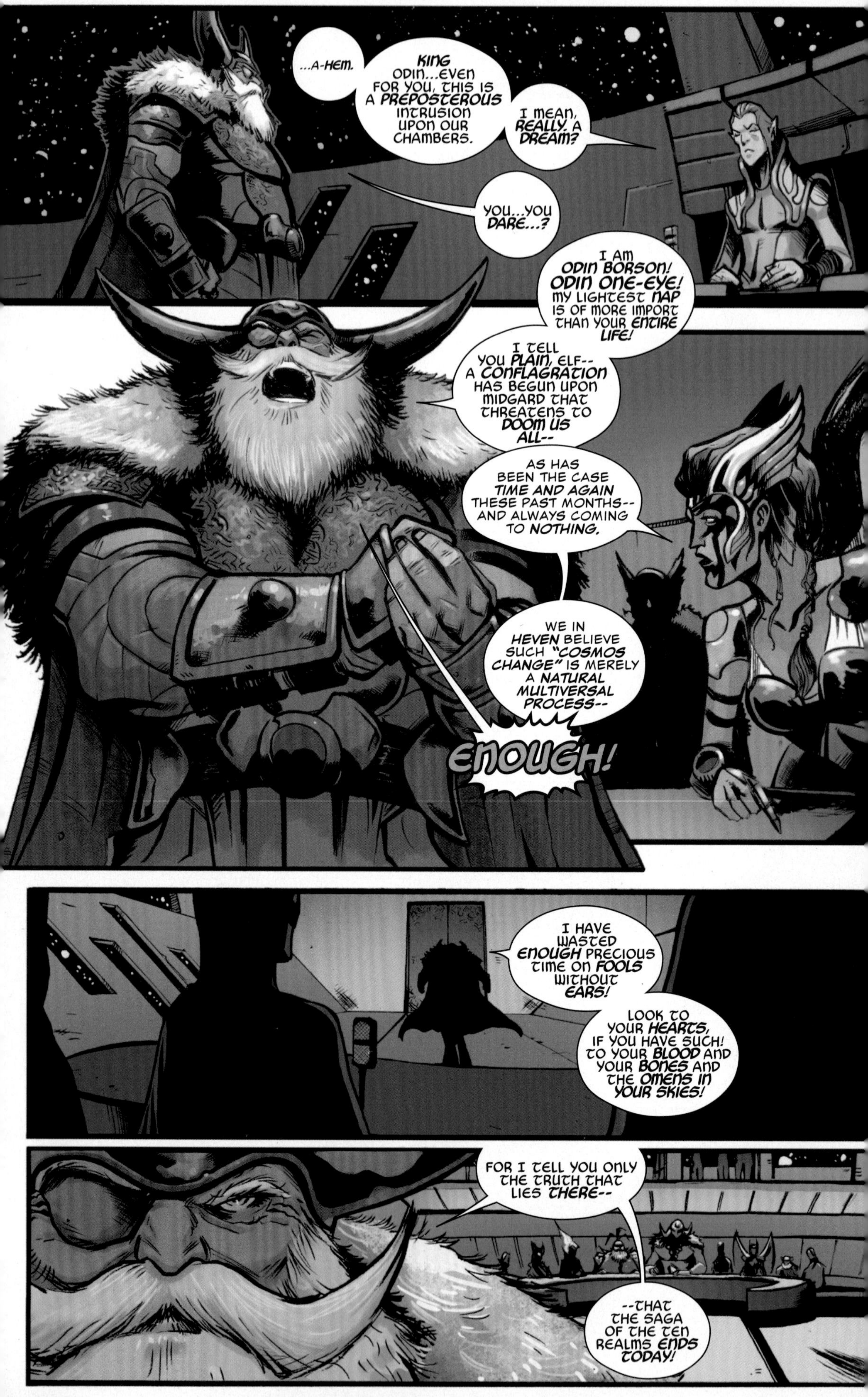
...A-HEM.
KING ODIN...EVEN FOR YOU, THIS IS A PREPOSTEROUS INTRUSION UPON OUR CHAMBERS.
I MEAN, REALLY. A DREAM?
YOU...YOU DARE...?
I AM ODIN BORSON! ODIN ONE-EYE! MY LIGHTEST NAP IS OF MORE IMPORT THAN YOUR ENTIRE LIFE!
I TELL YOU PLAIN, ELF--A CONFLAGRATION HAS BEGUN UPON MIDGARD THAT THREATENS TO DOOM US ALL--
AS HAS BEEN THE CASE TIME AND AGAIN THESE PAST MONTHS--AND ALWAYS COMING TO NOTHING.
WE IN HEVEN BELIEVE SUCH "COSMOS CHANGE" IS MERELY A NATURAL MULTIVERSAL PROCESS--
ENOUGH!
I HAVE WASTED ENOUGH PRECIOUS TIME ON FOOLS WITHOUT EARS!
LOOK TO YOUR HEARTS, IF YOU HAVE SUCH! TO YOUR BLOOD AND YOUR BONES AND THE OMENS IN YOUR SKIES!
FOR I TELL YOU ONLY THE TRUTH THAT LIES THERE--
--THAT THE SAGA OF THE TEN REALMS ENDS TODAY!

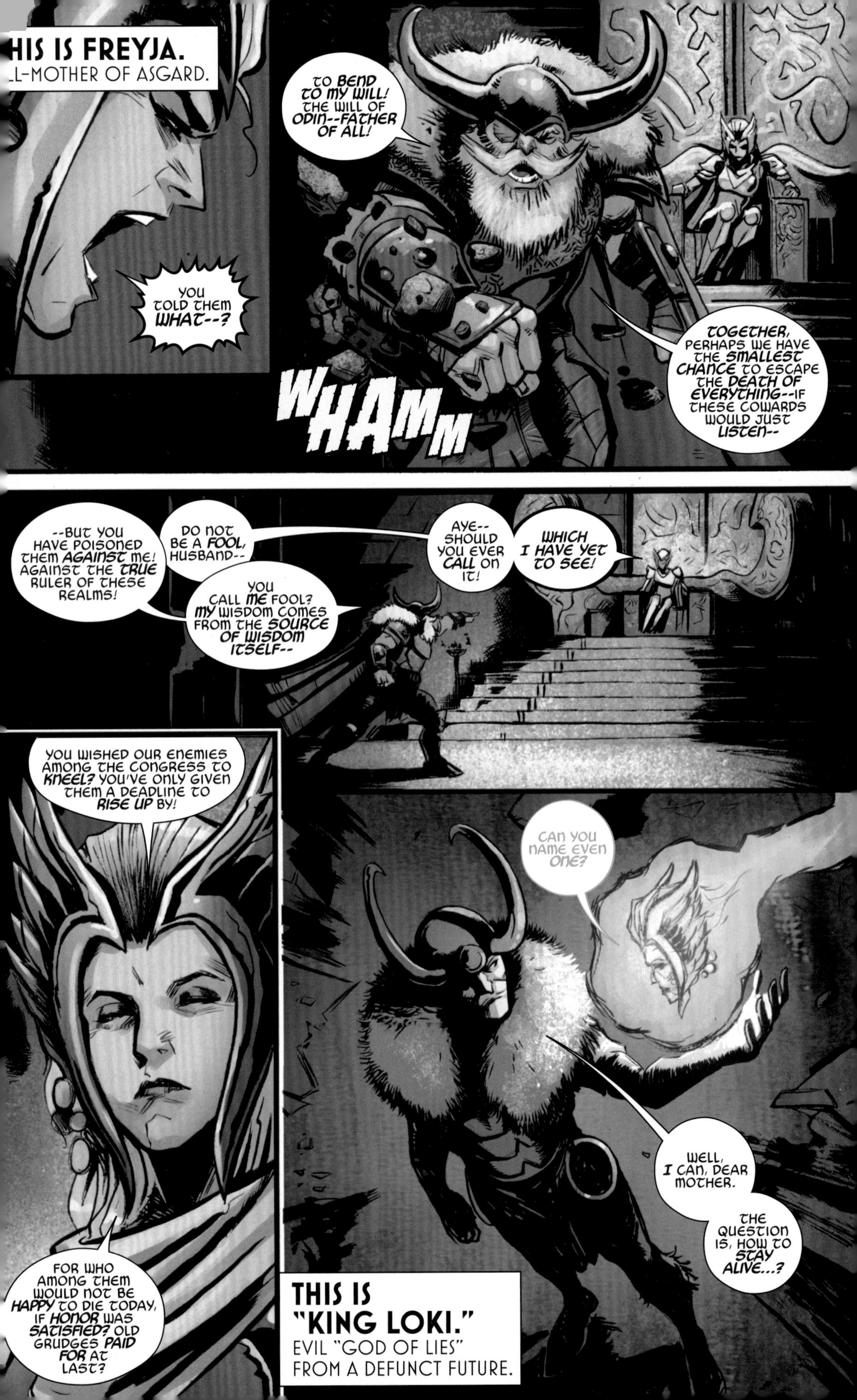

THIS IS FREYJA.
LL-MOTHER OF ASGARD.
TO BEND TO MY WILL! THE WILL OF ODIN--FATHER OF ALL!
YOU TOLD THEM WHAT--?
WHAMM
TOGETHER, PERHAPS WE HAVE THE SMALLEST CHANCE TO ESCAPE THE DEATH OF EVERYTHING--IF THESE COWARDS WOULD JUST LISTEN--
--BUT YOU HAVE POISONED THEM AGAINST ME! AGAINST THE TRUE RULER OF THESE REALMS!
DO NOT BE A FOOL, HUSBAND--
AYE--SHOULD YOU EVER CALL ON IT!
WHICH I HAVE YET TO SEE!
YOU CALL ME FOOL? MY WISDOM COMES FROM THE SOURCE OF WISDOM ITSELF--
YOU WISHED OUR ENEMIES AMONG THE CONGRESS TO KNEEL? YOU'VE ONLY GIVEN THEM A DEADLINE TO RISE UP BY!
FOR WHO AMONG THEM WOULD NOT BE HAPPY TO DIE TODAY, IF HONOR WAS SATISFIED? OLD GRUDGES PAID FOR AT LAST?
CAN YOU NAME EVEN ONE?
WELL, I CAN, DEAR MOTHER.
THE QUESTION IS, HOW TO STAY ALIVE...?
THIS IS "KING LOKI."
EVIL "GOD OF LIES" FROM A DEFUNCT FUTURE.

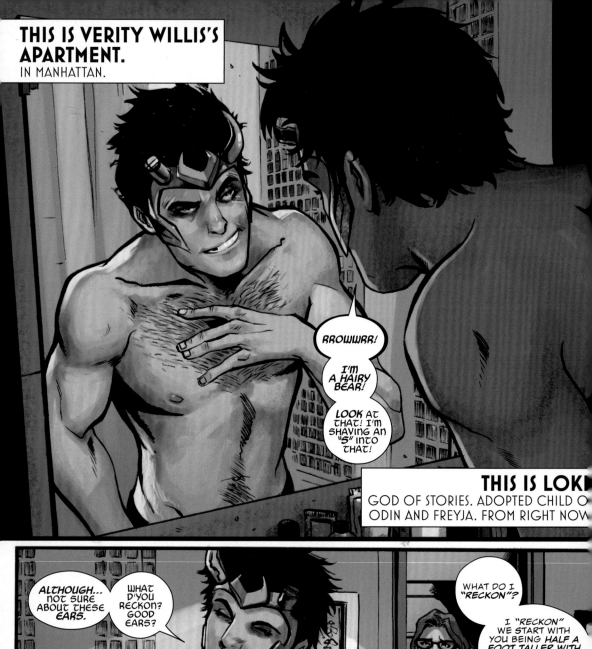

THIS IS VERITY WILLIS'S APARTMENT.
IN MANHATTAN.

BROWWRR!

I'M A HAIRY BEAR!

LOOK AT THAT! I'M SHAVING AN "S" INTO THAT!

THIS IS LOKI
GOD OF STORIES. ADOPTED CHILD O
ODIN AND FREYJA. FROM RIGHT NOW

ALTHOUGH... NOT SURE ABOUT THESE EARS.

WHAT D'YOU RECKON? GOOD EARS?

WHAT DO I "RECKON"?

I "RECKON" WE START WITH YOU BEING HALF A FOOT TALLER WITH A DIFFERENT VOICE! WHERE'S THE REAL LOKI?

THIS IS VERITY.
HUMAN LIE-DETECTOR.

ARE YOU HIM?

IS... IS HE DEAD?

DUNNO. IS SCHRÖDINGER'S CAT?

YOUR CHOICE.

EITHER WAY, HE'S OUT OF THAT BOX.

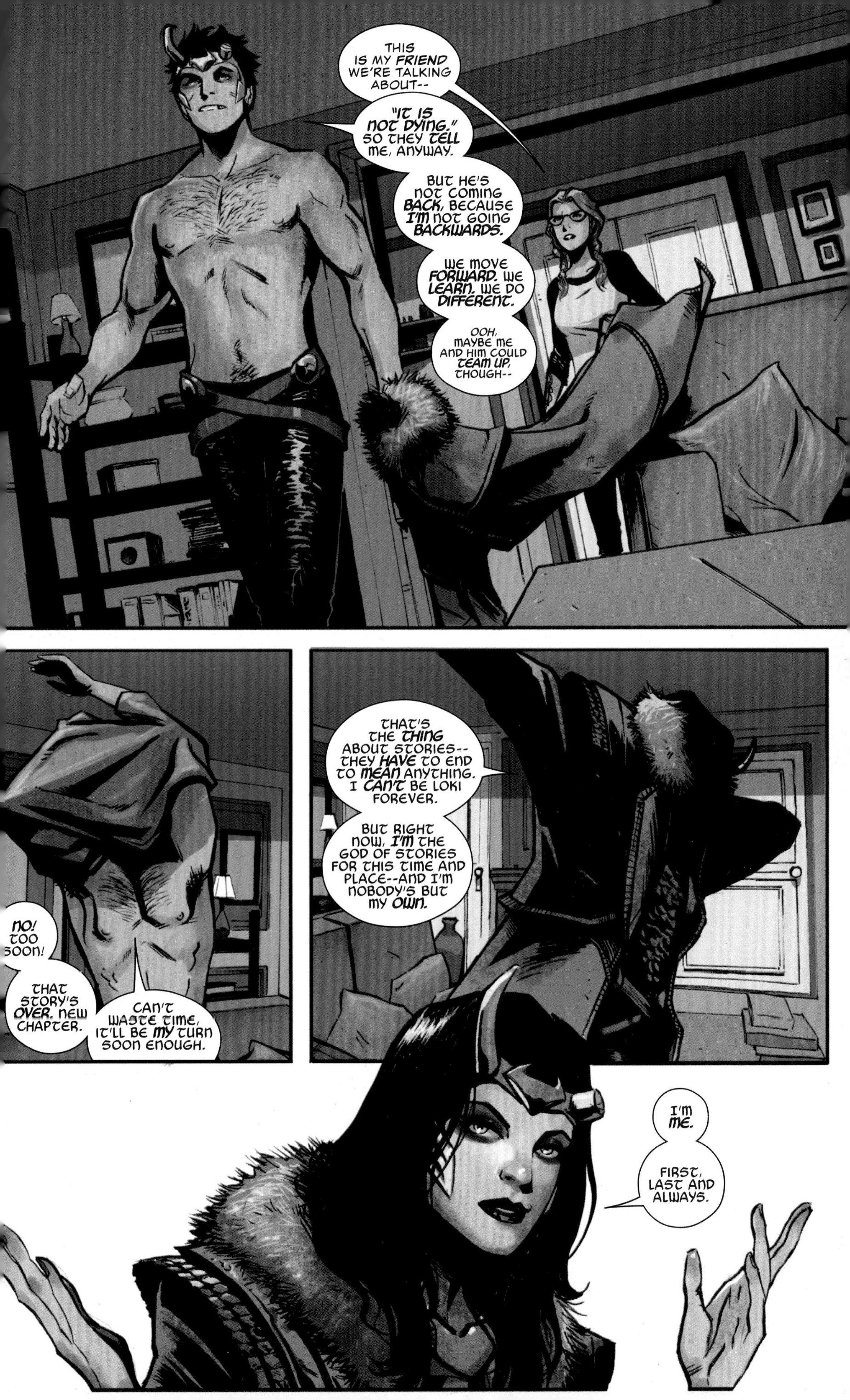
THIS IS MY FRIEND WE'RE TALKING ABOUT--
"IT IS NOT DYING." SO THEY TELL ME, ANYWAY.
BUT HE'S NOT COMING BACK, BECAUSE I'M NOT GOING BACKWARDS.
WE MOVE FORWARD. WE LEARN. WE DO DIFFERENT.
OOH, MAYBE ME AND HIM COULD TEAM UP, THOUGH--
NO! TOO SOON!
THAT STORY'S OVER. NEW CHAPTER.
CAN'T WASTE TIME, IT'LL BE MY TURN SOON ENOUGH.
THAT'S THE THING ABOUT STORIES--THEY HAVE TO END TO MEAN ANYTHING. I CAN'T BE LOKI FOREVER.
BUT RIGHT NOW, I'M THE GOD OF STORIES FOR THIS TIME AND PLACE--AND I'M NOBODY'S BUT MY OWN.
I'M ME.
FIRST, LAST AND ALWAYS.

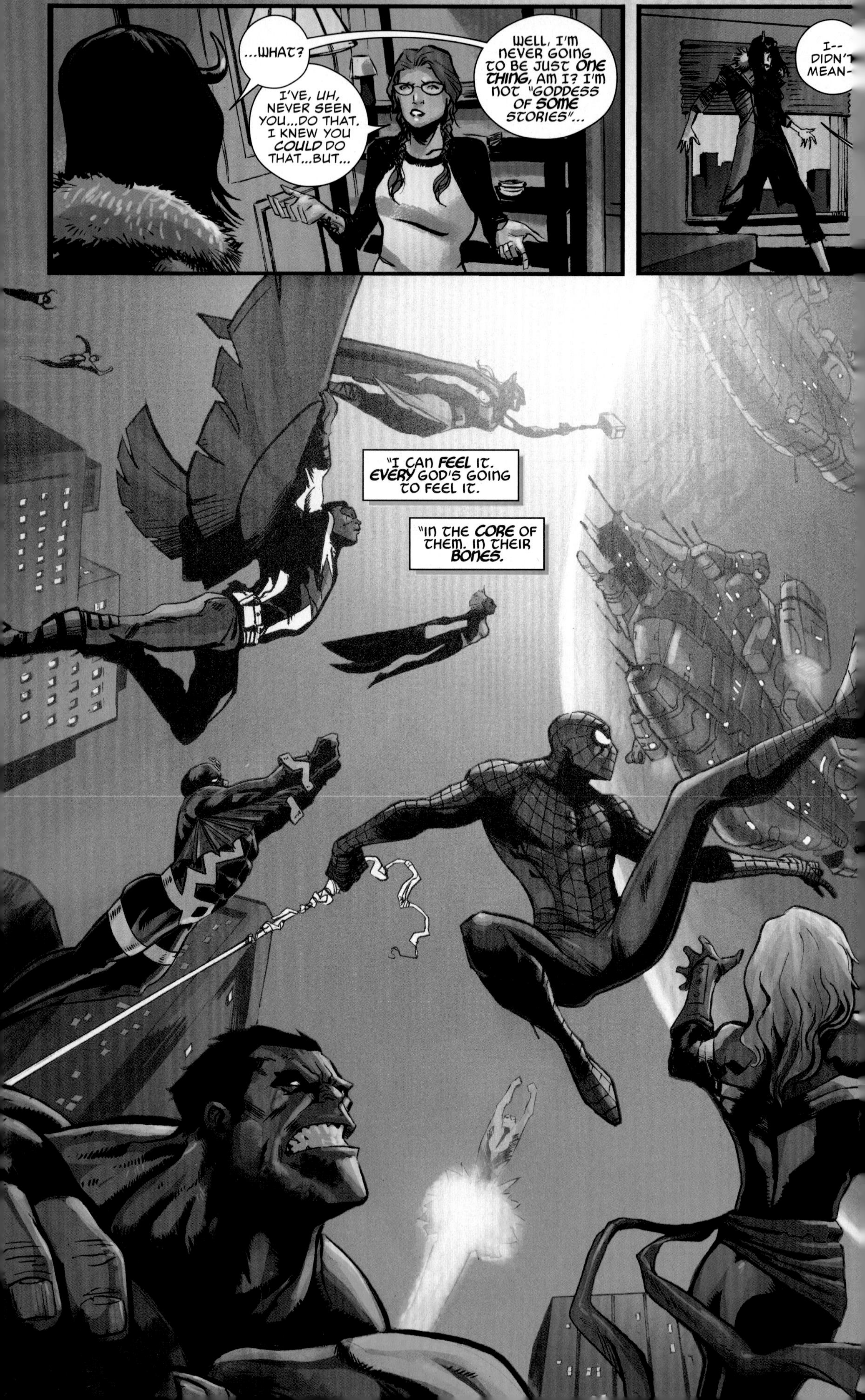
...WHAT?
I'VE, UH, NEVER SEEN YOU...DO THAT. I KNEW YOU COULD DO THAT...BUT...
WELL, I'M NEVER GOING TO BE JUST ONE THING, AM I? I'M NOT "GODDESS OF SOME STORIES"...
I-- DIDN'T MEAN-
"I CAN FEEL IT. EVERY GOD'S GOING TO FEEL IT.
"IN THE CORE OF THEM. IN THEIR BONES.

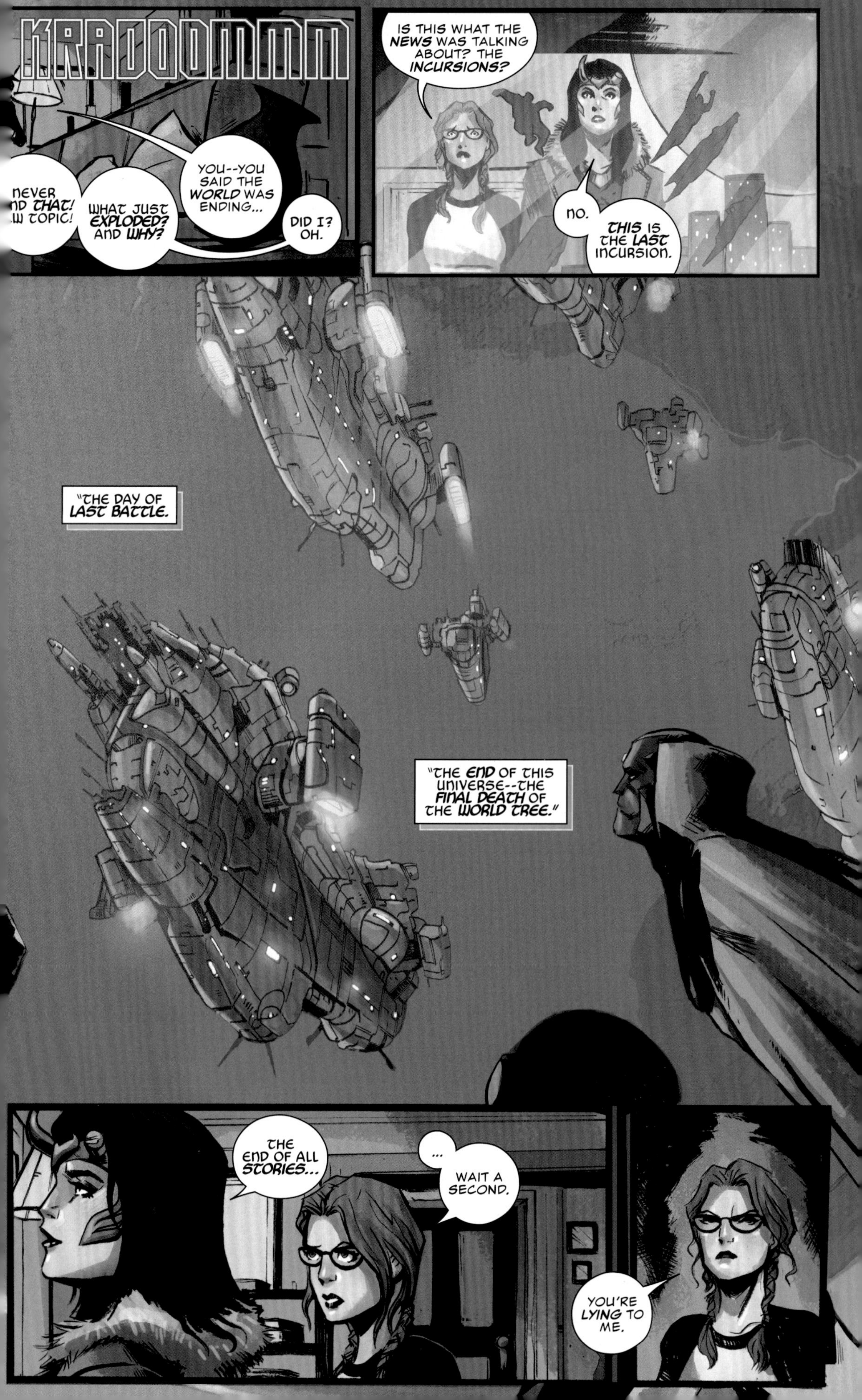
KRADOOMMM
YOU--YOU SAID THE WORLD WAS ENDING...
DID I? OH.
NEVER ...ND THAT! ...W TOPIC!
WHAT JUST EXPLODED? AND WHY?
IS THIS WHAT THE NEWS WAS TALKING ABOUT? THE INCURSIONS?
NO.
THIS IS THE LAST INCURSION.
"THE DAY OF LAST BATTLE.
"THE END OF THIS UNIVERSE--THE FINAL DEATH OF THE WORLD TREE."
THE END OF ALL STORIES...
...
WAIT A SECOND.
YOU'RE LYING TO ME.

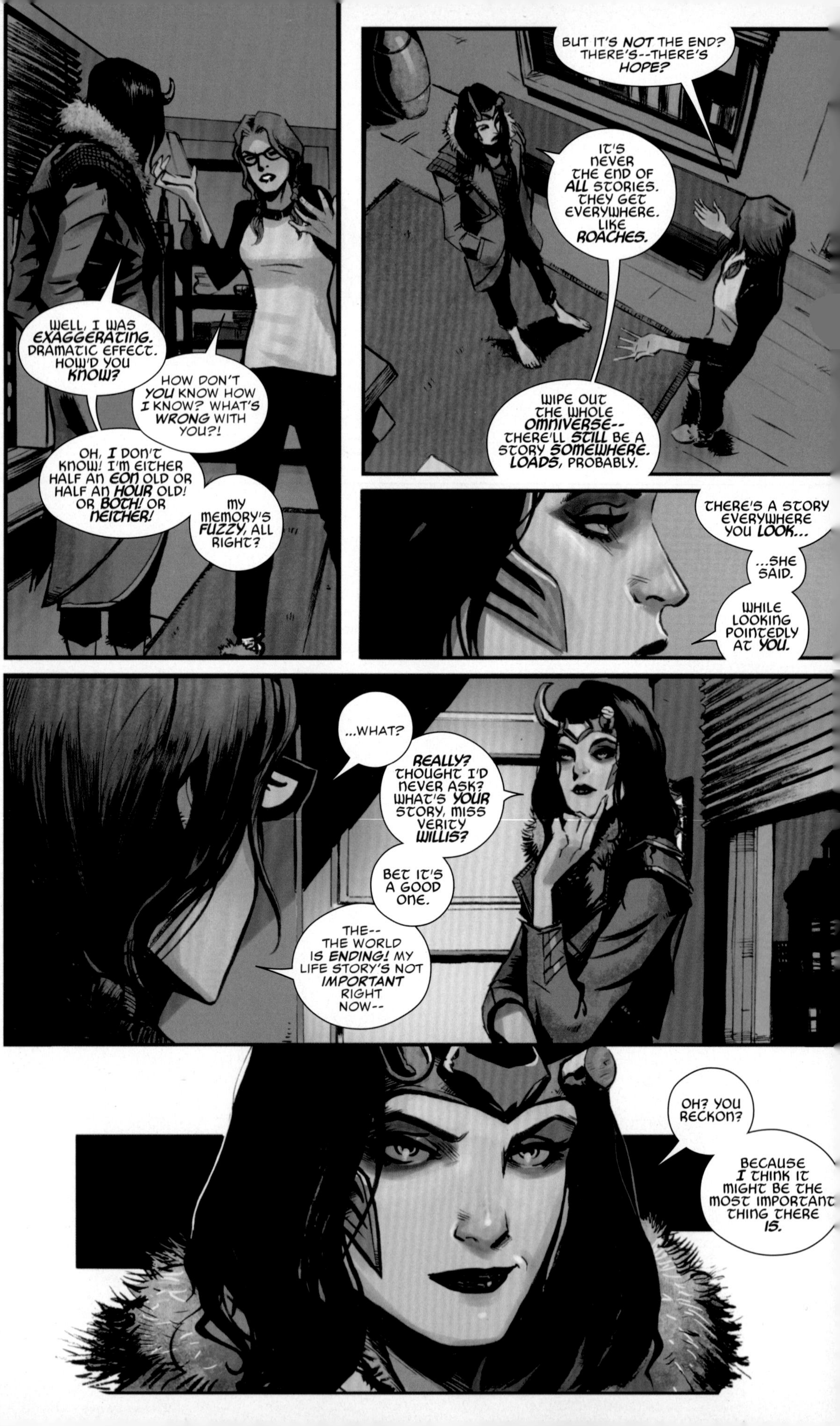
WELL, I WAS EXAGGERATING. DRAMATIC EFFECT. HOW'D YOU KNOW?
HOW DON'T YOU KNOW HOW I KNOW? WHAT'S WRONG WITH YOU?!
OH, I DON'T KNOW! I'M EITHER HALF AN EON OLD OR HALF AN HOUR OLD! OR BOTH! OR NEITHER!
MY MEMORY'S FUZZY, ALL RIGHT?
BUT IT'S NOT THE END? THERE'S--THERE'S HOPE?
IT'S NEVER THE END OF ALL STORIES. THEY GET EVERYWHERE. LIKE ROACHES.
WIPE OUT THE WHOLE OMNIVERSE-- THERE'LL STILL BE A STORY SOMEWHERE. LOADS, PROBABLY.
THERE'S A STORY EVERYWHERE YOU LOOK...
...SHE SAID.
WHILE LOOKING POINTEDLY AT YOU.
...WHAT?
REALLY? THOUGHT I'D NEVER ASK? WHAT'S YOUR STORY, MISS VERITY WILLIS?
BET IT'S A GOOD ONE.
THE-- THE WORLD IS ENDING! MY LIFE STORY'S NOT IMPORTANT RIGHT NOW--
OH? YOU RECKON?
BECAUSE I THINK IT MIGHT BE THE MOST IMPORTANT THING THERE IS.

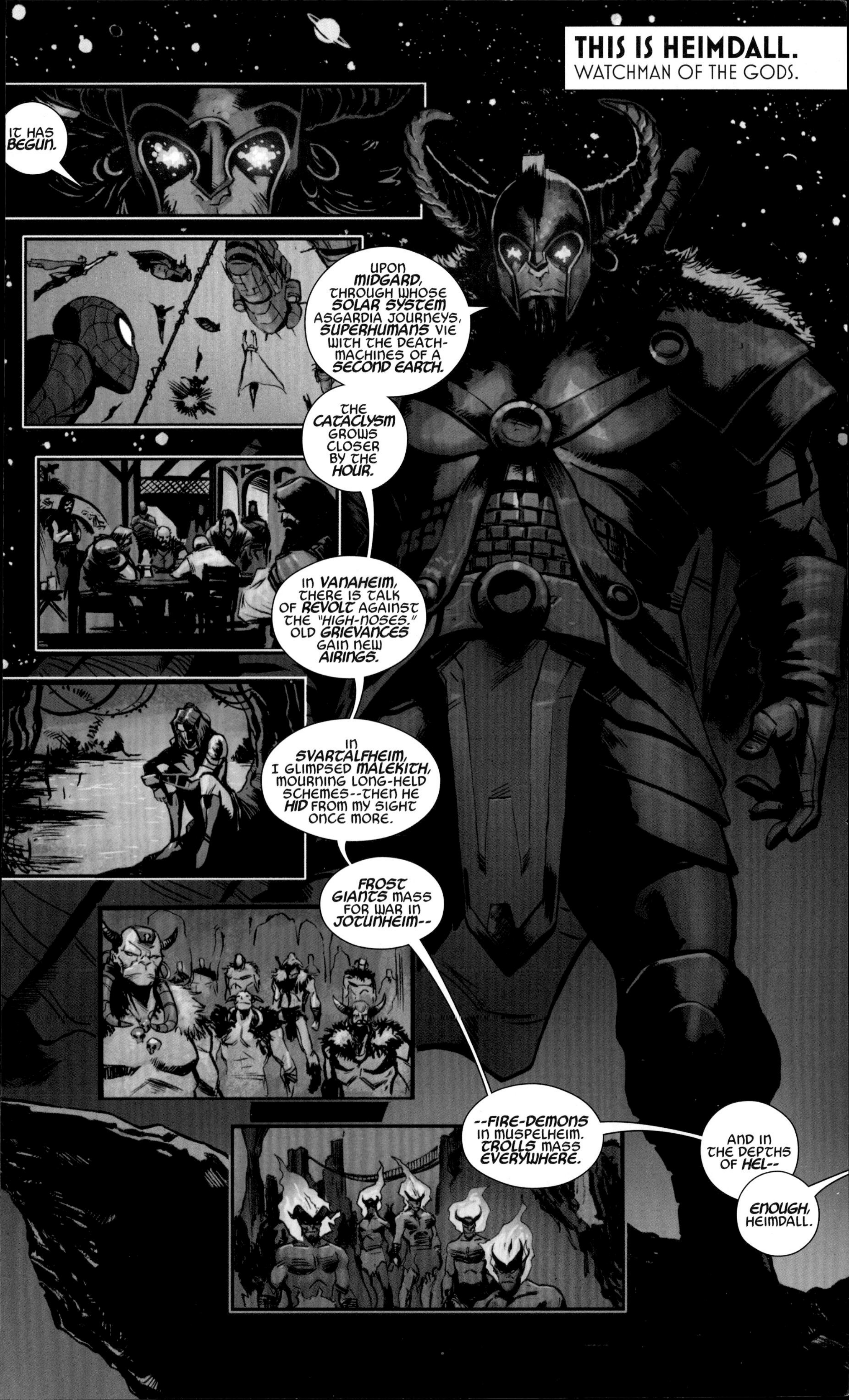
THIS IS HEIMDALL.
WATCHMAN OF THE GODS.
IT HAS BEGUN.
UPON MIDGARD, THROUGH WHOSE SOLAR SYSTEM ASGARDIA JOURNEYS, SUPERHUMANS VIE WITH THE DEATH-MACHINES OF A SECOND EARTH.
THE CATACLYSM GROWS CLOSER BY THE HOUR.
IN VANAHEIM, THERE IS TALK OF REVOLT AGAINST THE "HIGH-NOSES." OLD GRIEVANCES GAIN NEW AIRINGS.
IN SVARTALFHEIM, I GLIMPSED MALEKITH, MOURNING LONG-HELD SCHEMES--THEN HE HID FROM MY SIGHT ONCE MORE.
FROST GIANTS MASS FOR WAR IN JOTUNHEIM--
--FIRE-DEMONS IN MUSPELHEIM. TROLLS MASS EVERYWHERE.
AND IN THE DEPTHS OF HEL--
ENOUGH, HEIMDALL.

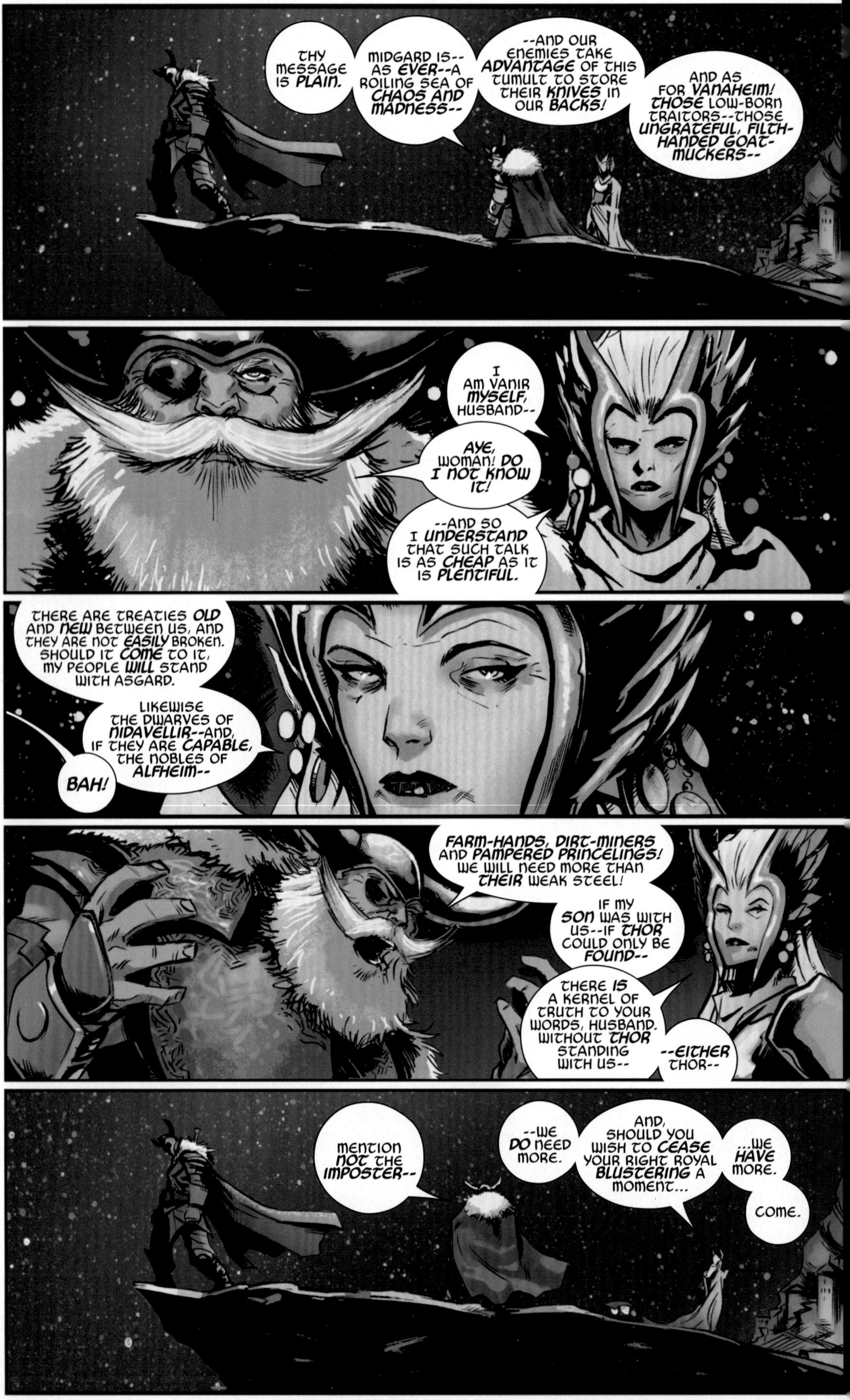
THY MESSAGE IS PLAIN.
MIDGARD IS-- AS EVER--A ROILING SEA OF CHAOS AND MADNESS--
--AND OUR ENEMIES TAKE ADVANTAGE OF THIS TUMULT TO STORE THEIR KNIVES IN OUR BACKS!
AND AS FOR VANAHEIM! THOSE LOW-BORN TRAITORS--THOSE UNGRATEFUL, FILTH-HANDED GOAT-MUCKERS--
I AM VANIR MYSELF, HUSBAND--
AYE, WOMAN! DO I NOT KNOW IT!
--AND SO I UNDERSTAND THAT SUCH TALK IS AS CHEAP AS IT IS PLENTIFUL.
THERE ARE TREATIES OLD AND NEW BETWEEN US, AND THEY ARE NOT EASILY BROKEN. SHOULD IT COME TO IT, MY PEOPLE WILL STAND WITH ASGARD.
LIKEWISE THE DWARVES OF NIDAVELLIR--AND, IF THEY ARE CAPABLE, THE NOBLES OF ALFHEIM--
BAH!
FARM-HANDS, DIRT-MINERS AND PAMPERED PRINCELINGS! WE WILL NEED MORE THAN THEIR WEAK STEEL!
IF MY SON WAS WITH US--IF THOR COULD ONLY BE FOUND--
THERE IS A KERNEL OF TRUTH TO YOUR WORDS, HUSBAND. WITHOUT THOR STANDING WITH US--
--EITHER THOR--
MENTION NOT THE IMPOSTER--
--WE DO NEED MORE.
AND, SHOULD YOU WISH TO CEASE YOUR RIGHT ROYAL BLUSTERING A MOMENT...
...WE HAVE MORE.
COME.

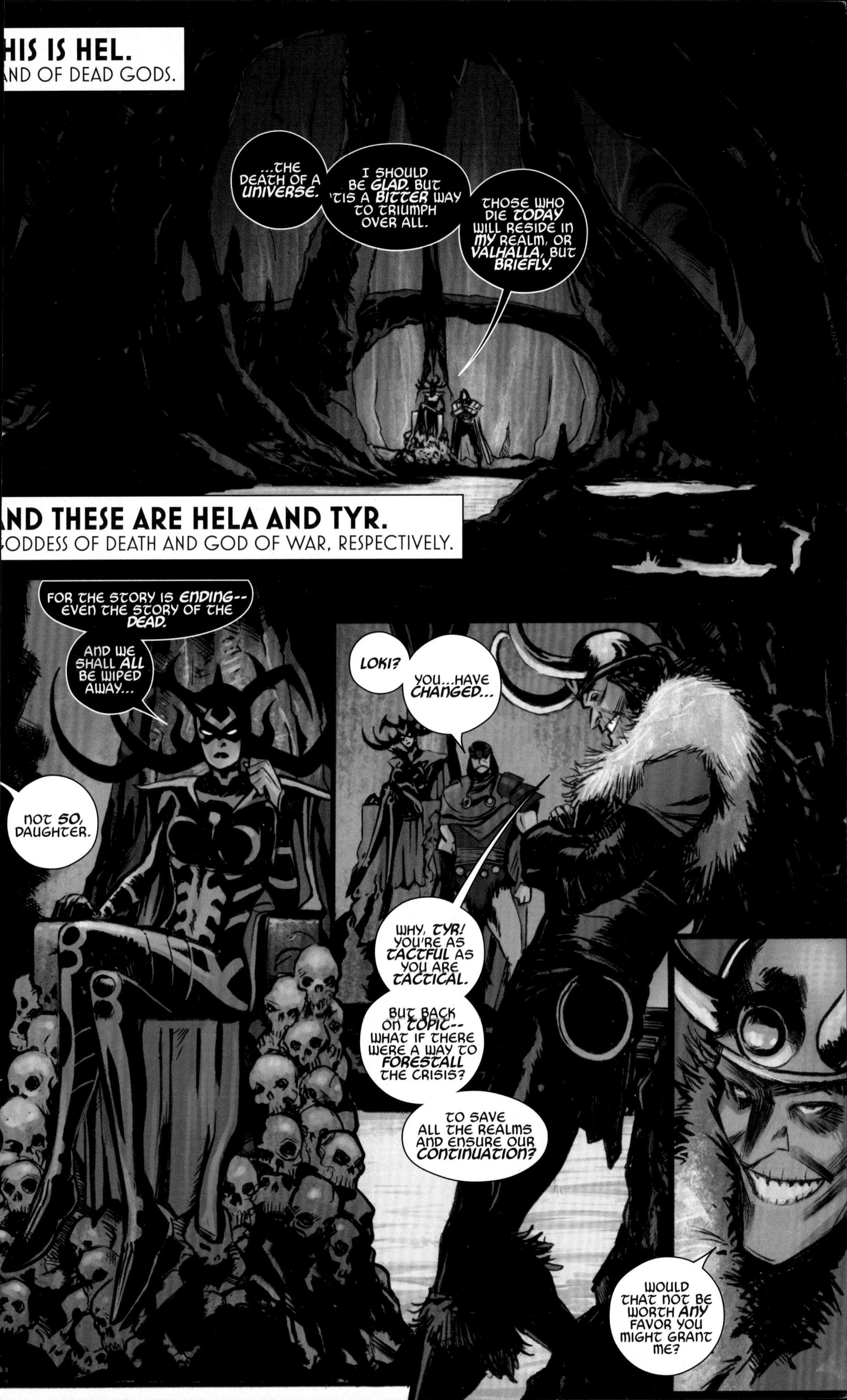

HIS IS HEL.
ND OF DEAD GODS.
...THE DEATH OF A UNIVERSE.
I SHOULD BE GLAD. BUT 'TIS A BITTER WAY TO TRIUMPH OVER ALL.
THOSE WHO DIE TODAY WILL RESIDE IN MY REALM, OR VALHALLA, BUT BRIEFLY.
ND THESE ARE HELA AND TYR.
ODDESS OF DEATH AND GOD OF WAR, RESPECTIVELY.
FOR THE STORY IS ENDING-- EVEN THE STORY OF THE DEAD.
AND WE SHALL ALL BE WIPED AWAY...
NOT SO, DAUGHTER.
LOKI?
YOU...HAVE CHANGED...
WHY, TYR! YOU'RE AS TACTFUL AS YOU ARE TACTICAL.
BUT BACK ON TOPIC-- WHAT IF THERE WERE A WAY TO FORESTALL THE CRISIS?
TO SAVE ALL THE REALMS AND ENSURE OUR CONTINUATION?
WOULD THAT NOT BE WORTH ANY FAVOR YOU MIGHT GRANT ME?

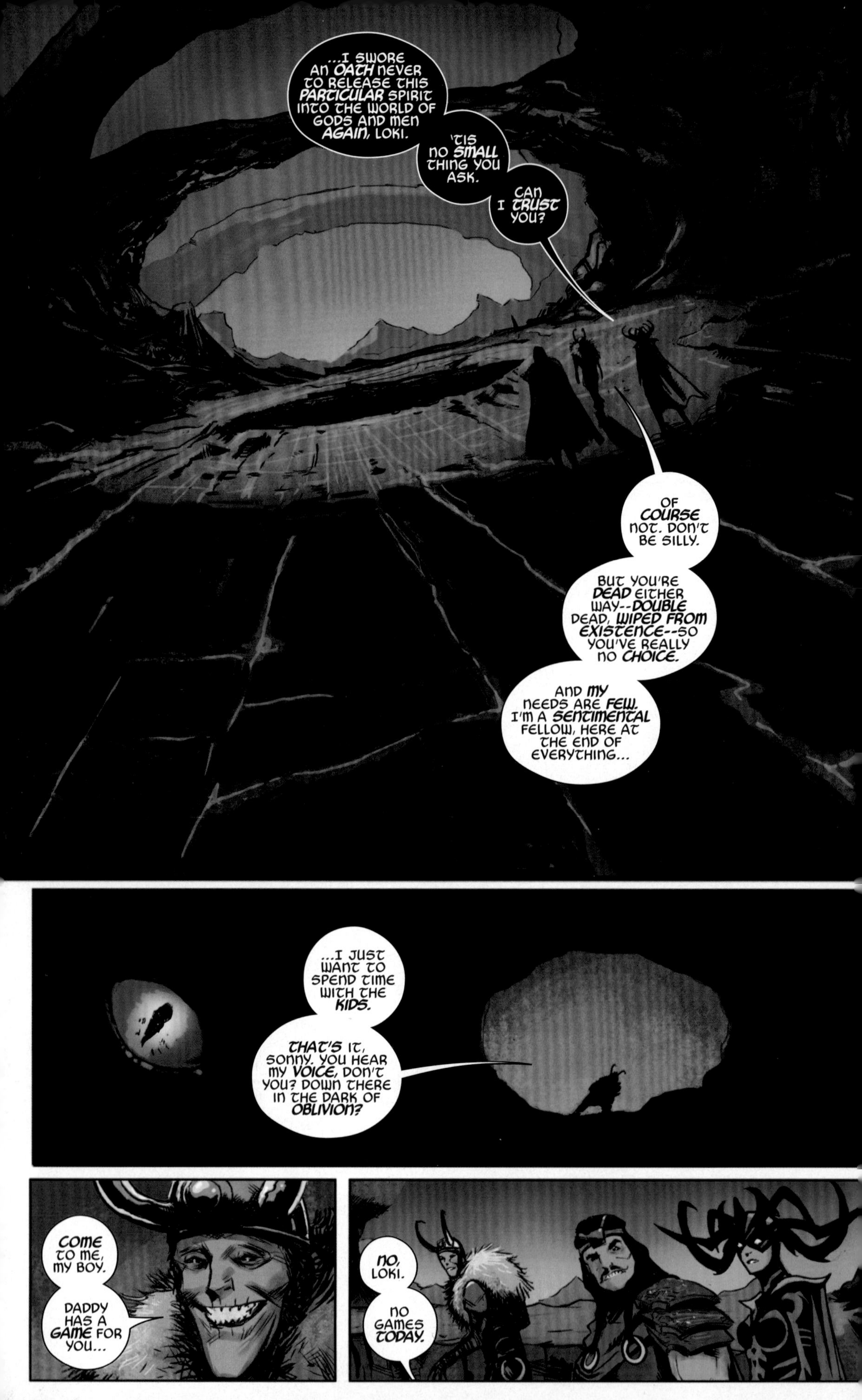
...I SWORE AN OATH NEVER TO RELEASE THIS PARTICULAR SPIRIT INTO THE WORLD OF GODS AND MEN AGAIN, LOKI.
'TIS NO SMALL THING YOU ASK.
CAN I TRUST YOU?
OF COURSE NOT. DON'T BE SILLY.
BUT YOU'RE DEAD EITHER WAY--DOUBLE DEAD, WIPED FROM EXISTENCE--SO YOU'VE REALLY NO CHOICE.
AND MY NEEDS ARE FEW. I'M A SENTIMENTAL FELLOW, HERE AT THE END OF EVERYTHING...
...I JUST WANT TO SPEND TIME WITH THE KIDS.
THAT'S IT, SONNY. YOU HEAR MY VOICE, DON'T YOU? DOWN THERE IN THE DARK OF OBLIVION?
COME TO ME, MY BOY.
DADDY HAS A GAME FOR YOU...
NO, LOKI.
NO GAMES TODAY.

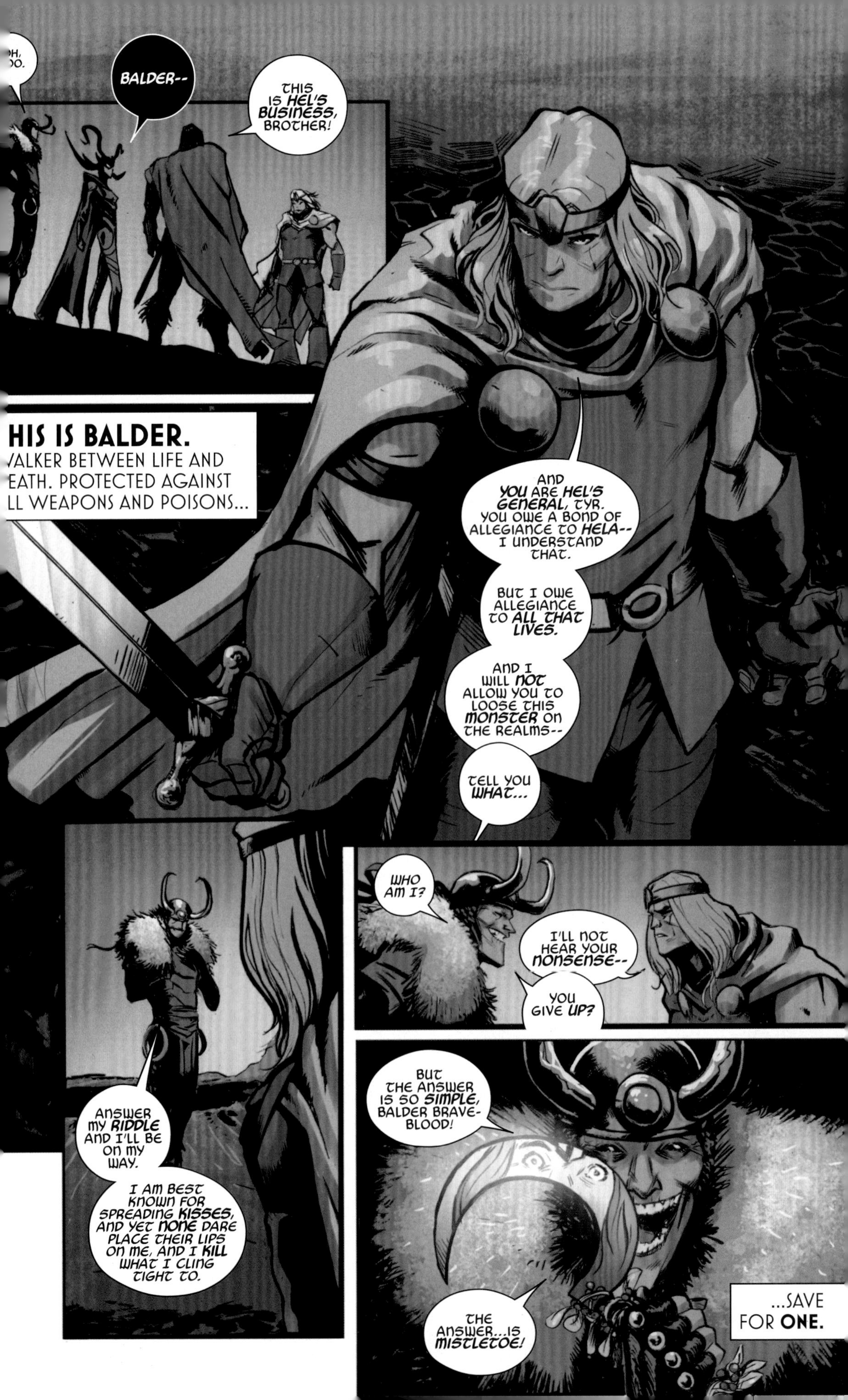

OH, ...OO.
BALDER--
THIS IS HEL'S BUSINESS, BROTHER!
HIS IS BALDER.
VALKER BETWEEN LIFE AND EATH. PROTECTED AGAINST LL WEAPONS AND POISONS...
AND YOU ARE HEL'S GENERAL, TYR. YOU OWE A BOND OF ALLEGIANCE TO HELA-- I UNDERSTAND THAT.
BUT I OWE ALLEGIANCE TO ALL THAT LIVES.
AND I WILL NOT ALLOW YOU TO LOOSE THIS MONSTER ON THE REALMS--
TELL YOU WHAT...
ANSWER MY RIDDLE AND I'LL BE ON MY WAY.
I AM BEST KNOWN FOR SPREADING KISSES, AND YET NONE DARE PLACE THEIR LIPS ON ME, AND I KILL WHAT I CLING TIGHT TO.
WHO AM I?
I'LL NOT HEAR YOUR NONSENSE--
YOU GIVE UP?
BUT THE ANSWER IS SO SIMPLE, BALDER BRAVE-BLOOD!
THE ANSWER...IS MISTLETOE!
...SAVE FOR ONE.

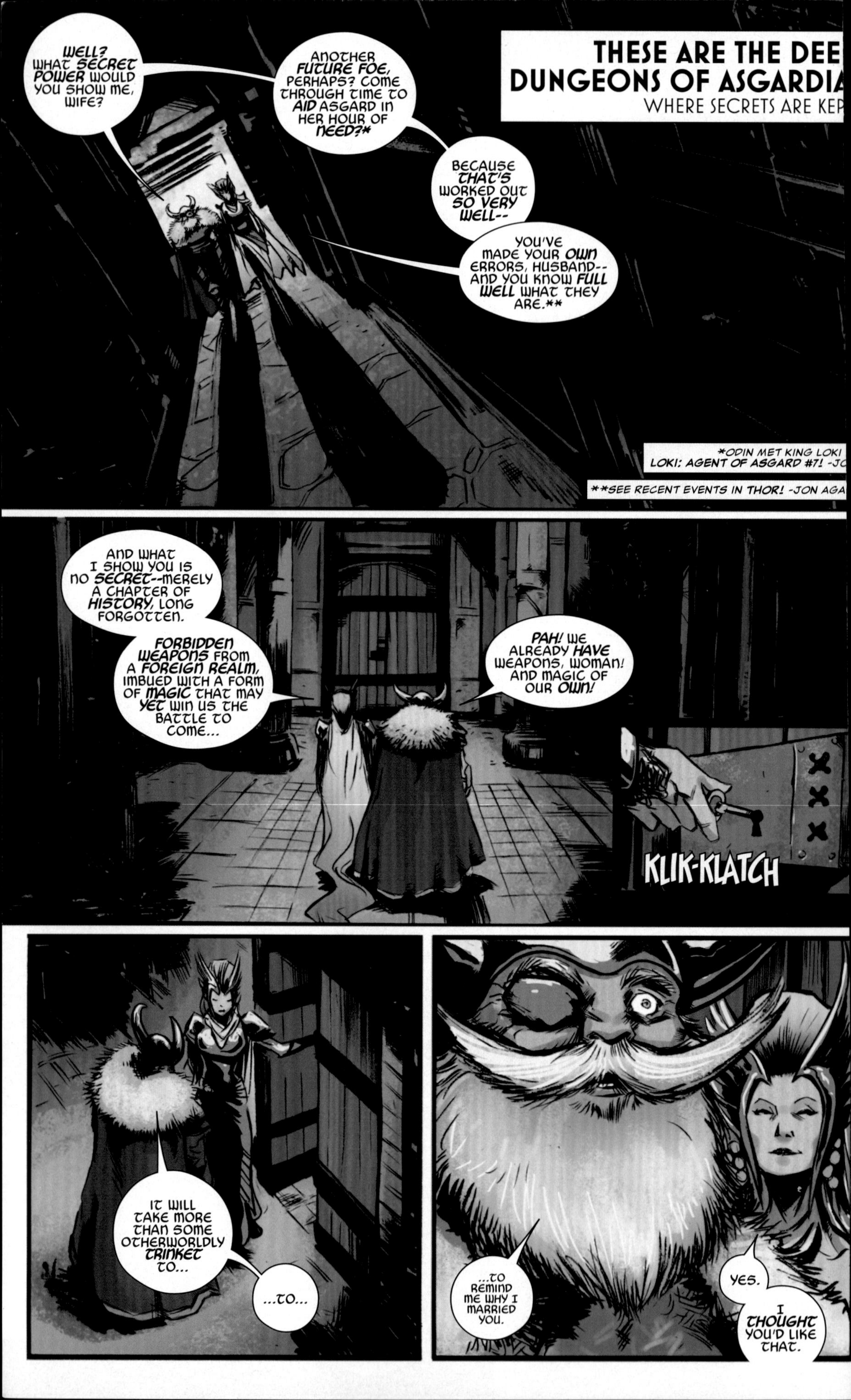

THESE ARE THE DEE
DUNGEONS OF ASGARDIA
WHERE SECRETS ARE KEP
WELL? WHAT SECRET POWER WOULD YOU SHOW ME, WIFE?
ANOTHER FUTURE FOE, PERHAPS? COME THROUGH TIME TO AID ASGARD IN HER HOUR OF NEED?*
BECAUSE THAT'S WORKED OUT SO VERY WELL--
YOU'VE MADE YOUR OWN ERRORS, HUSBAND-- AND YOU KNOW FULL WELL WHAT THEY ARE.**
*ODIN MET KING LOKI
LOKI: AGENT OF ASGARD #7! -JO
**SEE RECENT EVENTS IN THOR! -JON AGA
AND WHAT I SHOW YOU IS NO SECRET--MERELY A CHAPTER OF HISTORY, LONG FORGOTTEN.
FORBIDDEN WEAPONS FROM A FOREIGN REALM, IMBUED WITH A FORM OF MAGIC THAT MAY YET WIN US THE BATTLE TO COME...
PAH! WE ALREADY HAVE WEAPONS, WOMAN! AND MAGIC OF OUR OWN!
KLIK-KLATCH
IT WILL TAKE MORE THAN SOME OTHERWORLDLY TRINKET TO...
...TO...
...TO REMIND ME WHY I MARRIED YOU.
YES.
I THOUGHT YOU'D LIKE THAT.

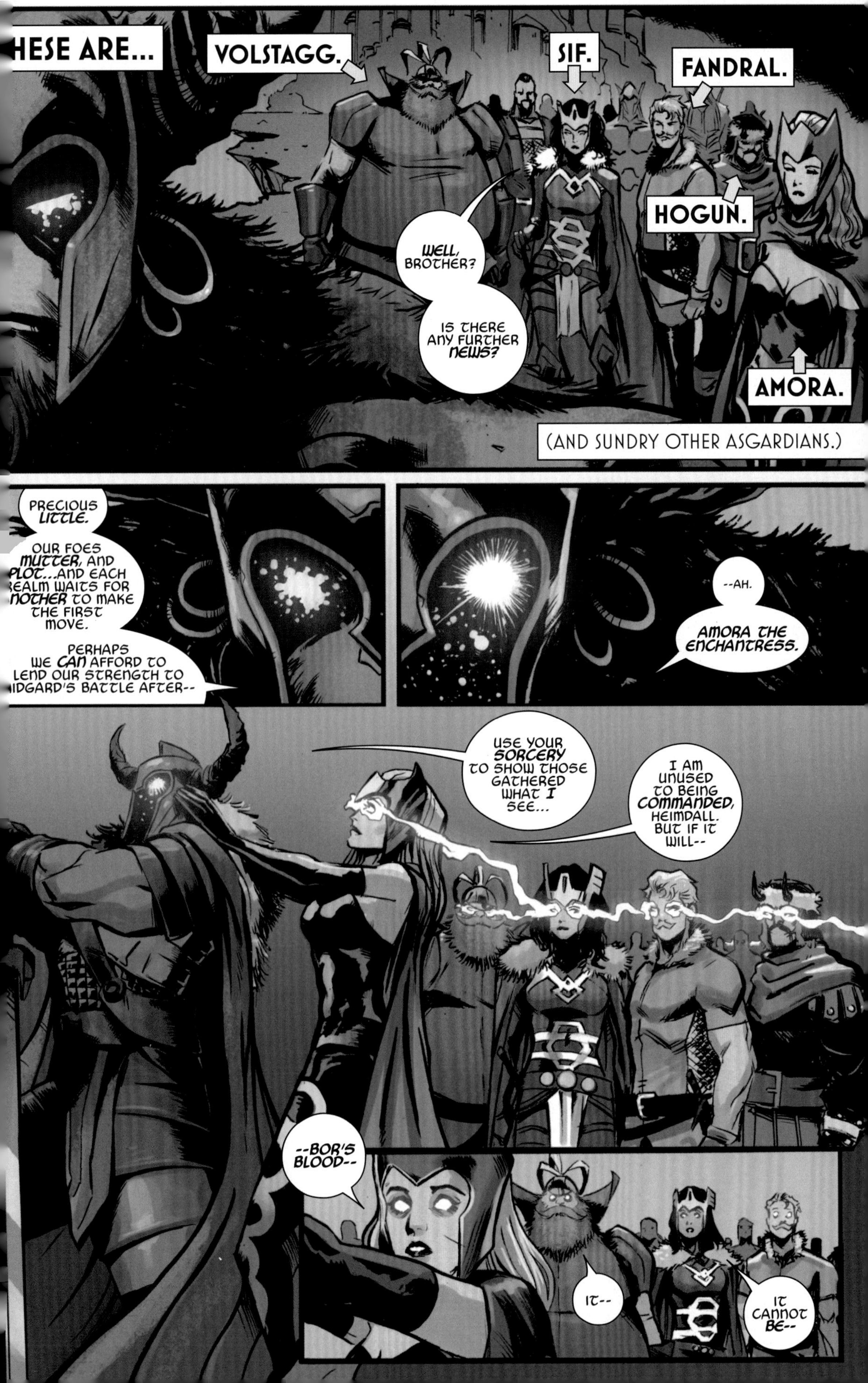
HESE ARE...
VOLSTAGG.
SIF.
FANDRAL.
WELL, BROTHER?
IS THERE ANY FURTHER NEWS?
HOGUN.
AMORA.
(AND SUNDRY OTHER ASGARDIANS.)
PRECIOUS LITTLE.
OUR FOES MUTTER, AND PLOT...AND EACH EALM WAITS FOR NOTHER TO MAKE THE FIRST MOVE.
PERHAPS WE CAN AFFORD TO LEND OUR STRENGTH TO IDGARD'S BATTLE AFTER--
--AH.
AMORA THE ENCHANTRESS.
USE YOUR SORCERY TO SHOW THOSE GATHERED WHAT I SEE...
I AM UNUSED TO BEING COMMANDED, HEIMDALL. BUT IF IT WILL--
--BOR'S BLOOD--
IT--
IT CANNOT BE--

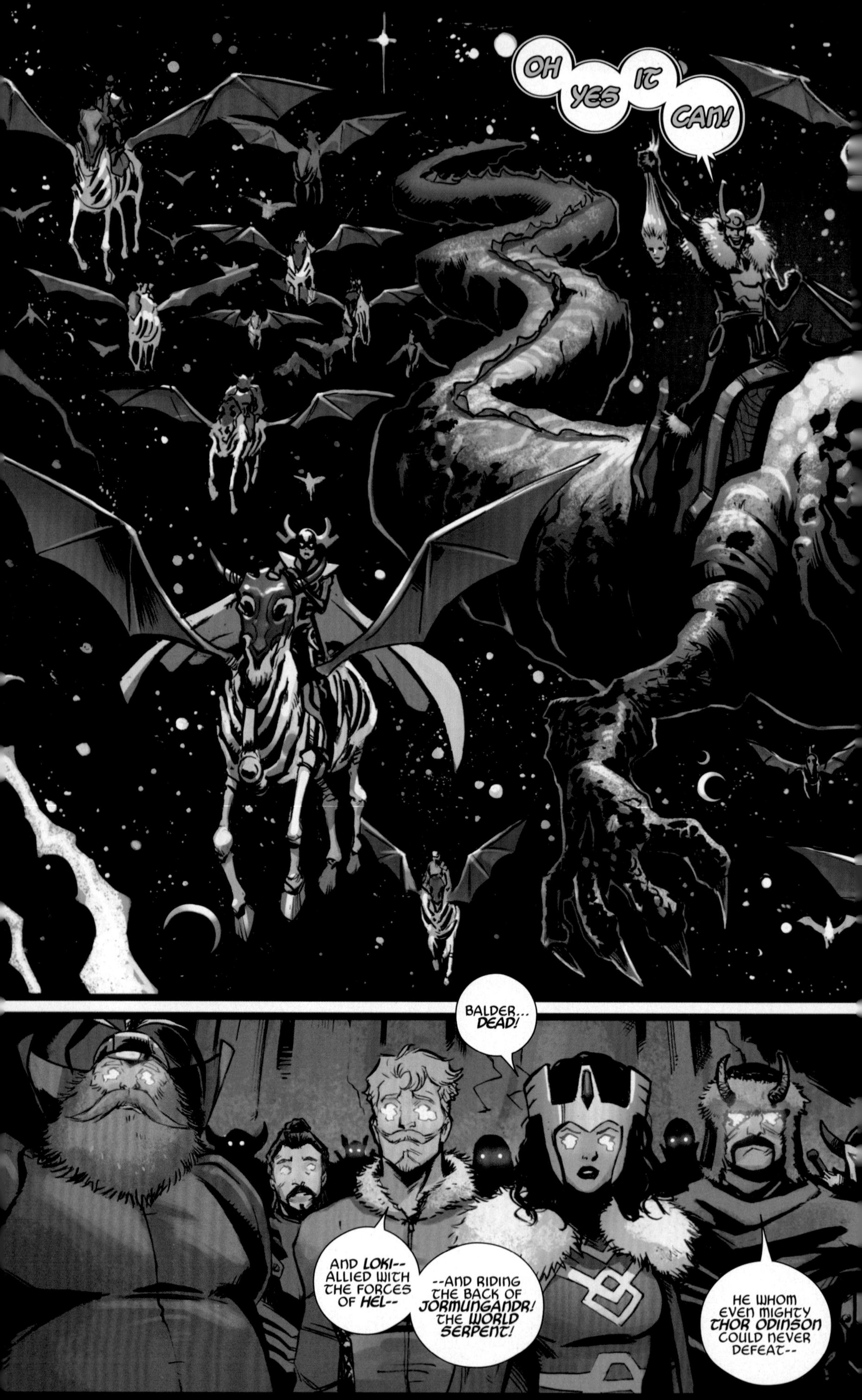
OH YES IT CAN!
BALDER... DEAD!
AND LOKI-- ALLIED WITH THE FORCES OF HEL--
--AND RIDING THE BACK OF JORMUNGANDR! THE WORLD SERPENT!
HE WHOM EVEN MIGHTY THOR ODINSON COULD NEVER DEFEAT--

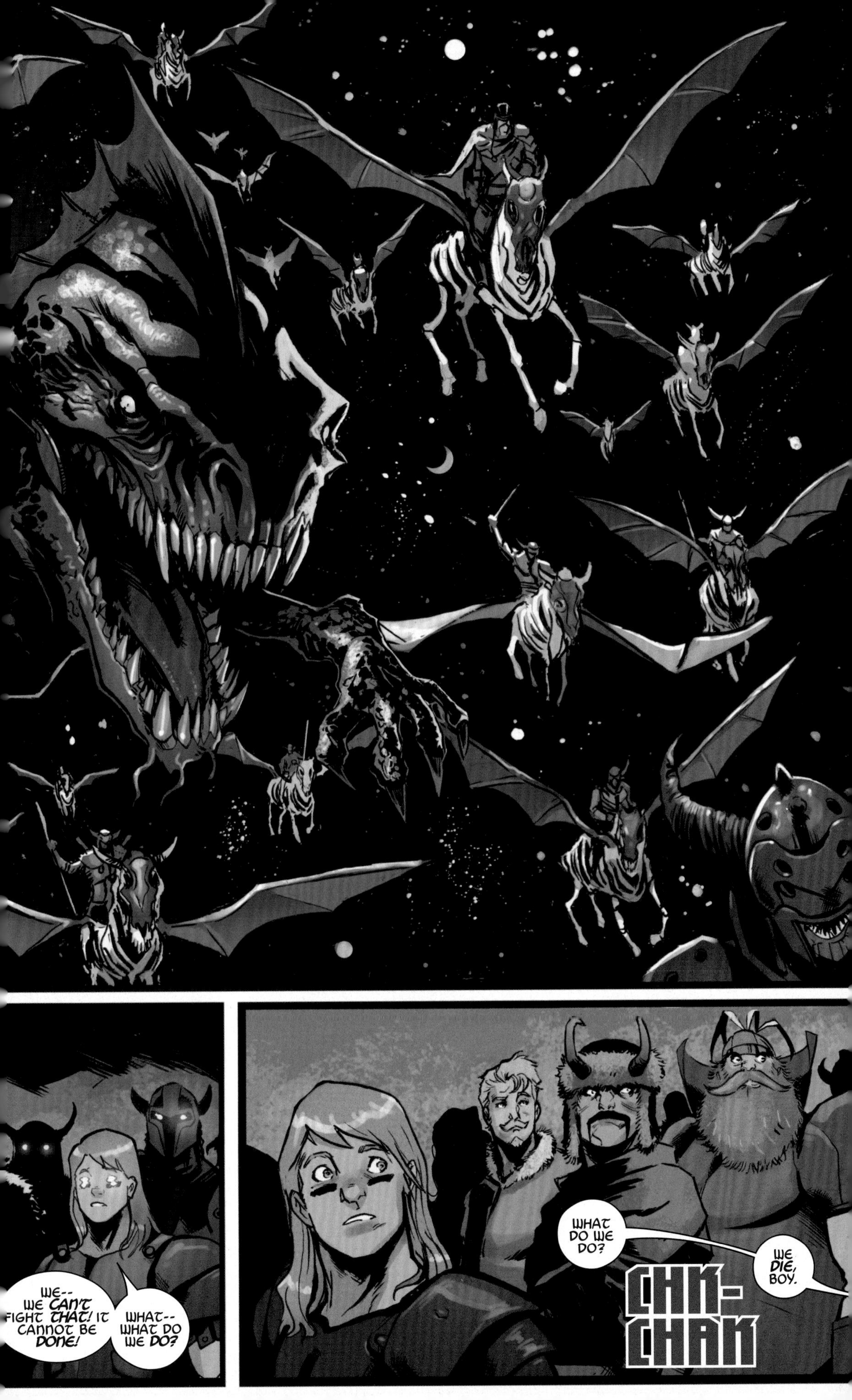
WE-- WE CAN'T FIGHT THAT! IT CANNOT BE DONE!
WHAT-- WHAT DO WE DO?
WHAT DO WE DO?
WE DIE, BOY.
CHK-CHAK

FOR ASGARD--
--WE DIE LIKE GODS!
BORN ONE MORNING
AND THE SUN DIDN'T SHINE

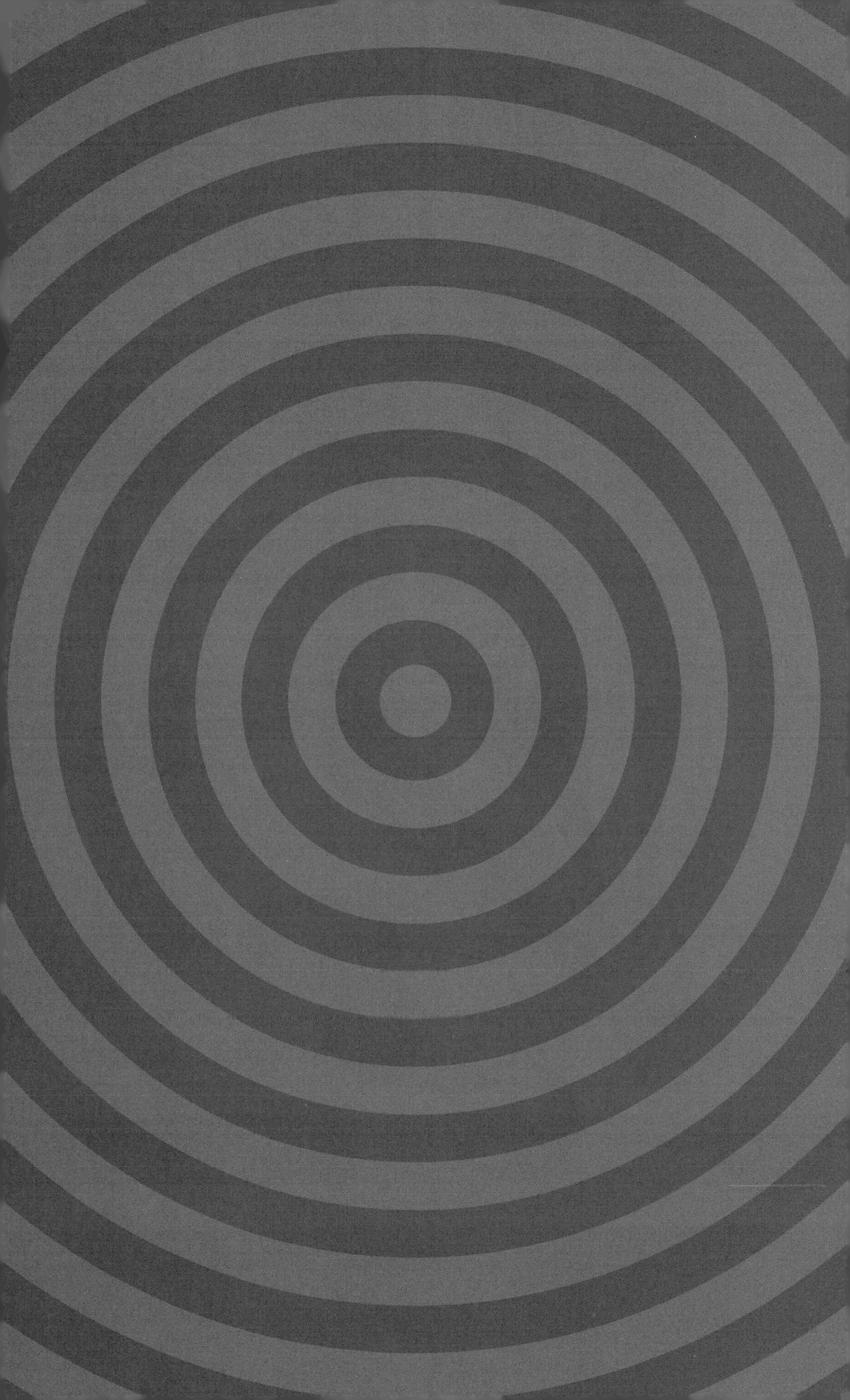

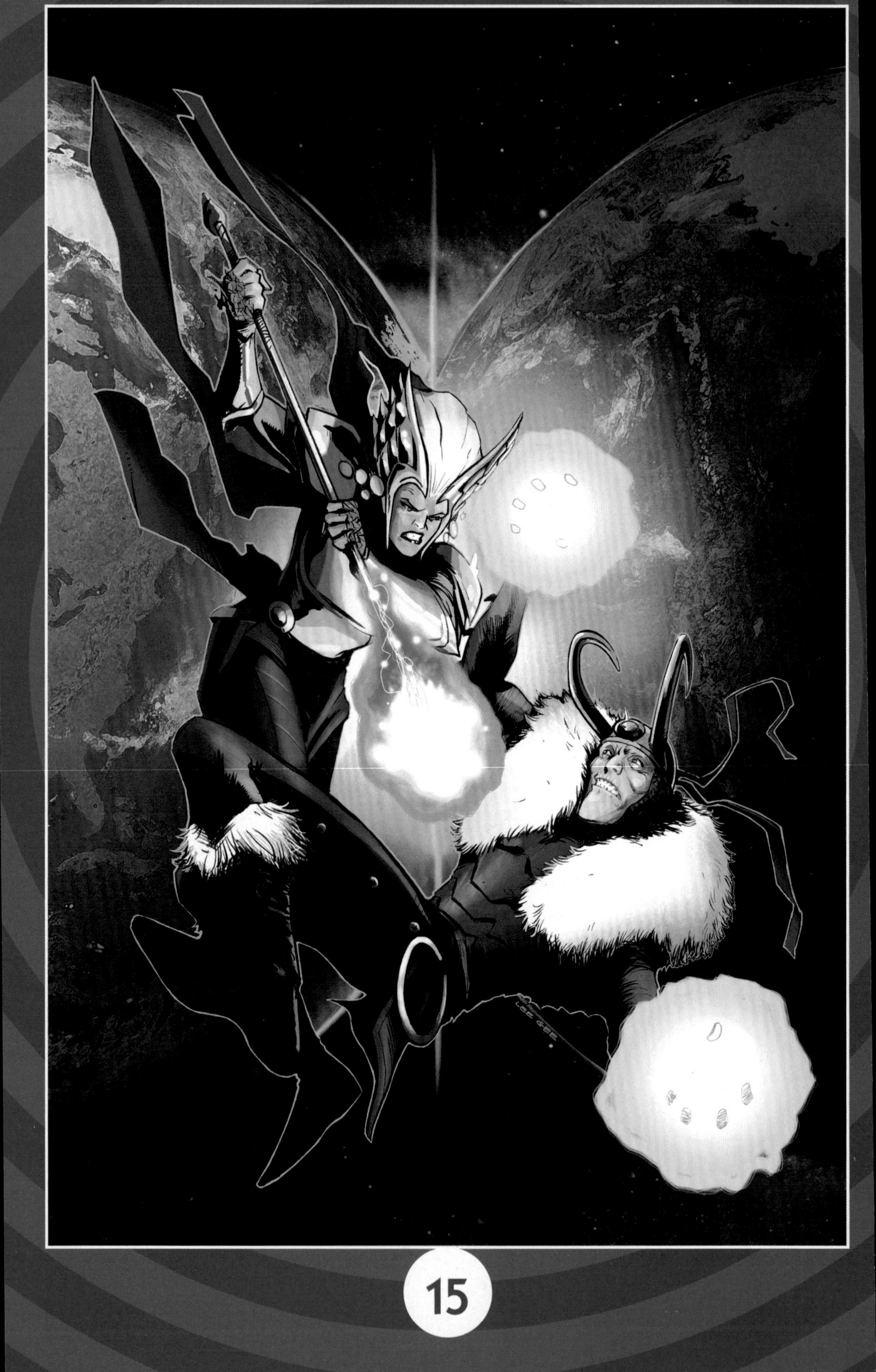

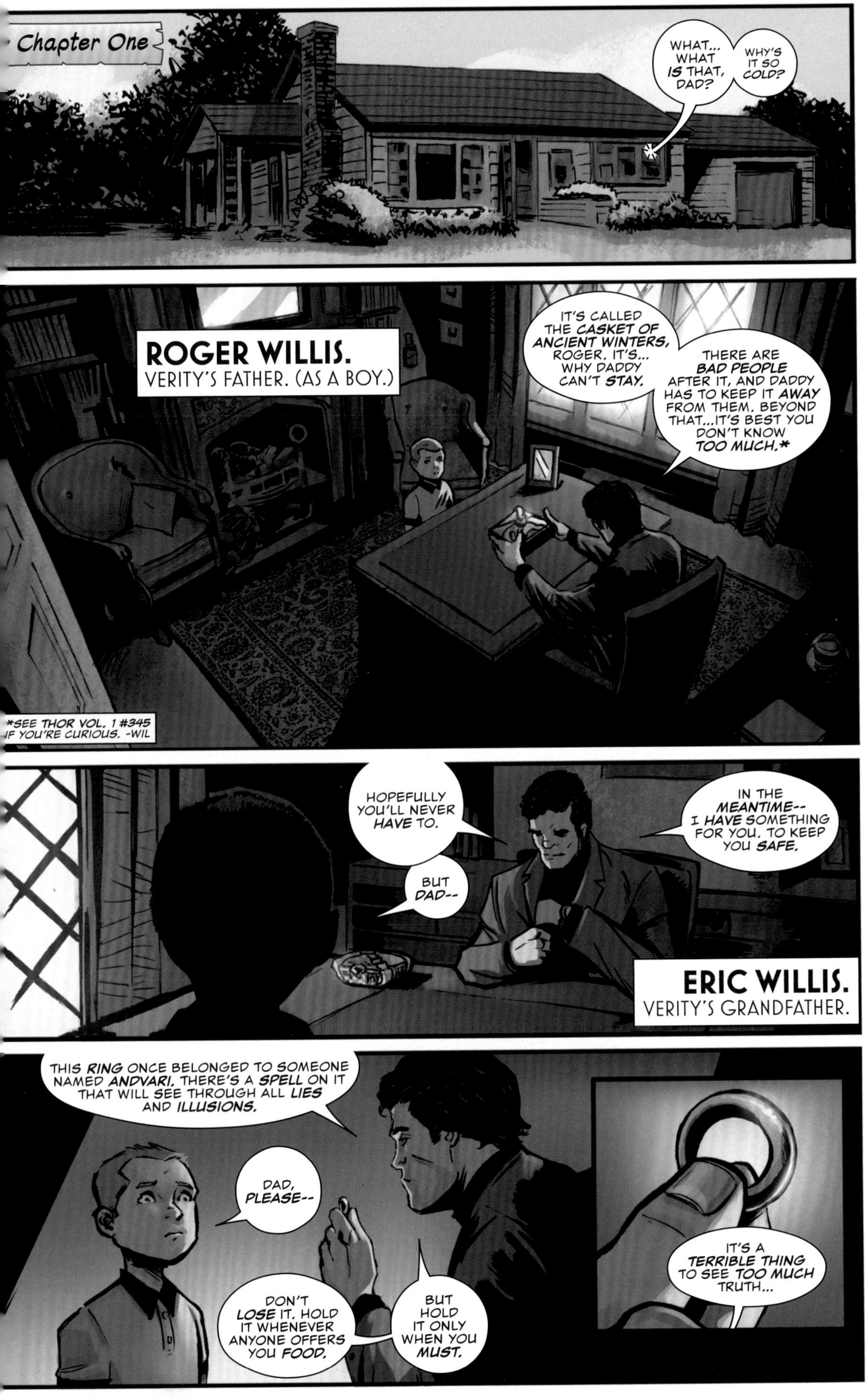
Chapter One
WHAT... WHAT IS THAT, DAD?
WHY'S IT SO COLD?
ROGER WILLIS.
VERITY'S FATHER. (AS A BOY.)
IT'S CALLED THE CASKET OF ANCIENT WINTERS, ROGER. IT'S... WHY DADDY CAN'T STAY.
THERE ARE BAD PEOPLE AFTER IT, AND DADDY HAS TO KEEP IT AWAY FROM THEM. BEYOND THAT...IT'S BEST YOU DON'T KNOW TOO MUCH.*
*SEE THOR VOL. 1 #345 IF YOU'RE CURIOUS. -WIL
HOPEFULLY YOU'LL NEVER HAVE TO.
BUT DAD--
IN THE MEANTIME-- I HAVE SOMETHING FOR YOU. TO KEEP YOU SAFE.
ERIC WILLIS.
VERITY'S GRANDFATHER.
THIS RING ONCE BELONGED TO SOMEONE NAMED ANDVARI. THERE'S A SPELL ON IT THAT WILL SEE THROUGH ALL LIES AND ILLUSIONS.
DAD, PLEASE--
DON'T LOSE IT. HOLD IT WHENEVER ANYONE OFFERS YOU FOOD.
BUT HOLD IT ONLY WHEN YOU MUST.
IT'S A TERRIBLE THING TO SEE TOO MUCH TRUTH...

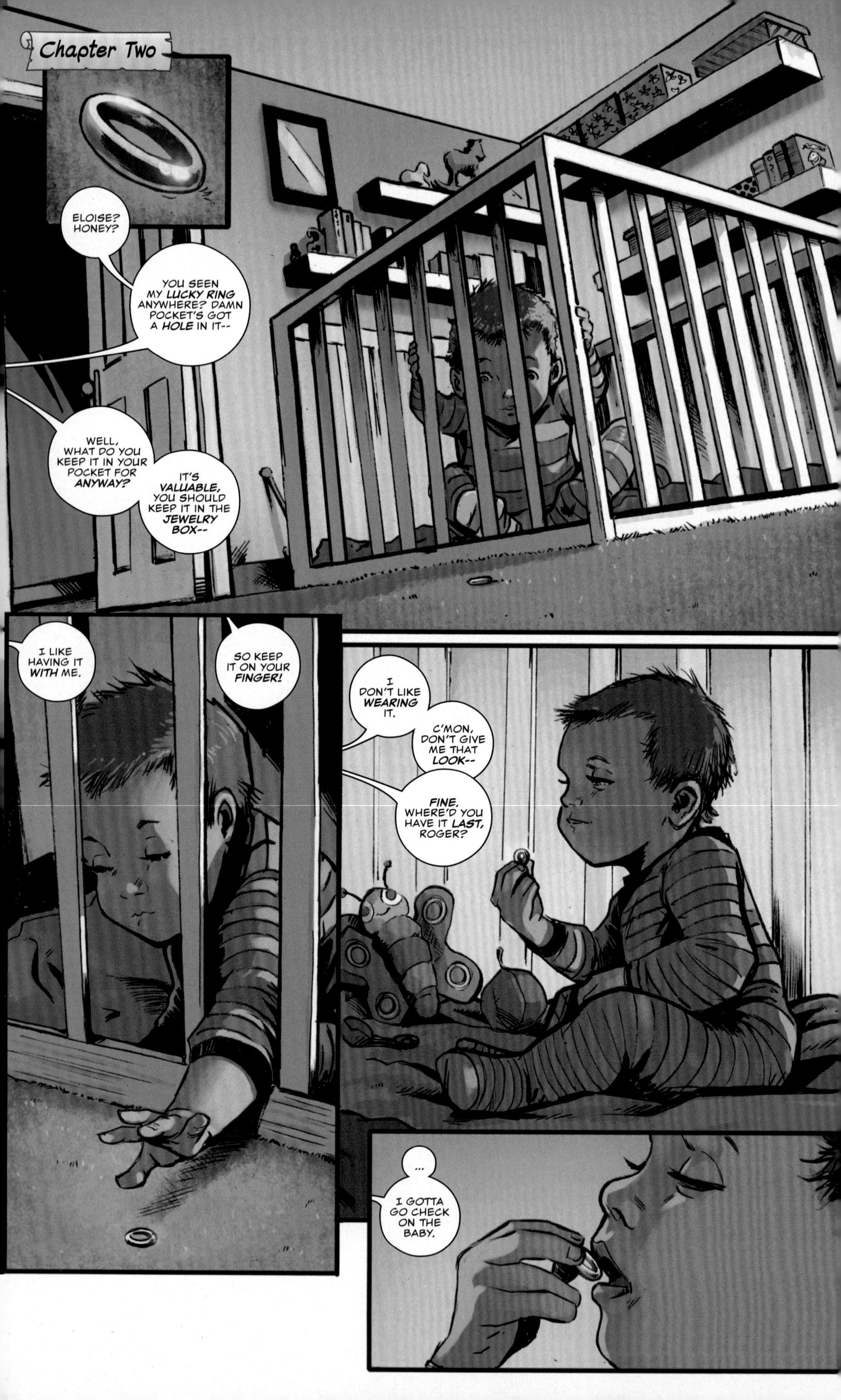
Chapter Two
ELOISE? HONEY?
YOU SEEN MY LUCKY RING ANYWHERE? DAMN POCKET'S GOT A HOLE IN IT--
WELL, WHAT DO YOU KEEP IT IN YOUR POCKET FOR ANYWAY?
IT'S VALUABLE, YOU SHOULD KEEP IT IN THE JEWELRY BOX--
I LIKE HAVING IT WITH ME.
SO KEEP IT ON YOUR FINGER!
I DON'T LIKE WEARING IT.
C'MON, DON'T GIVE ME THAT LOOK--
FINE. WHERE'D YOU HAVE IT LAST, ROGER?
...
I GOTTA GO CHECK ON THE BABY.

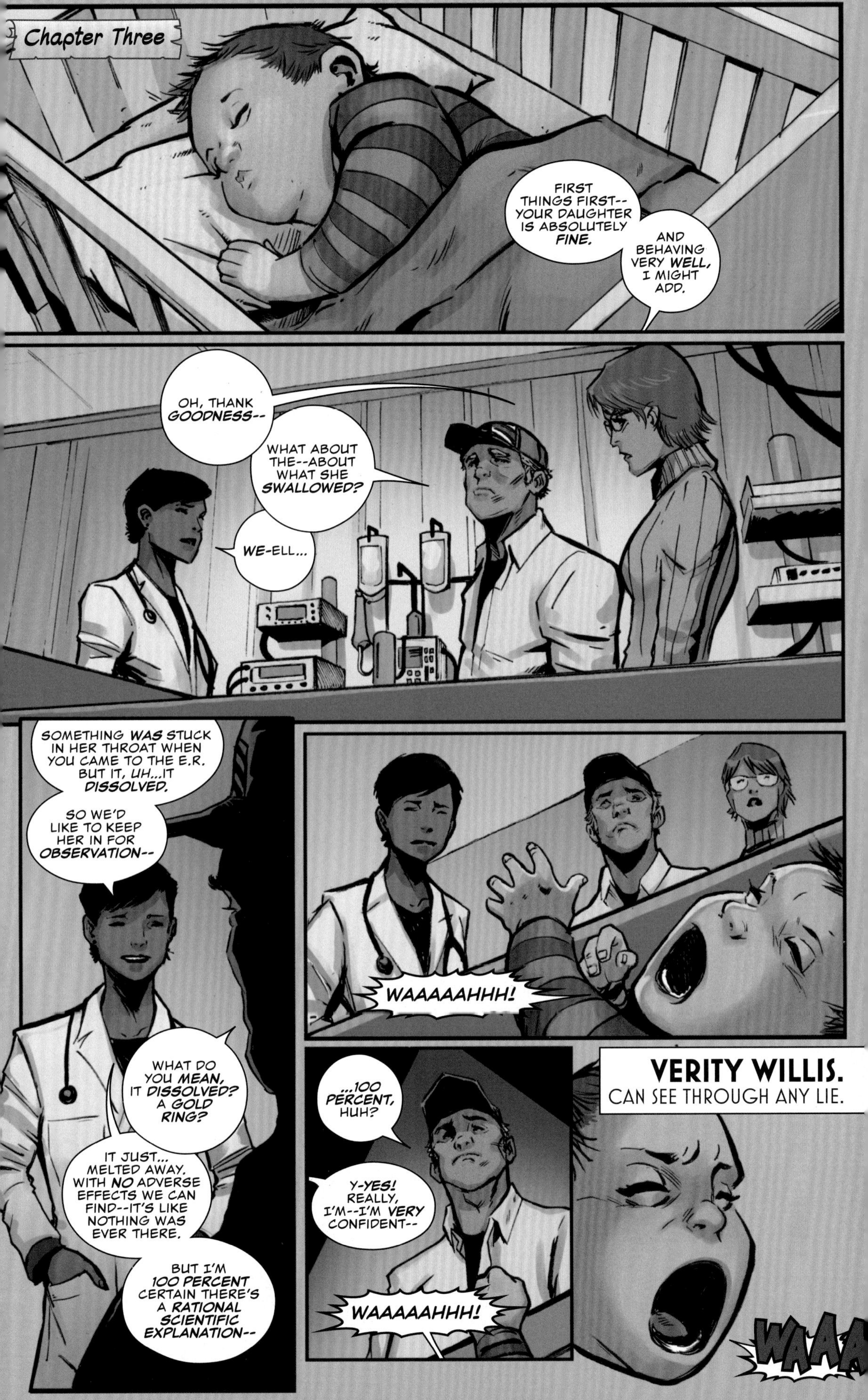
Chapter Three
FIRST THINGS FIRST-- YOUR DAUGHTER IS ABSOLUTELY FINE.
AND BEHAVING VERY WELL, I MIGHT ADD.
OH, THANK GOODNESS--
WHAT ABOUT THE--ABOUT WHAT SHE SWALLOWED?
WE-ELL...
SOMETHING WAS STUCK IN HER THROAT WHEN YOU CAME TO THE E.R. BUT IT, UH...IT DISSOLVED.
SO WE'D LIKE TO KEEP HER IN FOR OBSERVATION--
WAAAAAHHH!
WHAT DO YOU MEAN, IT DISSOLVED? A GOLD RING?
IT JUST... MELTED AWAY. WITH NO ADVERSE EFFECTS WE CAN FIND--IT'S LIKE NOTHING WAS EVER THERE.
BUT I'M 100 PERCENT CERTAIN THERE'S A RATIONAL SCIENTIFIC EXPLANATION--
...100 PERCENT, HUH?
Y-YES! REALLY, I'M--I'M VERY CONFIDENT--
WAAAAAHHH!
VERITY WILLIS.
CAN SEE THROUGH ANY LIE.
WAAA

ASGARDIA.
A VERY DIFFERENT STORY.
SPIT STEEL AND FIRE, O GOD OF MIDGARD!
YE WHOSE ENDLESS METAL THUNDER THE MORTALS CHOSE TO WORSHIP OVER JUSTICE!
PIT YOUR RED-HANDED HORROR AGAINST THE HORROR WE FACE! SCREAM YOUR BLOODY MURDER! BELLOW YOUR SONG OF MINDLESS IRE!
ODIN ONE-EYE COMMANDS YOU!
ODIN,
THE ALL-FATHER.
AIM FOR THE HEAD! SHORT BURSTS!
YOUR AMMUNITION HAS A LIMIT--
I--I CANNOT FATHOM THIS MORTAL MAGIC--
THEN LEARN FAST, BOY!

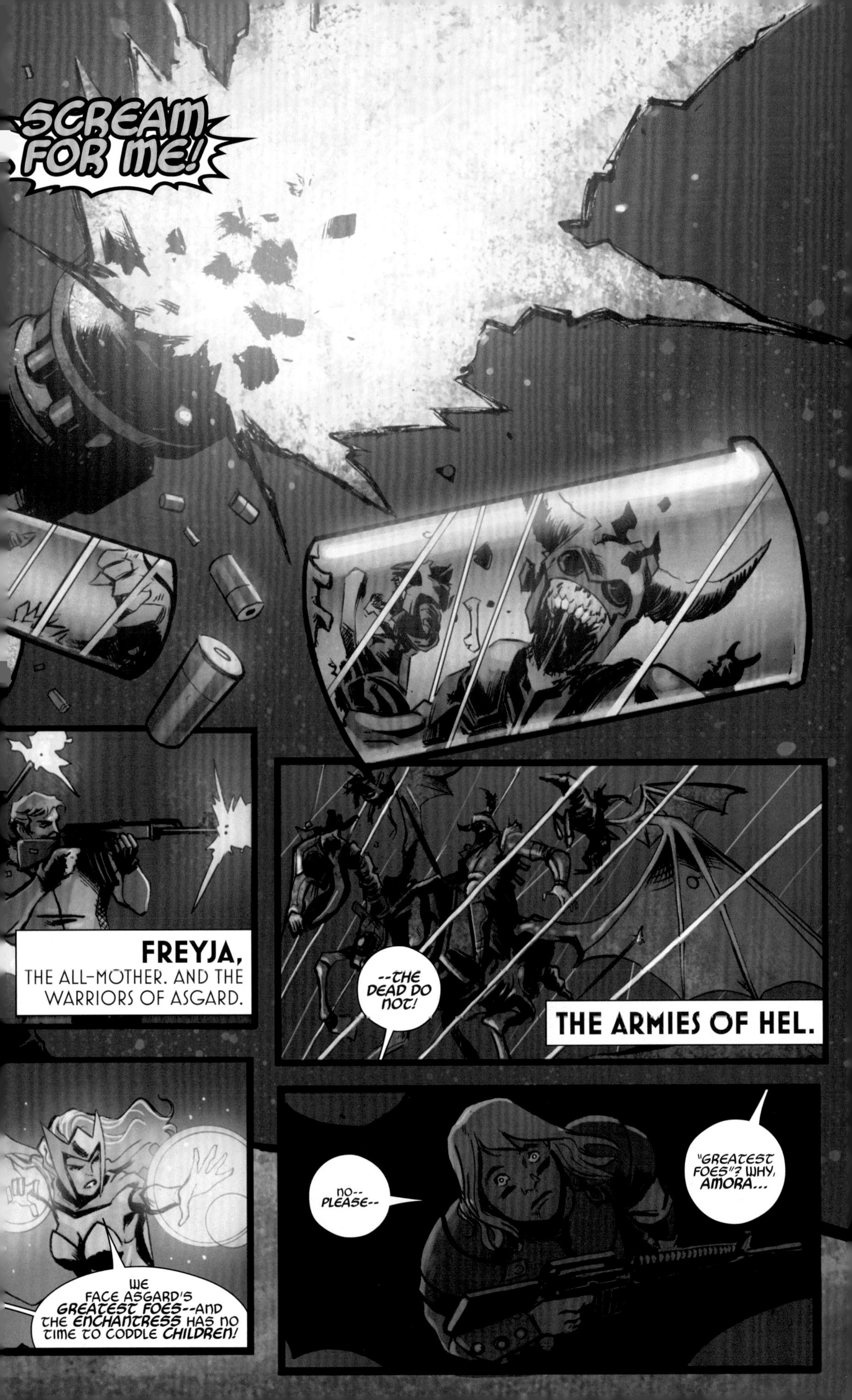
SCREAM FOR ME!
FREYJA, THE ALL-MOTHER. AND THE WARRIORS OF ASGARD.
--THE DEAD DO NOT!
THE ARMIES OF HEL.
WE FACE ASGARD'S GREATEST FOES--AND THE ENCHANTRESS HAS NO TIME TO CODDLE CHILDREN!
NO-- PLEASE--
"GREATEST FOES"? WHY, AMORA...

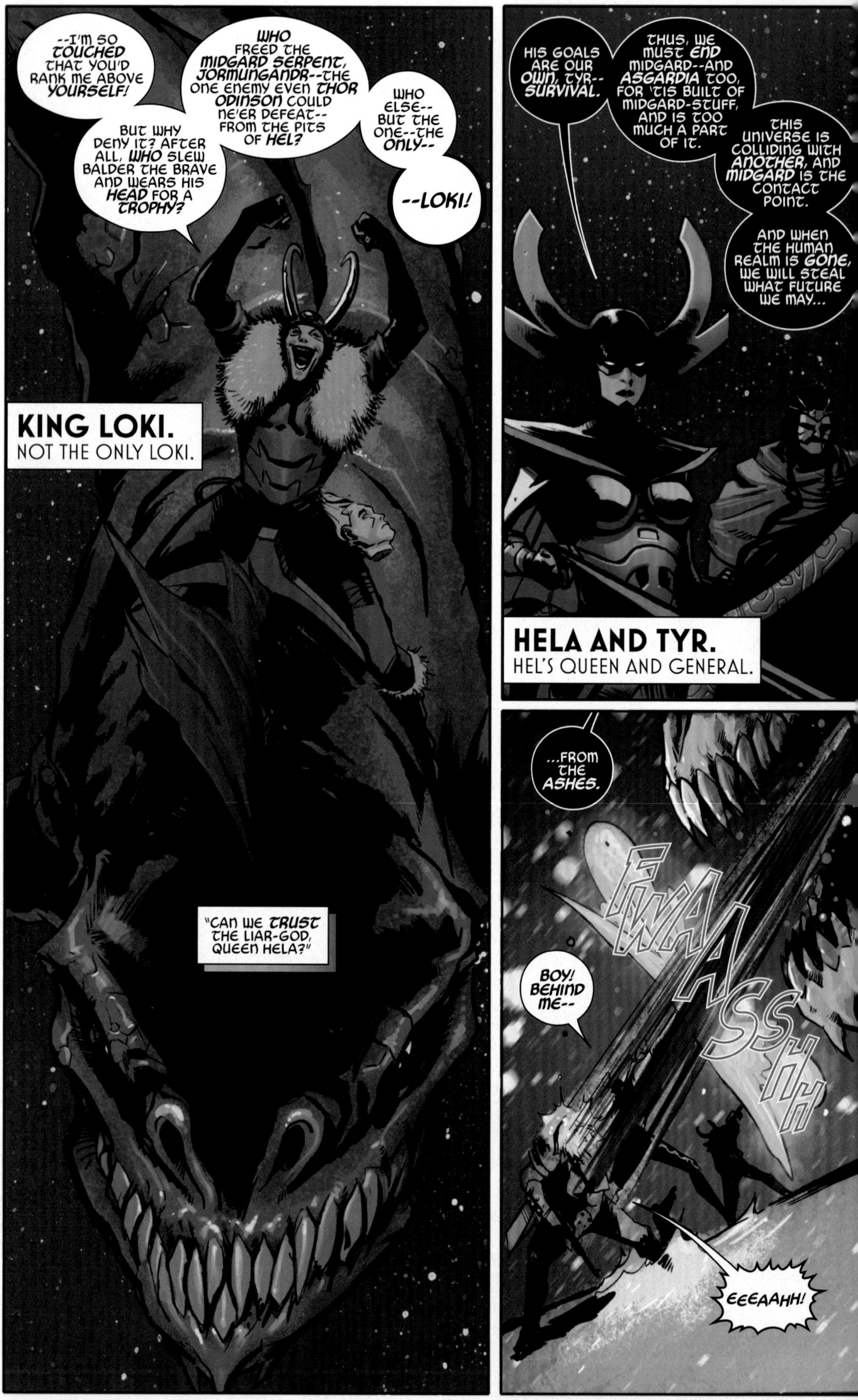
--I'M SO TOUCHED THAT YOU'D RANK ME ABOVE YOURSELF!
BUT WHY DENY IT? AFTER ALL, WHO SLEW BALDER THE BRAVE AND WEARS HIS HEAD FOR A TROPHY?
WHO FREED THE MIDGARD SERPENT, JORMUNGANDR--THE ONE ENEMY EVEN THOR ODINSON COULD NE'ER DEFEAT--FROM THE PITS OF HEL?
WHO ELSE--BUT THE ONE--THE ONLY--
--LOKI!
KING LOKI.
NOT THE ONLY LOKI.
"CAN WE TRUST THE LIAR-GOD, QUEEN HELA?"
HIS GOALS ARE OUR OWN, TYR--SURVIVAL.
THUS, WE MUST END MIDGARD--AND ASGARDIA TOO, FOR 'TIS BUILT OF MIDGARD-STUFF, AND IS TOO MUCH A PART OF IT.
THIS UNIVERSE IS COLLIDING WITH ANOTHER, AND MIDGARD IS THE CONTACT POINT.
AND WHEN THE HUMAN REALM IS GONE, WE WILL STEAL WHAT FUTURE WE MAY...
HELA AND TYR.
HEL'S QUEEN AND GENERAL.
...FROM THE ASHES.
FWAASSHH
BOY! BEHIND ME--
EEEAAHH!

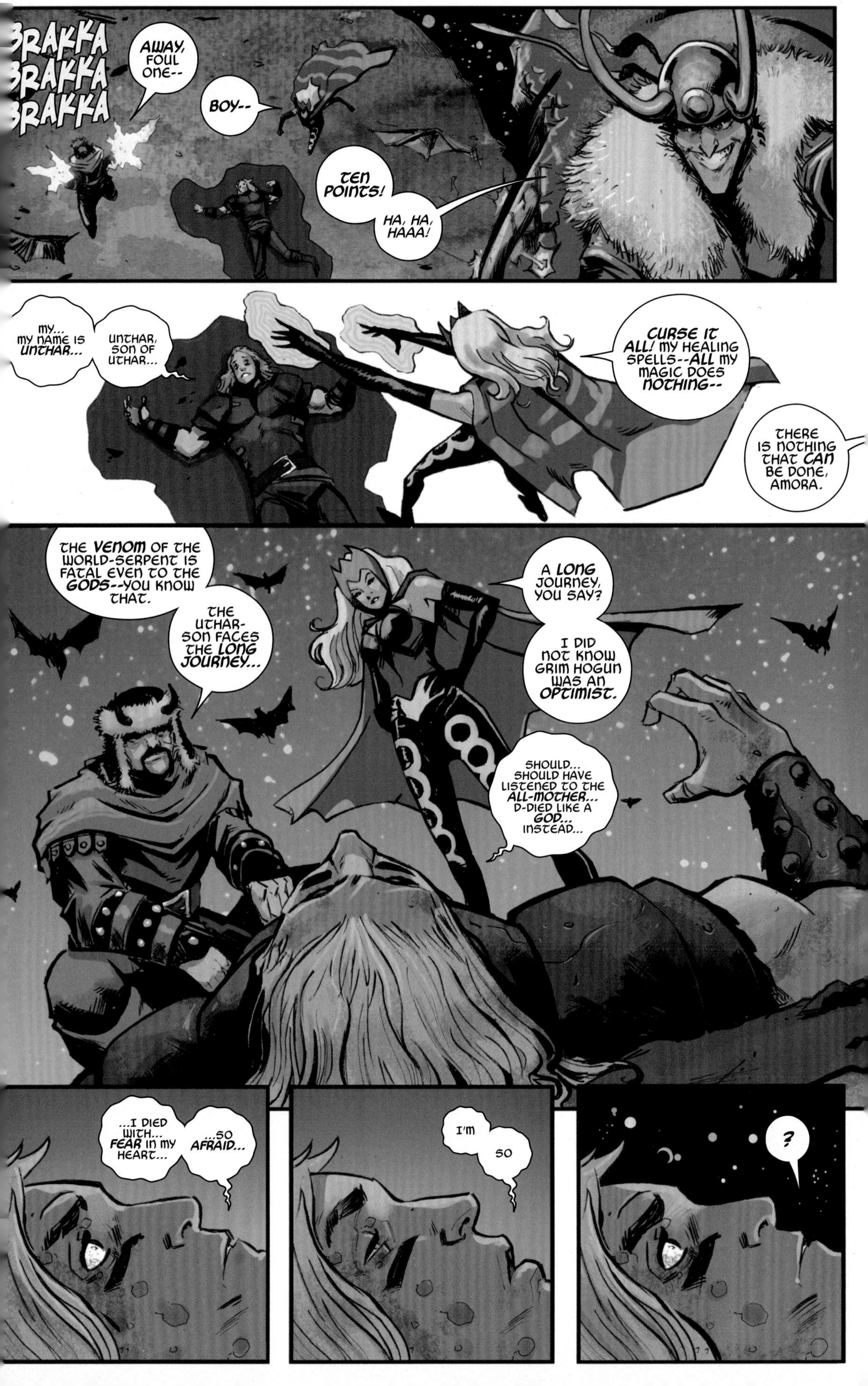
BRAKKA
BRAKKA
BRAKKA
AWAY, FOUL ONE--
BOY--
TEN POINTS!
HA, HA, HAAA!
MY... MY NAME IS UNTHAR...
UNTHAR, SON OF UTHAR...
CURSE IT ALL! MY HEALING SPELLS--ALL MY MAGIC DOES NOTHING--
THERE IS NOTHING THAT CAN BE DONE, AMORA.
THE VENOM OF THE WORLD-SERPENT IS FATAL EVEN TO THE GODS--YOU KNOW THAT.
THE UTHAR-SON FACES THE LONG JOURNEY...
A LONG JOURNEY, YOU SAY?
I DID NOT KNOW GRIM HOGUN WAS AN OPTIMIST.
SHOULD... SHOULD HAVE LISTENED TO THE ALL-MOTHER... D-DIED LIKE A GOD... INSTEAD...
...I DIED WITH... FEAR IN MY HEART...
...SO AFRAID...
I'M
SO
?

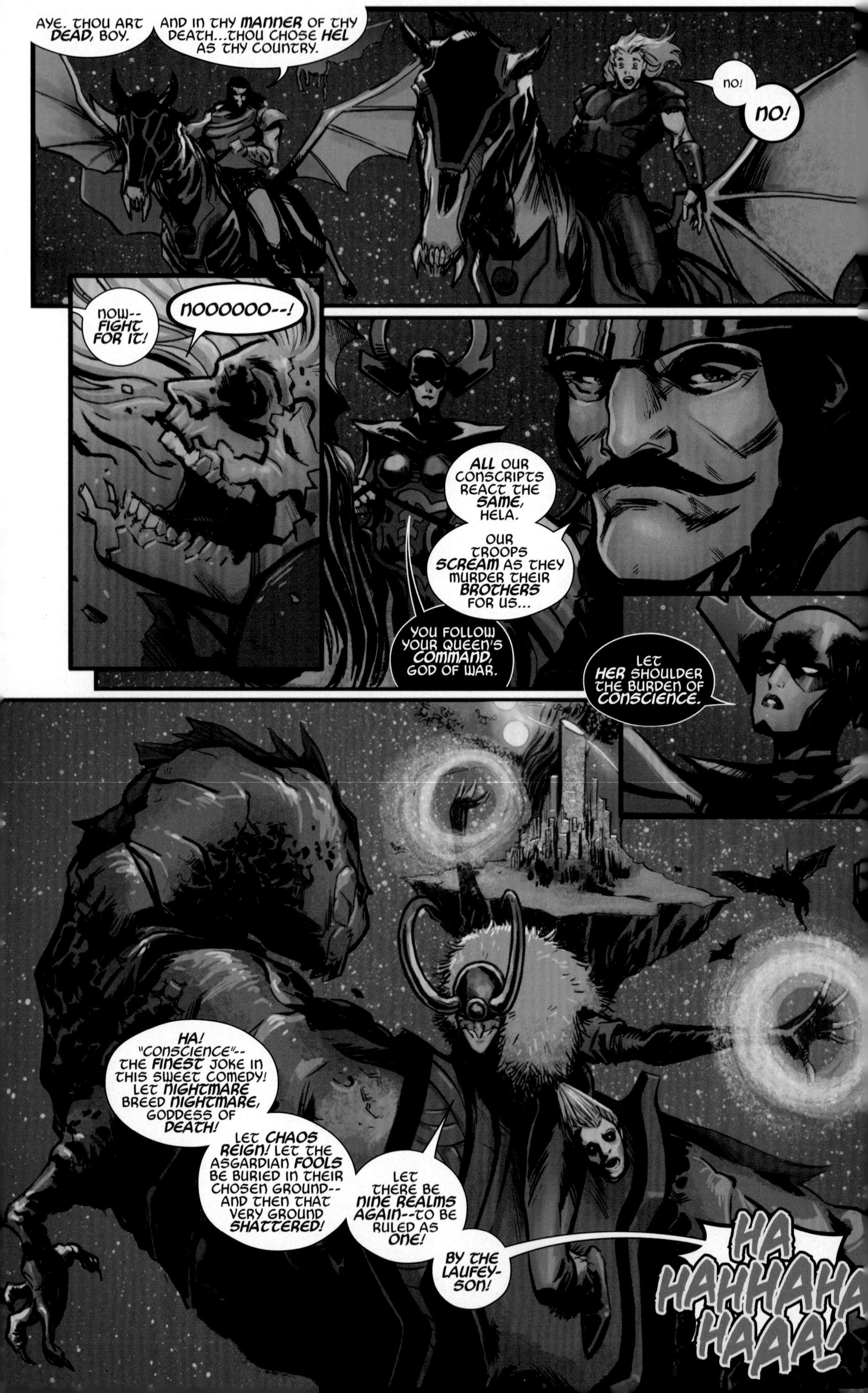
AYE. THOU ART DEAD, BOY.
AND IN THY MANNER OF THY DEATH...THOU CHOSE HEL AS THY COUNTRY.
NO!
NO!
NOW-- FIGHT FOR IT!
NOOOOOO--!
ALL OUR CONSCRIPTS REACT THE SAME, HELA.
OUR TROOPS SCREAM AS THEY MURDER THEIR BROTHERS FOR US...
YOU FOLLOW YOUR QUEEN'S COMMAND, GOD OF WAR.
LET HER SHOULDER THE BURDEN OF CONSCIENCE.
HA! "CONSCIENCE"-- THE FINEST JOKE IN THIS SWEET COMEDY! LET NIGHTMARE BREED NIGHTMARE, GODDESS OF DEATH!
LET CHAOS REIGN! LET THE ASGARDIAN FOOLS BE BURIED IN THEIR CHOSEN GROUND-- AND THEN THAT VERY GROUND SHATTERED!
LET THERE BE NINE REALMS AGAIN--TO BE RULED AS ONE!
BY THE LAUFEY-SON!
HA HAHHAHA HAAA!

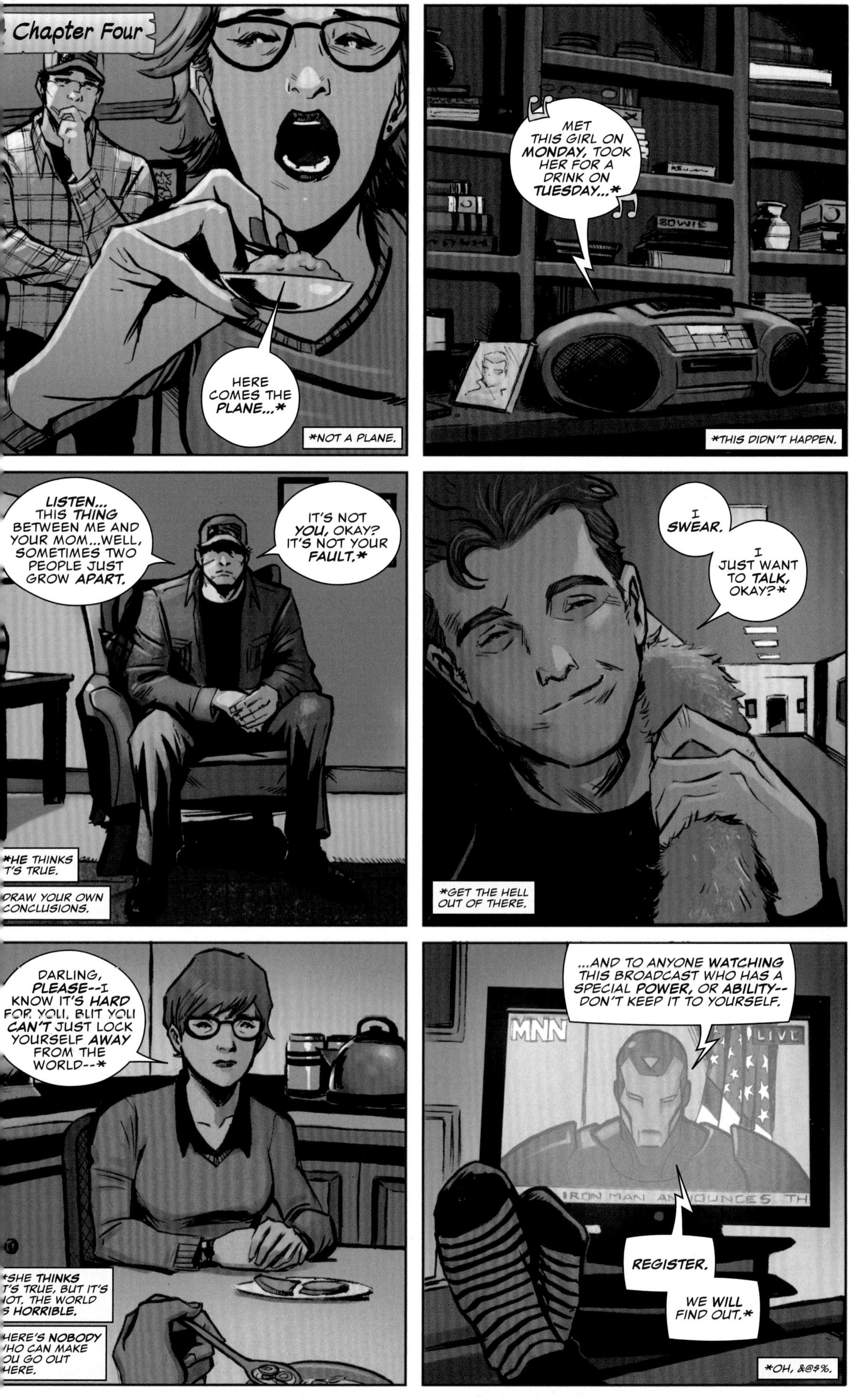
Chapter Four
HERE COMES THE PLANE...*
*NOT A PLANE.
MET THIS GIRL ON MONDAY, TOOK HER FOR A DRINK ON TUESDAY...*
BOWIE
*THIS DIDN'T HAPPEN.
LISTEN... THIS THING BETWEEN ME AND YOUR MOM...WELL, SOMETIMES TWO PEOPLE JUST GROW APART.
IT'S NOT YOU, OKAY? IT'S NOT YOUR FAULT.*
*HE THINKS 'T'S TRUE.
DRAW YOUR OWN CONCLUSIONS.
I SWEAR.
I JUST WANT TO TALK, OKAY?*
*GET THE HELL OUT OF THERE.
DARLING, PLEASE--I KNOW IT'S HARD FOR YOU, BUT YOU CAN'T JUST LOCK YOURSELF AWAY FROM THE WORLD--*
*SHE THINKS 'T'S TRUE, BUT IT'S NOT. THE WORLD S HORRIBLE.
HERE'S NOBODY WHO CAN MAKE OU GO OUT HERE.
...AND TO ANYONE WATCHING THIS BROADCAST WHO HAS A SPECIAL POWER, OR ABILITY--DON'T KEEP IT TO YOURSELF.
MNN
LIVE
IRON MAN ANNOUNCES TH
REGISTER.
WE WILL FIND OUT.*
*OH, &@$%.

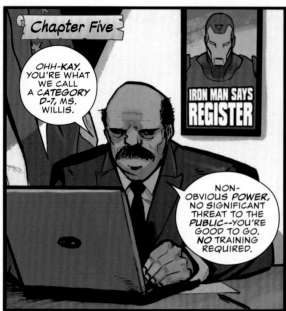

Chapter Five

OHH-KAY. YOU'RE WHAT WE CALL A *CATEGORY D-7*, MS. WILLIS.

IRON MAN SAYS REGISTER

NON-OBVIOUS *POWER*, NO SIGNIFICANT THREAT TO THE *PUBLIC*--YOU'RE GOOD TO GO. *NO TRAINING REQUIRED.*

YOU COULD JOIN A SUPERTEAM *TOMORROW* IF YOU WANTED.

THAT'S WHAT PEOPLE *DO* WITH SUPERPOWERS, RIGHT?

IRON REGISTER

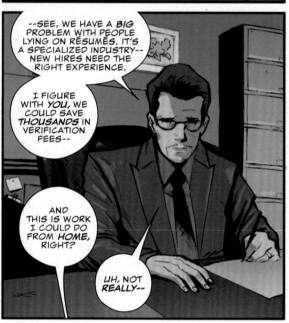

--SEE, WE HAVE A *BIG* PROBLEM WITH PEOPLE LYING ON RÉSUMÉS. IT'S A SPECIALIZED INDUSTRY-- NEW HIRES NEED THE RIGHT EXPERIENCE.

I FIGURE WITH *YOU*, WE COULD SAVE *THOUSANDS* IN VERIFICATION FEES--

AND THIS IS WORK I COULD DO FROM *HOME*, RIGHT?

UH, NOT *REALLY*--

WHAT I'D REALLY LIKE TO USE YOU FOR IS THE *POLITICAL* AND *BUSINESS SECTIONS*--HAVE YOU READ THROUGH A FEW *OFFICIAL STATEMENTS.*

FACT-CHECKING.

AND THIS IS WORK I COULD DO FROM *HOME*, RIGHT?

WE'D NEED YOU ON A *DESK*, I'M AFRAID.

OUR SURVEYS ARE *COMPLETELY ANONYMOUS*--THERE'S NO *REASON* TO LIE ON THEM ABOUT, SAY, YOUR *AGE*, OR YOUR *WEIGHT.*

BUT PEOPLE *DO*, ALL THE TIME. NOW, IF WE COULD *ELIMINATE* THAT *BAD DATA*...

AND THIS IS WORK I COULD DO FROM *HOME*, RIGHT?

I DON'T SEE WHY NOT.

HERE WE ARE.

WELCOME TO YOUR NEW *HOME*, MS. WILLIS.

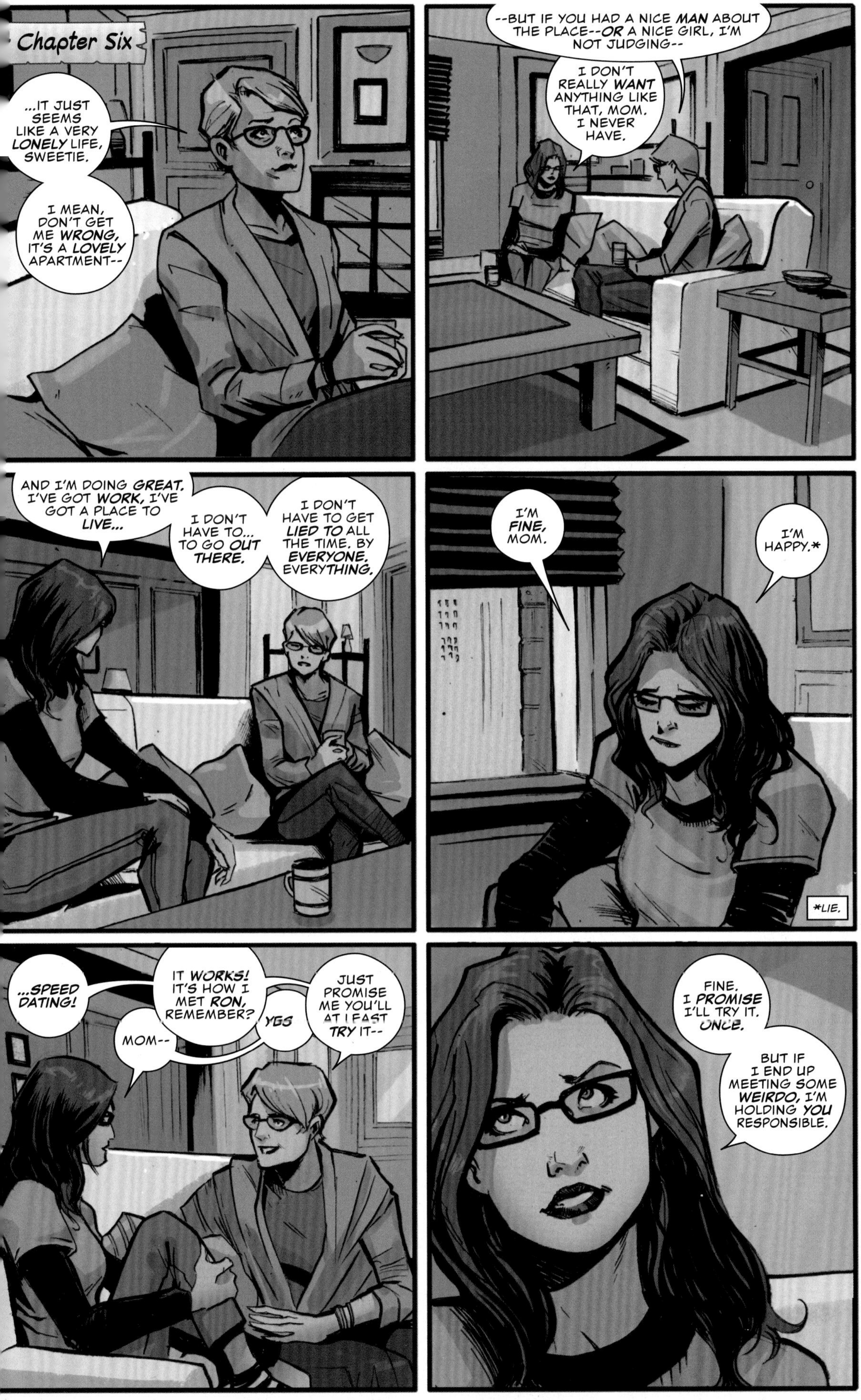
Chapter Six
...IT JUST SEEMS LIKE A VERY LONELY LIFE, SWEETIE.
I MEAN, DON'T GET ME WRONG, IT'S A LOVELY APARTMENT--
--BUT IF YOU HAD A NICE MAN ABOUT THE PLACE--OR A NICE GIRL, I'M NOT JUDGING--
I DON'T REALLY WANT ANYTHING LIKE THAT, MOM. I NEVER HAVE.
AND I'M DOING GREAT. I'VE GOT WORK, I'VE GOT A PLACE TO LIVE...
I DON'T HAVE TO... TO GO OUT THERE.
I DON'T HAVE TO GET LIED TO ALL THE TIME. BY EVERYONE. EVERYTHING.
I'M FINE, MOM.
I'M HAPPY.*
*LIE.
...SPEED DATING!
MOM--
IT WORKS! IT'S HOW I MET RON, REMEMBER?
YES
JUST PROMISE ME YOU'LL AT LEAST TRY IT--
FINE. I PROMISE I'LL TRY IT. ONCE.
BUT IF I END UP MEETING SOME WEIRDO, I'M HOLDING YOU RESPONSIBLE.

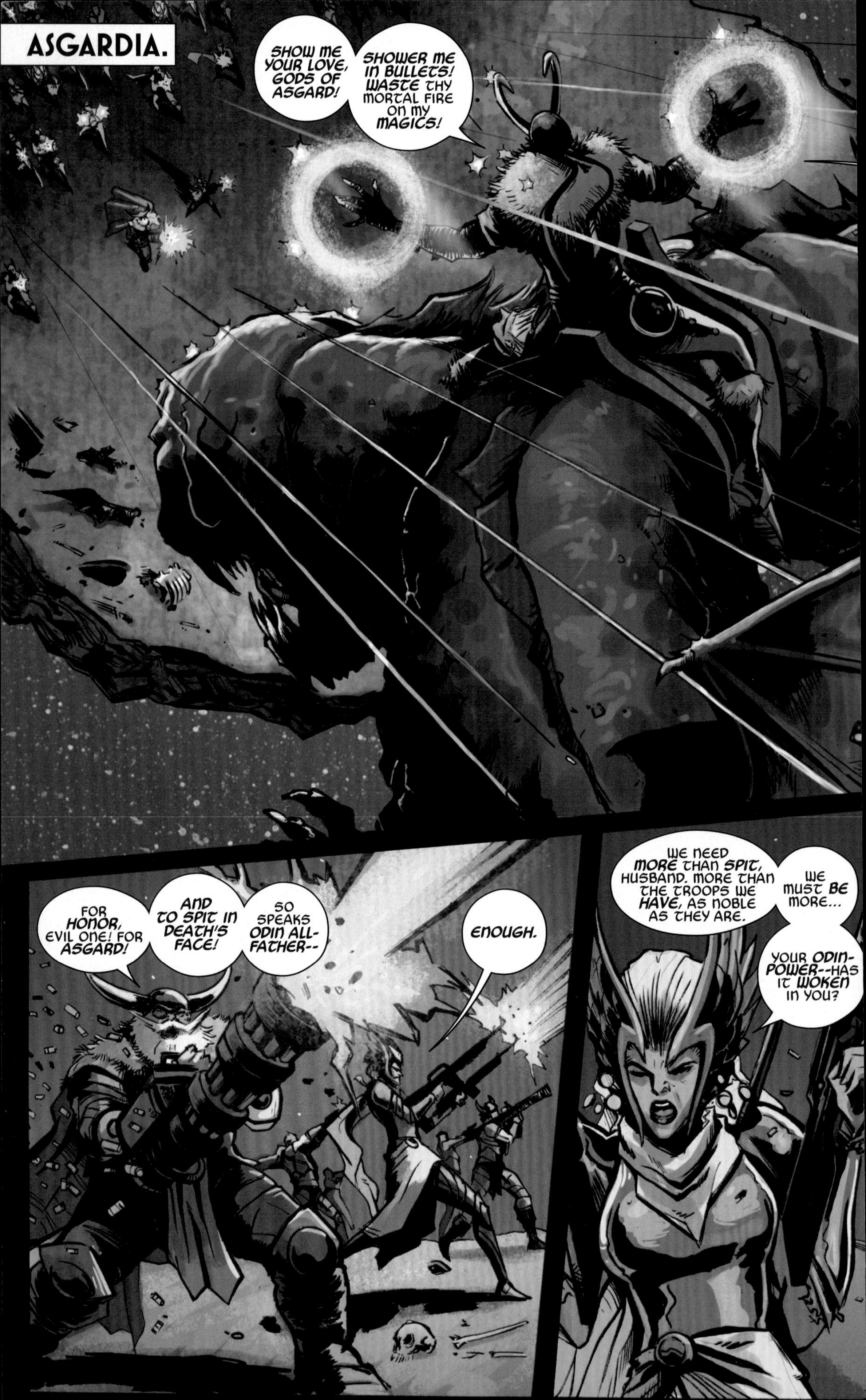
ASGARDIA.
SHOW ME YOUR LOVE, GODS OF ASGARD!
SHOWER ME IN BULLETS! WASTE THY MORTAL FIRE ON MY MAGICS!
FOR HONOR, EVIL ONE! FOR ASGARD!
AND TO SPIT IN DEATH'S FACE!
SO SPEAKS ODIN ALL-FATHER--
ENOUGH.
WE NEED MORE THAN SPIT, HUSBAND. MORE THAN THE TROOPS WE HAVE, AS NOBLE AS THEY ARE.
WE MUST BE MORE...
YOUR ODIN-POWER--HAS IT WOKEN IN YOU?

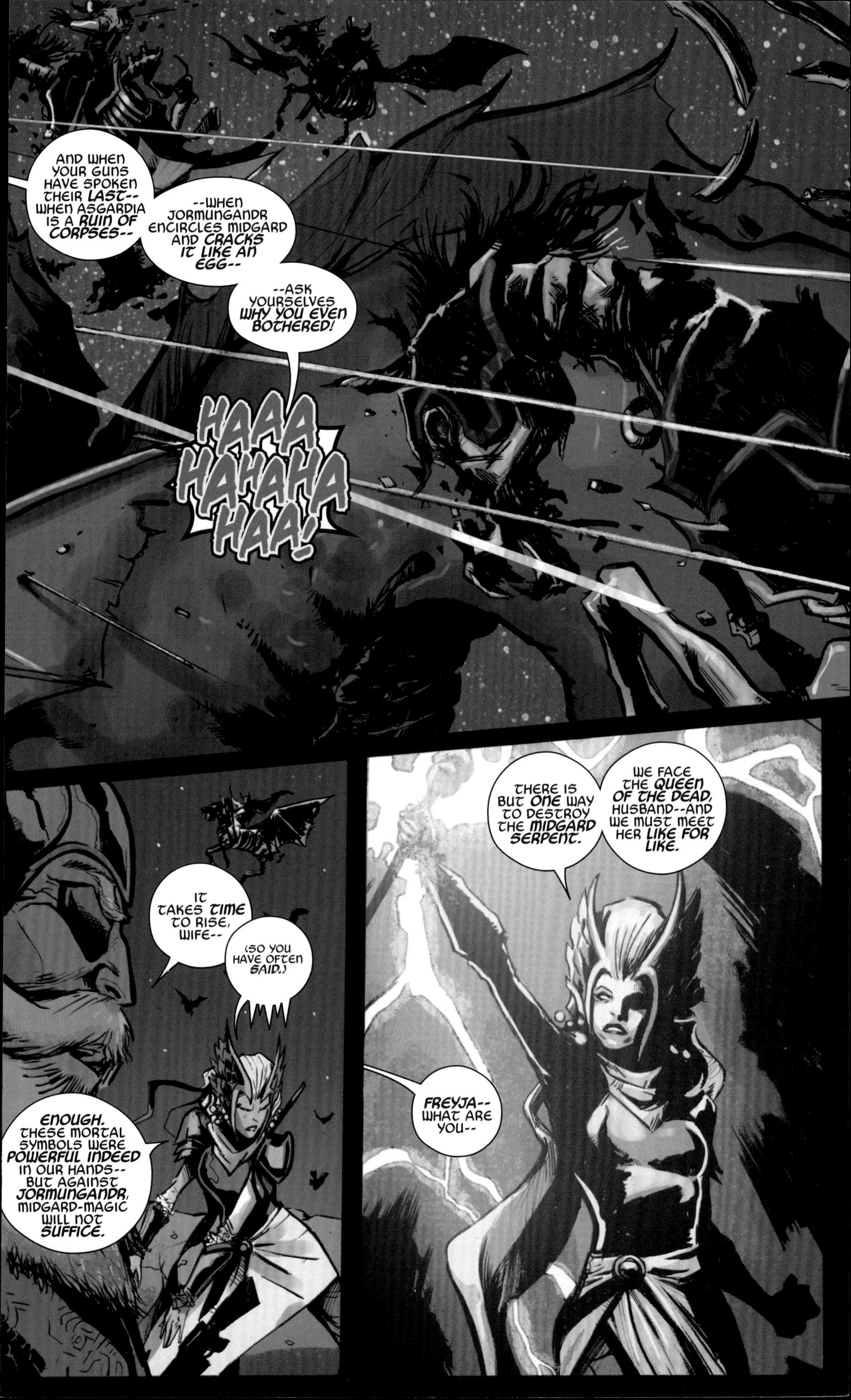

AND WHEN YOUR GUNS HAVE SPOKEN THEIR LAST-- WHEN ASGARDIA IS A RUIN OF CORPSES--
--WHEN JORMUNGANDR ENCIRCLES MIDGARD AND CRACKS IT LIKE AN EGG--
--ASK YOURSELVES WHY YOU EVEN BOTHERED!
HAAA HAHAHA HAA!
IT TAKES TIME TO RISE, WIFE--
(SO YOU HAVE OFTEN SAID.)
ENOUGH. THESE MORTAL SYMBOLS WERE POWERFUL INDEED IN OUR HANDS-- BUT AGAINST JORMUNGANDR, MIDGARD-MAGIC WILL NOT SUFFICE.
THERE IS BUT ONE WAY TO DESTROY THE MIDGARD SERPENT.
WE FACE THE QUEEN OF THE DEAD, HUSBAND--AND WE MUST MEET HER LIKE FOR LIKE.
FREYJA-- WHAT ARE YOU--

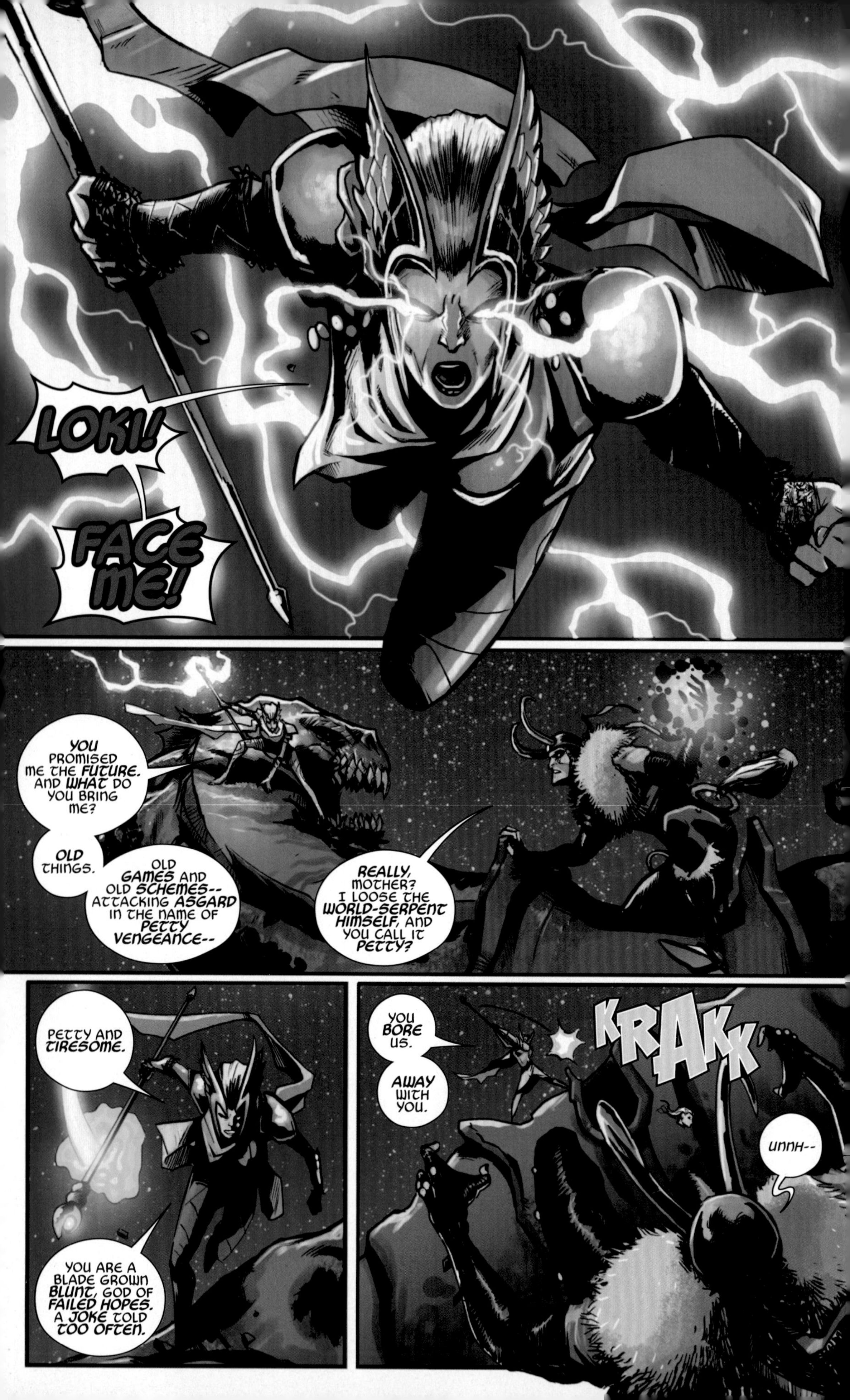

LOKI!
FACE ME!
YOU PROMISED ME THE FUTURE. AND WHAT DO YOU BRING ME?
OLD THINGS.
OLD GAMES AND OLD SCHEMES-- ATTACKING ASGARD IN THE NAME OF PETTY VENGEANCE--
REALLY, MOTHER? I LOOSE THE WORLD-SERPENT HIMSELF, AND YOU CALL IT PETTY?
PETTY AND TIRESOME.
YOU ARE A BLADE GROWN BLUNT, GOD OF FAILED HOPES. A JOKE TOLD TOO OFTEN.
YOU BORE US.
AWAY WITH YOU.
KRAKK
UNNH--

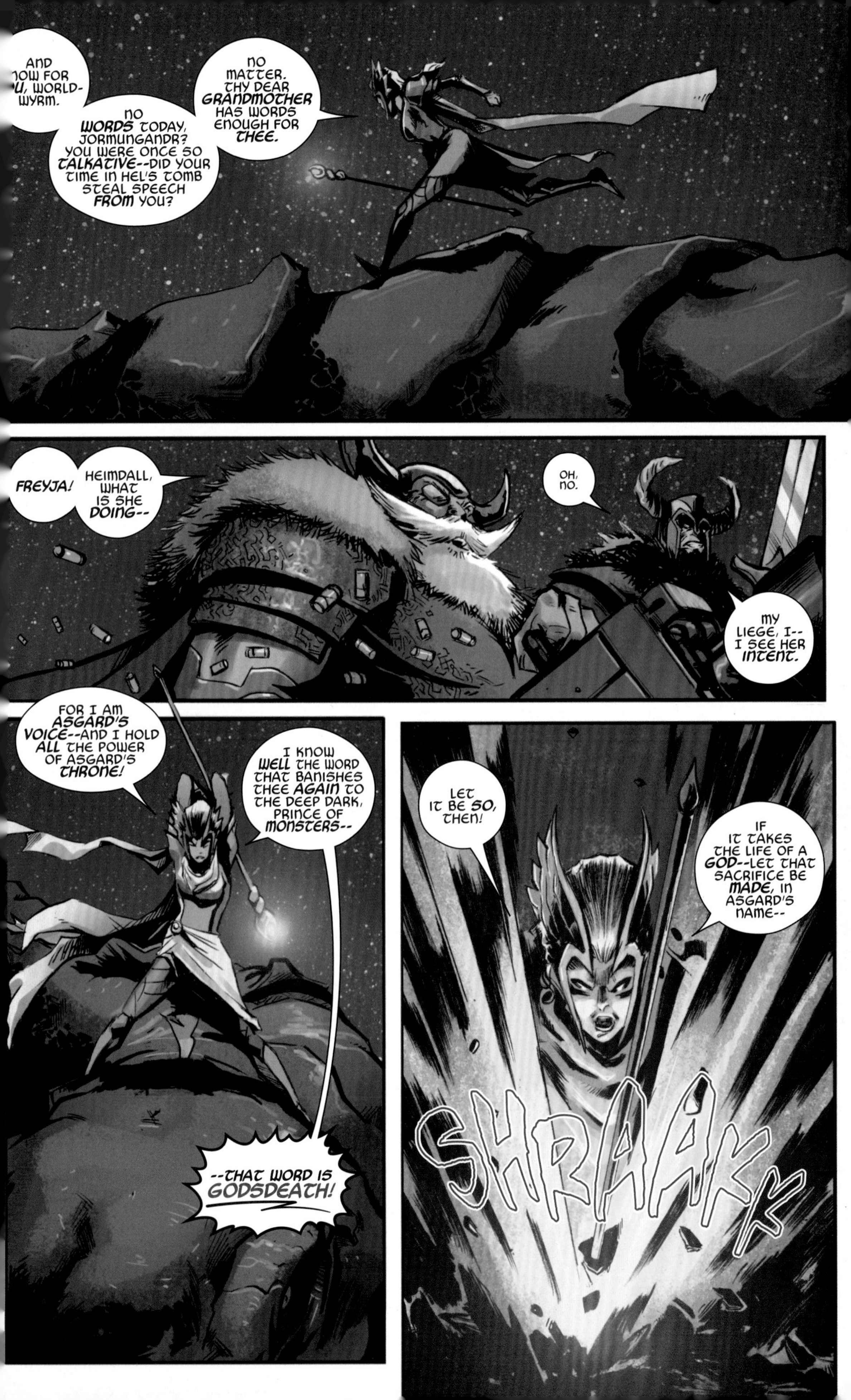
AND NOW FOR YOU, WORLD-WYRM.
NO WORDS TODAY, JORMUNGANDR? YOU WERE ONCE SO TALKATIVE--DID YOUR TIME IN HEL'S TOMB STEAL SPEECH FROM YOU?
NO MATTER. THY DEAR GRANDMOTHER HAS WORDS ENOUGH FOR THEE.
FREYJA!
HEIMDALL, WHAT IS SHE DOING--
OH, NO.
MY LIEGE, I-- I SEE HER INTENT.
FOR I AM ASGARD'S VOICE--AND I HOLD ALL THE POWER OF ASGARD'S THRONE!
I KNOW WELL THE WORD THAT BANISHES THEE AGAIN TO THE DEEP DARK, PRINCE OF MONSTERS--
--THAT WORD IS GODSDEATH!
LET IT BE SO, THEN!
IF IT TAKES THE LIFE OF A GOD--LET THAT SACRIFICE BE MADE, IN ASGARD'S NAME--
SHRAAKK

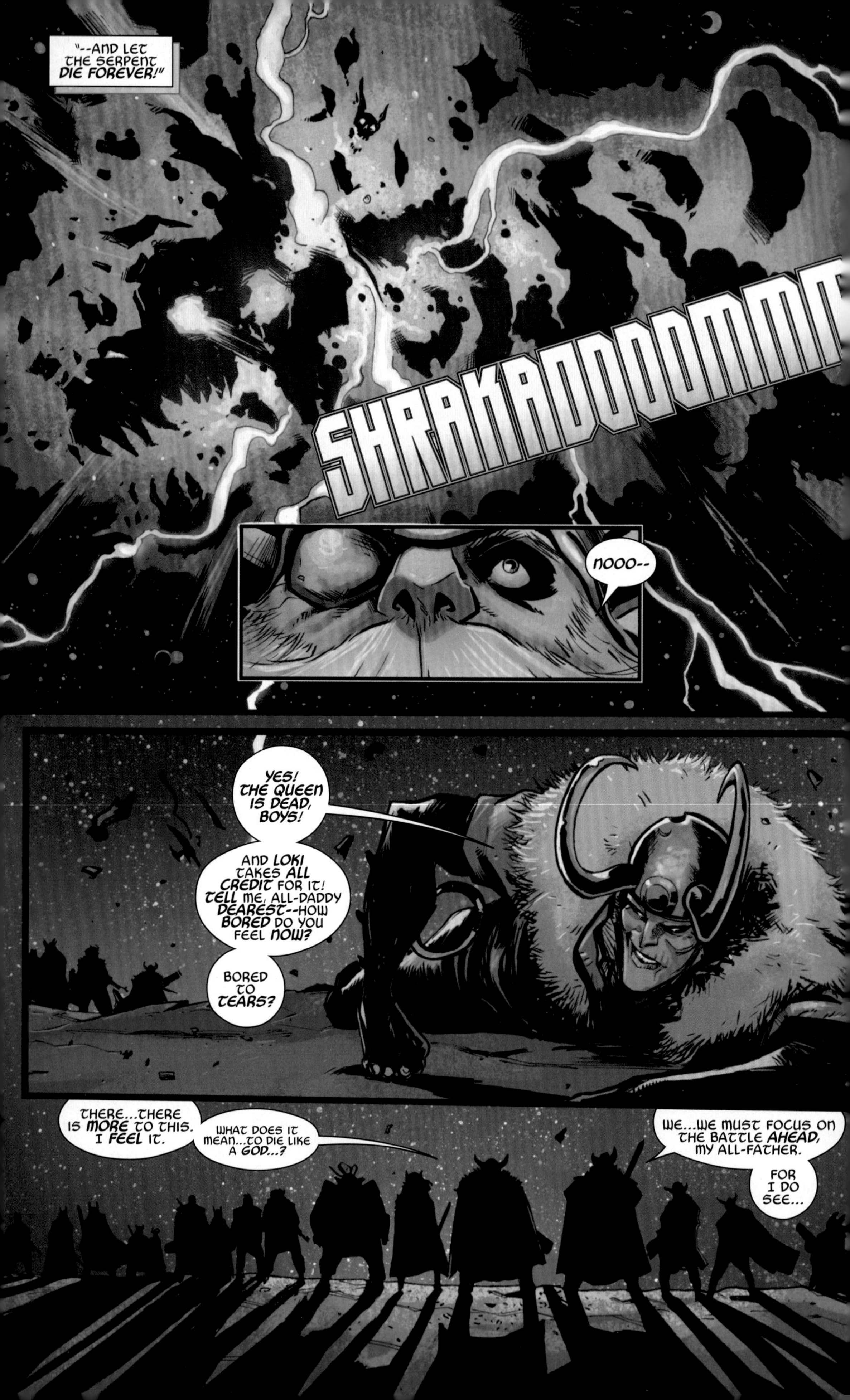
"--AND LET THE SERPENT DIE FOREVER!"
SHRAKADOOOMMM
NOOO--
YES! THE QUEEN IS DEAD, BOYS!
AND LOKI TAKES ALL CREDIT FOR IT! TELL ME, ALL-DADDY DEAREST--HOW BORED DO YOU FEEL NOW?
BORED TO TEARS?
THERE...THERE IS MORE TO THIS. I FEEL IT.
WHAT DOES IT MEAN...TO DIE LIKE A GOD...?
WE...WE MUST FOCUS ON THE BATTLE AHEAD, MY ALL-FATHER.
FOR I DO SEE...

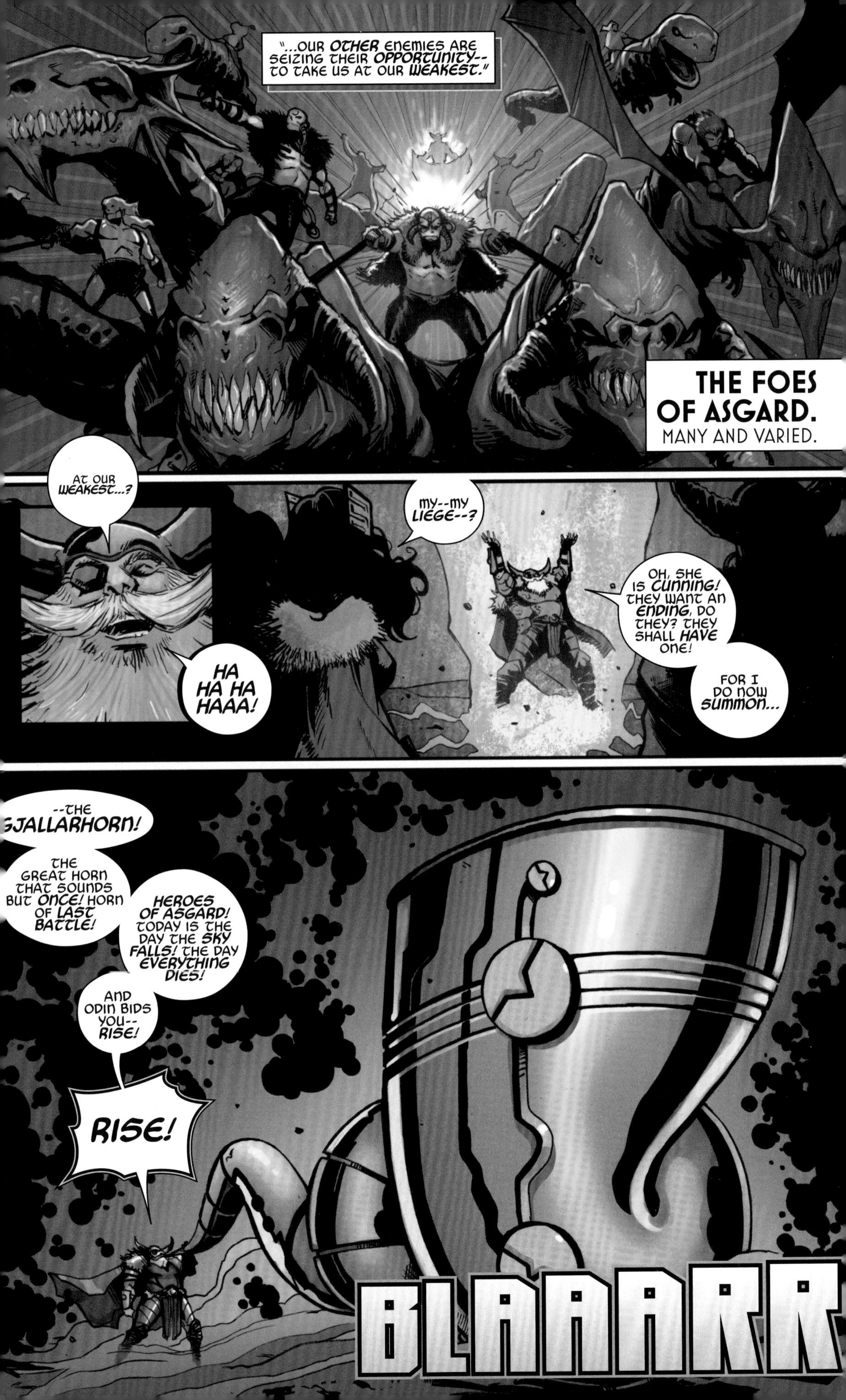
"...OUR OTHER ENEMIES ARE SEIZING THEIR OPPORTUNITY-- TO TAKE US AT OUR WEAKEST."
THE FOES OF ASGARD.
MANY AND VARIED.
AT OUR WEAKEST...?
HA HA HA HAAA!
MY--MY LIEGE--?
OH, SHE IS CUNNING! THEY WANT AN ENDING, DO THEY? THEY SHALL HAVE ONE!
FOR I DO NOW SUMMON...
--THE GJALLARHORN!
THE GREAT HORN THAT SOUNDS BUT ONCE! HORN OF LAST BATTLE!
HEROES OF ASGARD! TODAY IS THE DAY THE SKY FALLS! THE DAY EVERYTHING DIES!
AND ODIN BIDS YOU--RISE!
RISE!
BLAAARR

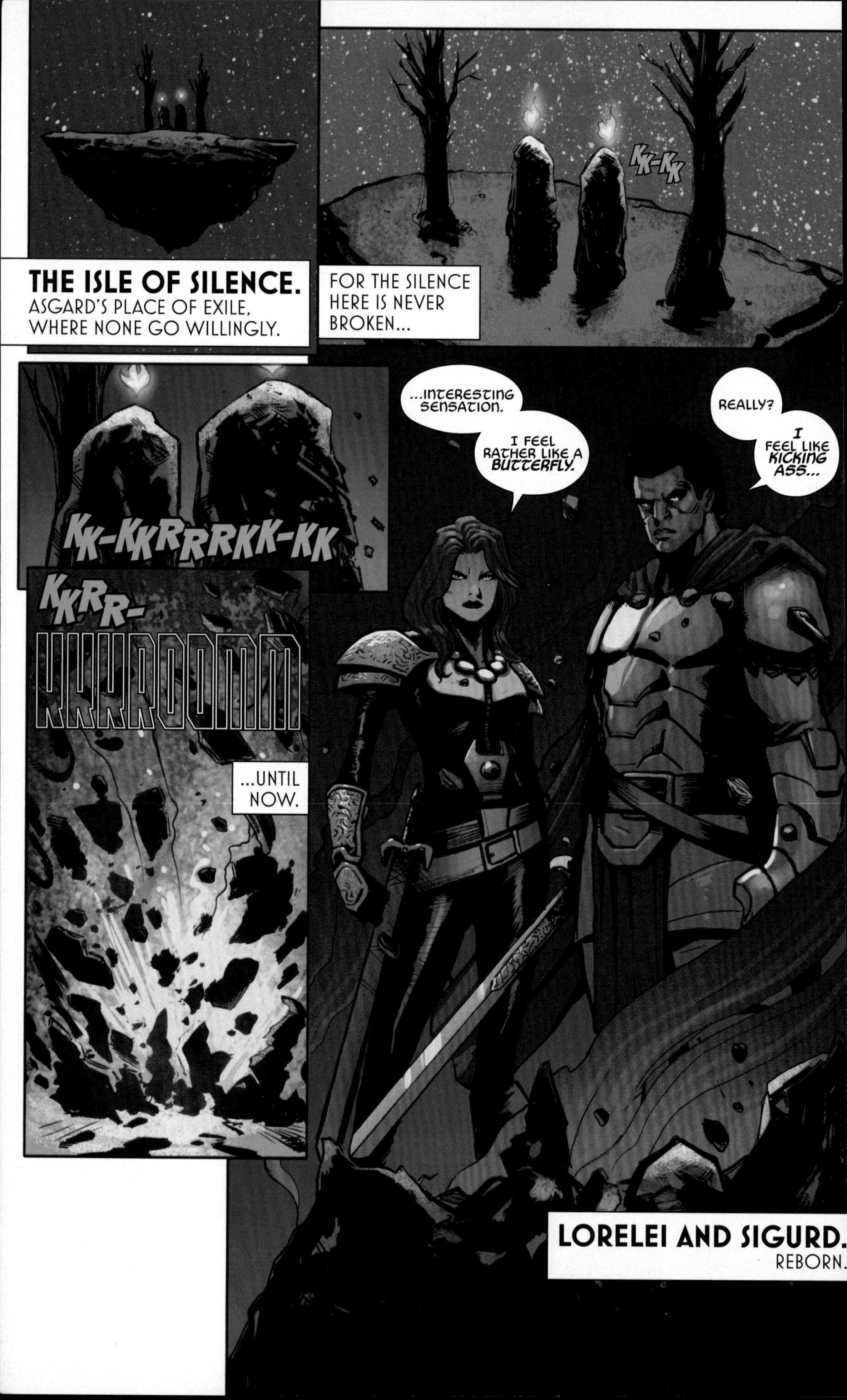

THE ISLE OF SILENCE.
ASGARD'S PLACE OF EXILE, WHERE NONE GO WILLINGLY.
FOR THE SILENCE HERE IS NEVER BROKEN...
KK-KK
KK-KKRRRKK-KK
KKRR-
KKKROOMM
...UNTIL NOW.
...INTERESTING SENSATION.
I FEEL RATHER LIKE A BUTTERFLY.
REALLY?
I FEEL LIKE KICKING ASS...
LORELEI AND SIGURD.
REBORN.

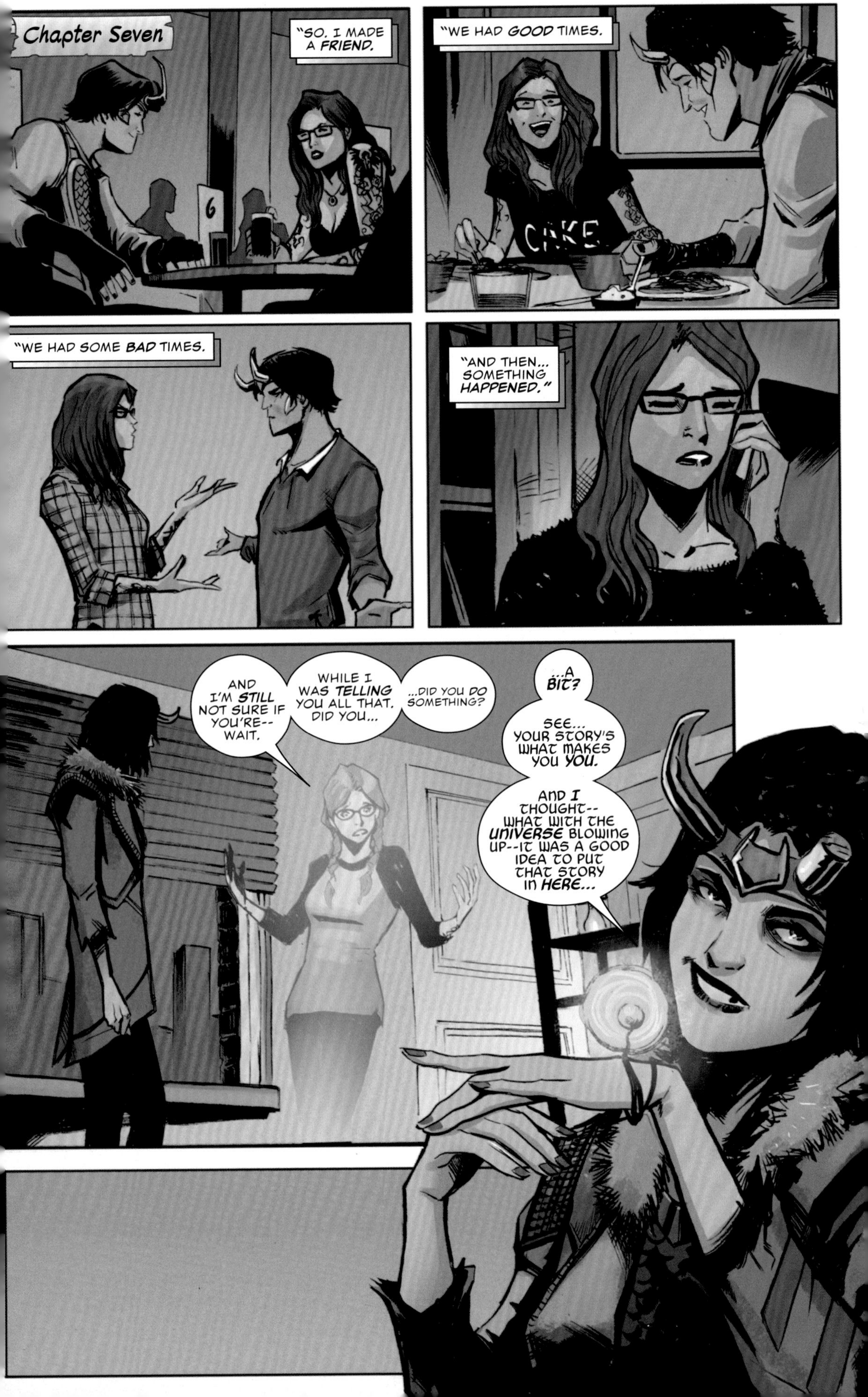
Chapter Seven
"SO, I MADE A FRIEND.
"WE HAD GOOD TIMES.
"WE HAD SOME BAD TIMES.
"AND THEN... SOMETHING HAPPENED."
AND I'M STILL NOT SURE IF YOU'RE-- WAIT.
WHILE I WAS TELLING YOU ALL THAT, DID YOU...
...DID YOU DO SOMETHING?
...A BIT?
SEE... YOUR STORY'S WHAT MAKES YOU YOU.
AND I THOUGHT-- WHAT WITH THE UNIVERSE BLOWING UP--IT WAS A GOOD IDEA TO PUT THAT STORY IN HERE...

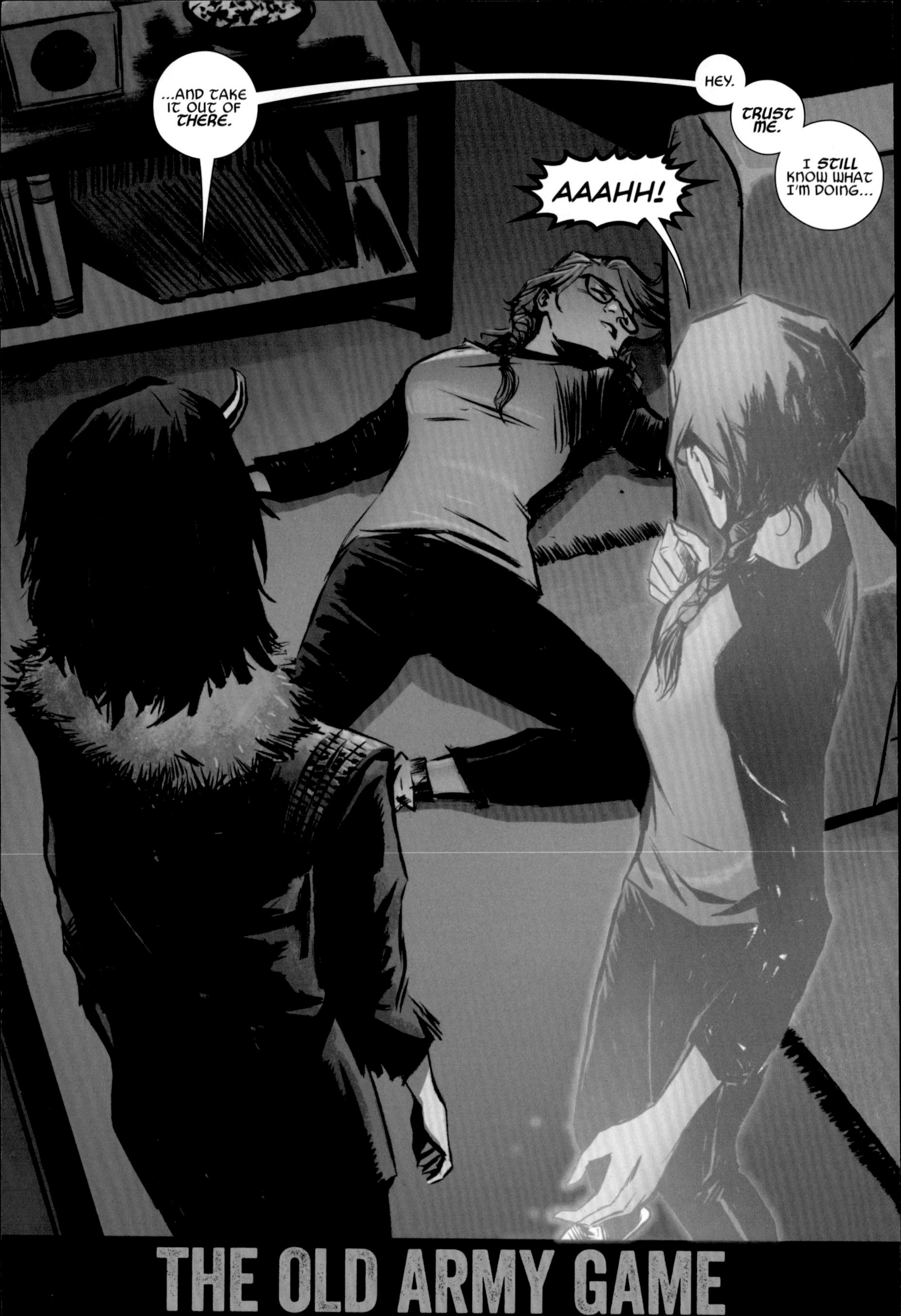
...AND TAKE IT OUT OF THERE.
HEY.
TRUST ME.
I STILL KNOW WHAT I'M DOING...
AAAHH!
THE OLD ARMY GAME

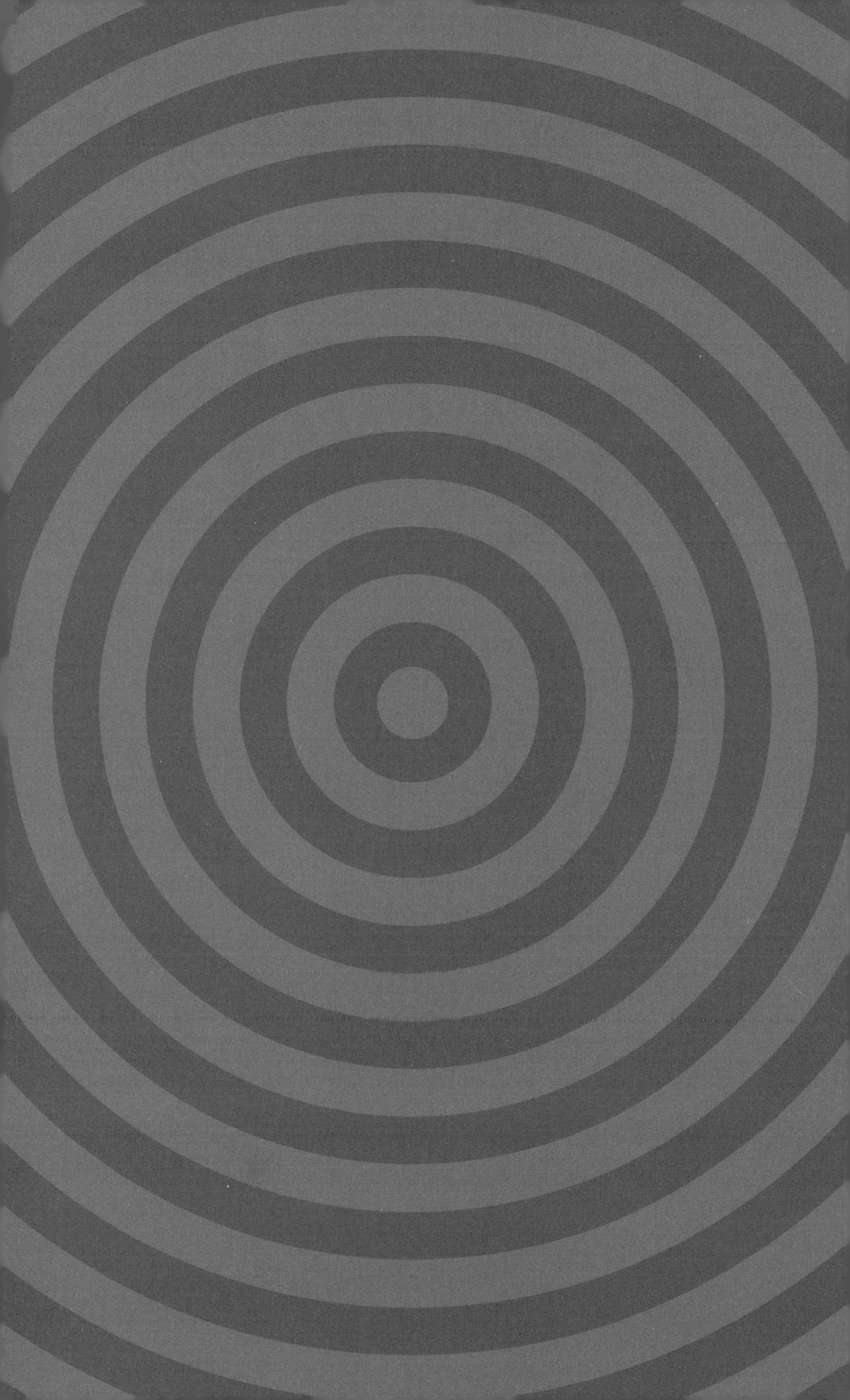

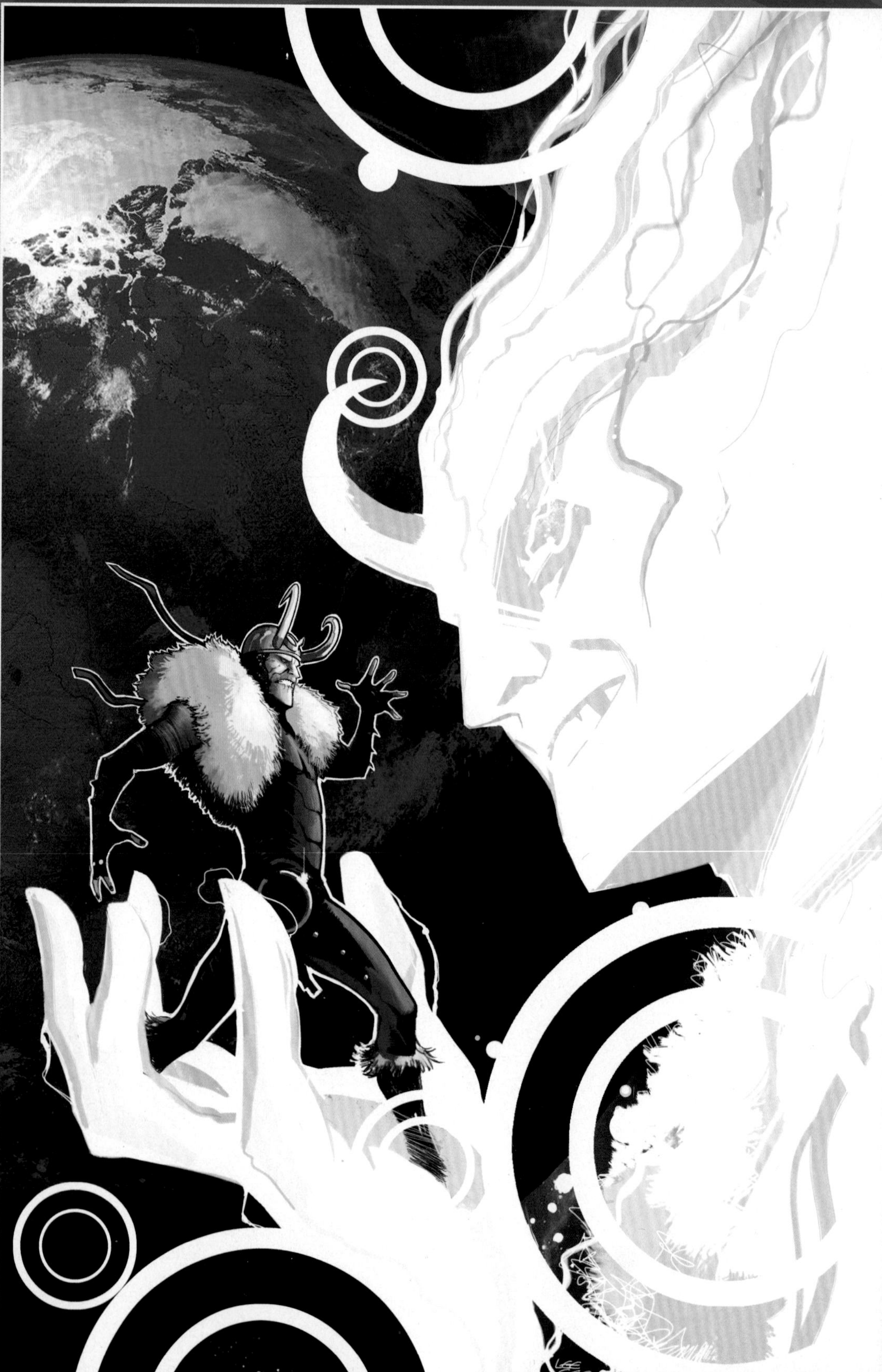

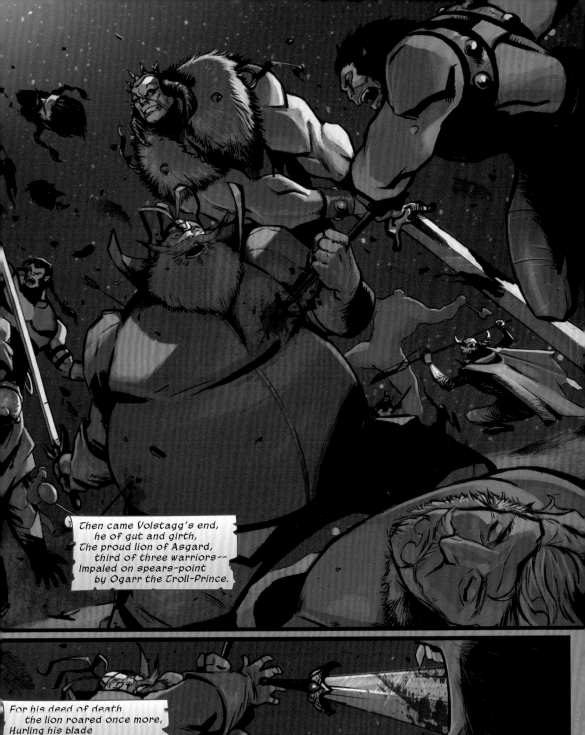

Then came Volstagg's end,
    he of gut and girth,
The proud lion of Asgard,
    third of three warriors--
Impaled on spears-point
    by Ogarr the Troll-Prince.

For his deed of death
    the lion roared once more,
Hurling his blade
    to cleave the troll's heart.

Then brave Volstagg fell,
    let go his last breath--

--and woke anew--

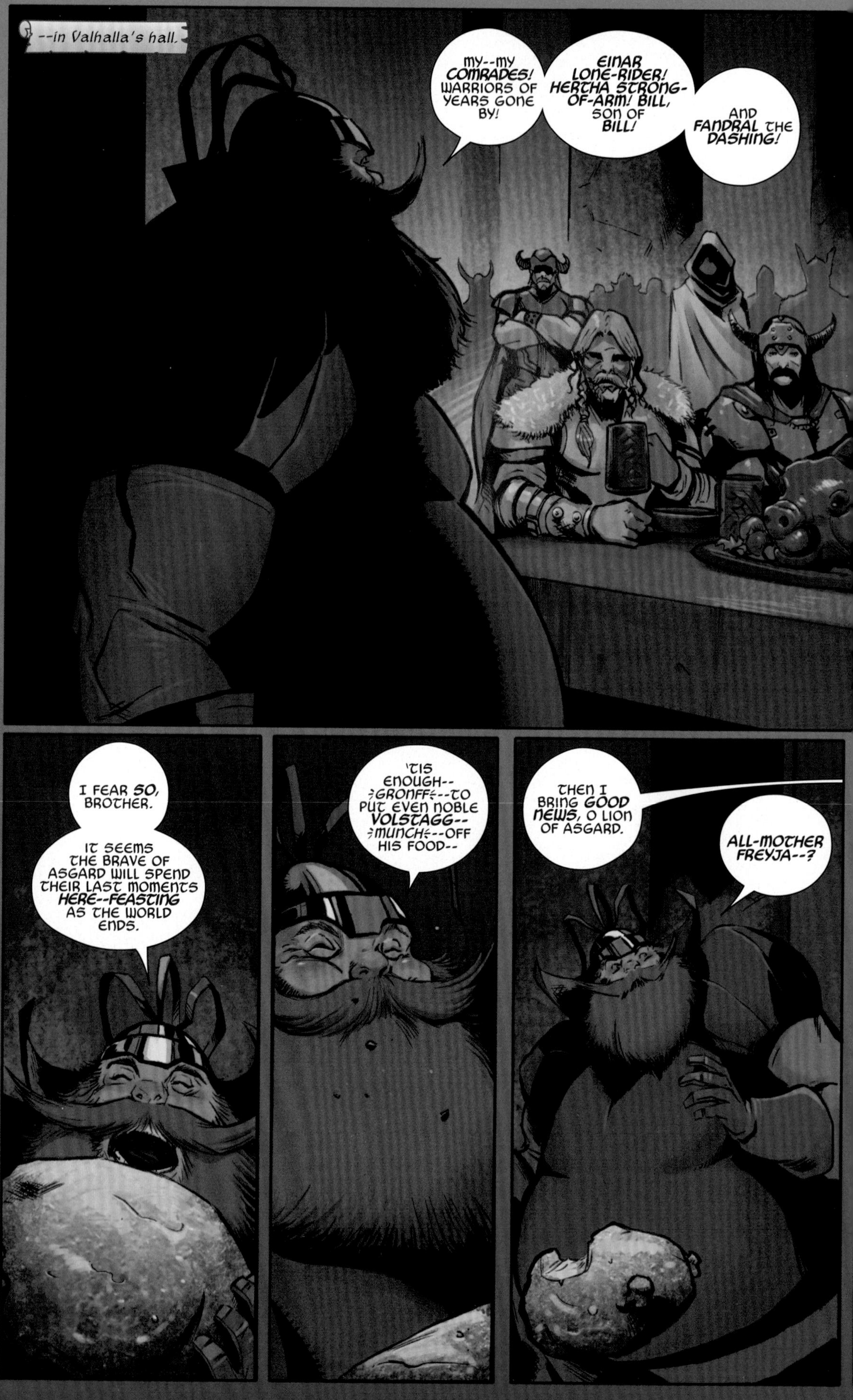
--in Valhalla's hall.
My--my COMRADES! Warriors of years gone by!
EINAR LONE-RIDER! HERTHA STRONG-OF-ARM! BILL, SON OF BILL!
And FANDRAL the DASHING!
I fear SO, brother.
It seems the brave of Asgard will spend their last moments HERE--FEASTING as the world ends.
'Tis enough-- *gronff*--to put even noble VOLSTAGG-- *munch*--off his food--
Then I bring GOOD NEWS, O Lion of Asgard.
ALL-MOTHER FREYJA--?

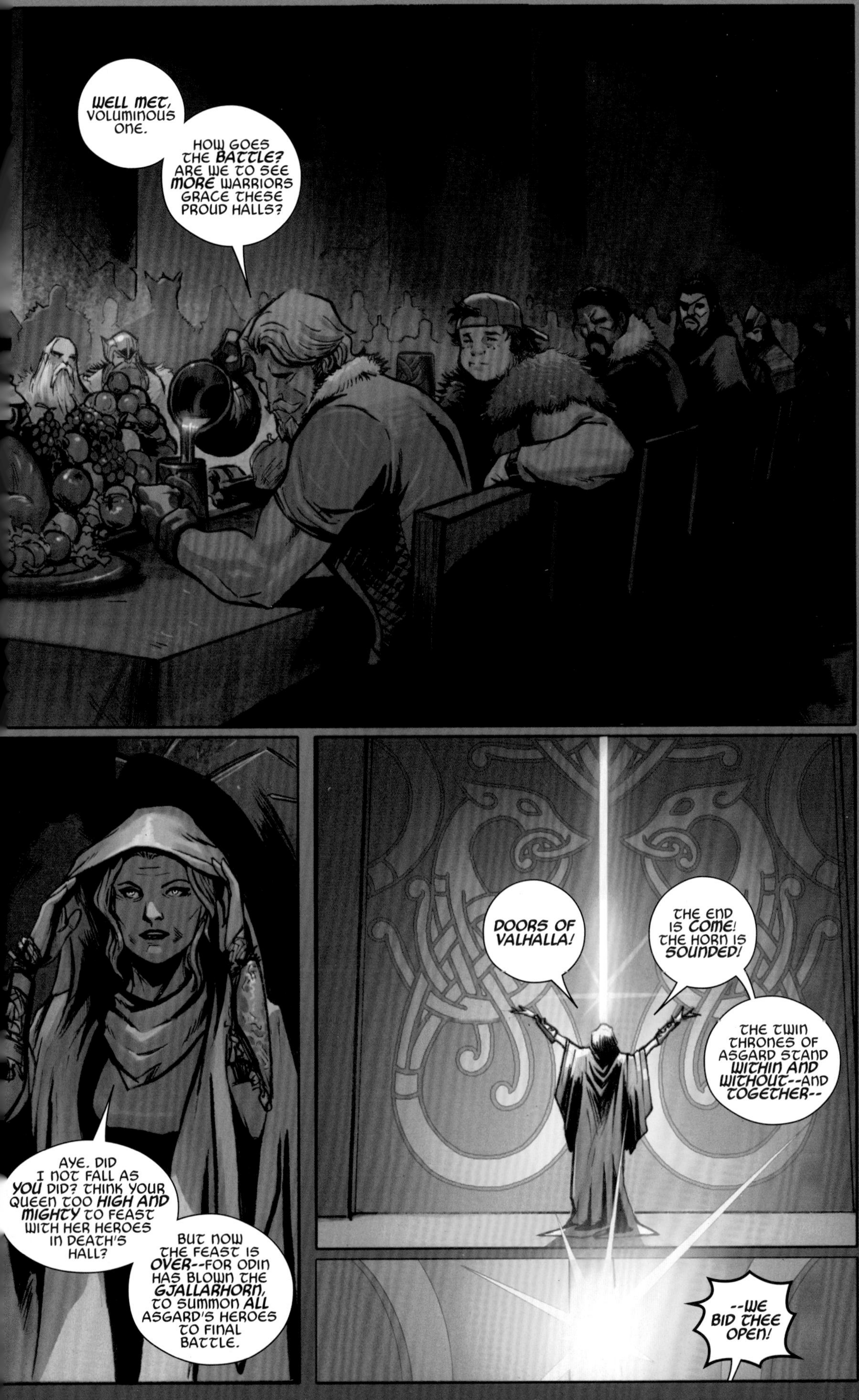
WELL MET, VOLUMINOUS ONE.
HOW GOES THE BATTLE? ARE WE TO SEE MORE WARRIORS GRACE THESE PROUD HALLS?
AYE. DID I NOT FALL AS YOU DID? THINK YOUR QUEEN TOO HIGH AND MIGHTY TO FEAST WITH HER HEROES IN DEATH'S HALL?
BUT NOW THE FEAST IS OVER--FOR ODIN HAS BLOWN THE GJALLARHORN, TO SUMMON ALL ASGARD'S HEROES TO FINAL BATTLE.
DOORS OF VALHALLA!
THE END IS COME! THE HORN IS SOUNDED!
THE TWIN THRONES OF ASGARD STAND WITHIN AND WITHOUT--AND TOGETHER--
--WE BID THEE OPEN!

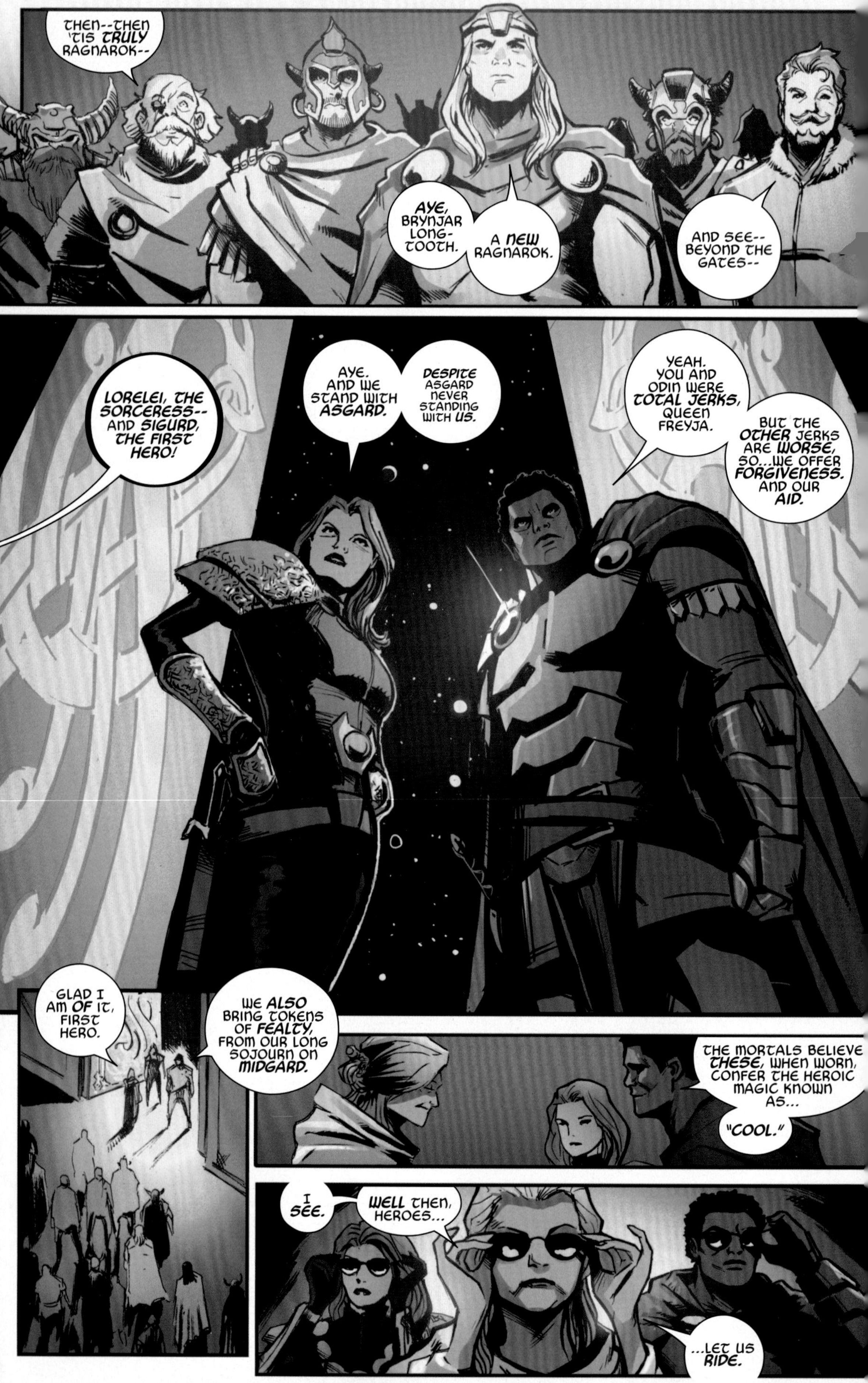

THEN--THEN 'TIS TRULY RAGNAROK--
AYE, BRYNJAR LONG-TOOTH.
A NEW RAGNAROK.
AND SEE--BEYOND THE GATES--
LORELEI, THE SORCERESS--AND SIGURD, THE FIRST HERO!
AYE. AND WE STAND WITH ASGARD.
DESPITE ASGARD NEVER STANDING WITH US.
YEAH. YOU AND ODIN WERE TOTAL JERKS, QUEEN FREYJA.
BUT THE OTHER JERKS ARE WORSE, SO...WE OFFER FORGIVENESS. AND OUR AID.
GLAD I AM OF IT, FIRST HERO.
WE ALSO BRING TOKENS OF FEALTY, FROM OUR LONG SOJOURN ON MIDGARD.
THE MORTALS BELIEVE THESE, WHEN WORN, CONFER THE HEROIC MAGIC KNOWN AS...
"COOL."
I SEE.
WELL THEN, HEROES...
...LET US RIDE.

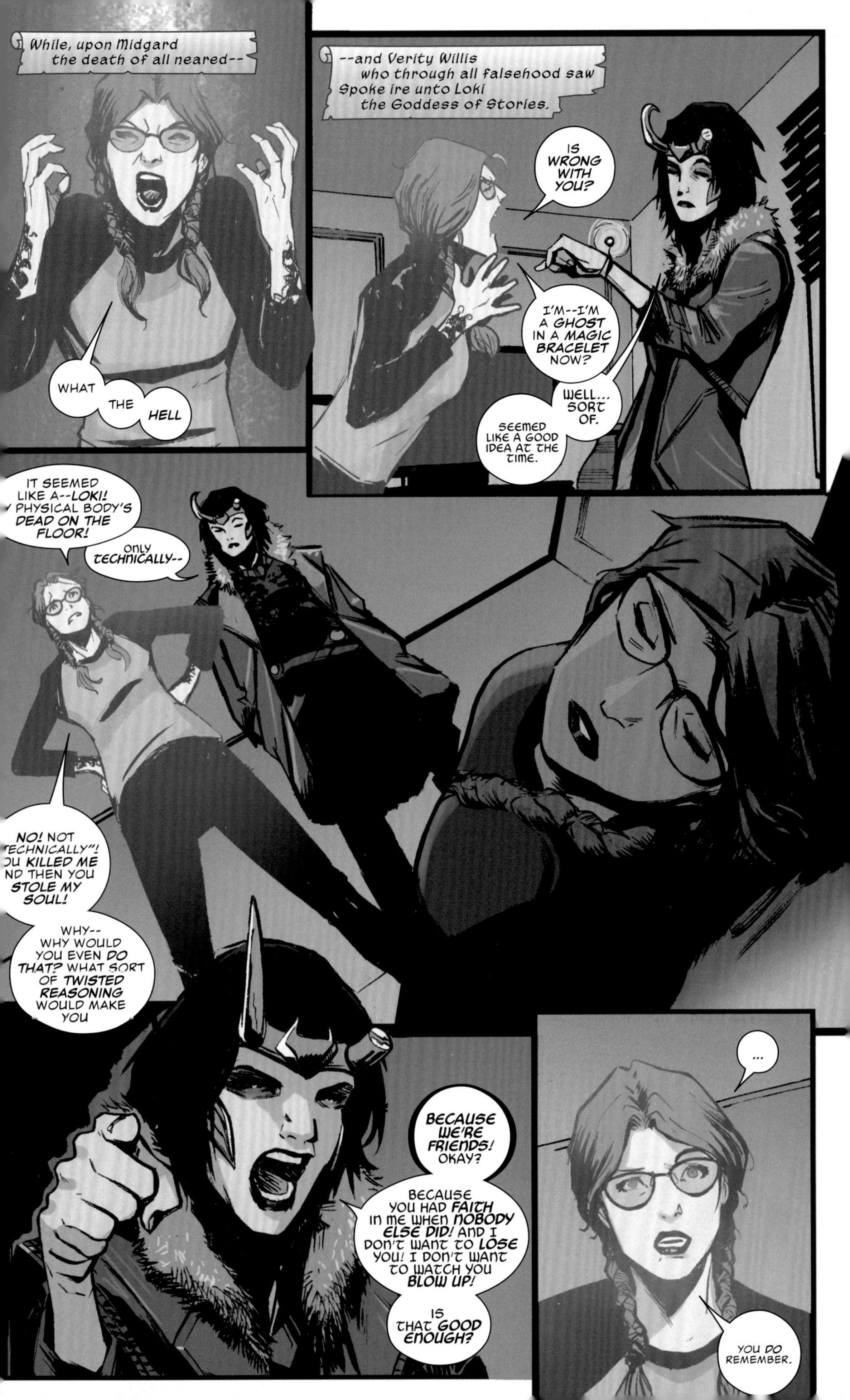
While, upon Midgard the death of all neared--
WHAT THE HELL
--and Verity Willis who through all falsehood saw Spoke ire unto Loki the Goddess of Stories.
IS WRONG WITH YOU?
I'M--I'M A GHOST IN A MAGIC BRACELET NOW?
WELL... SORT OF.
SEEMED LIKE A GOOD IDEA AT THE TIME.
IT SEEMED LIKE A--LOKI! Y PHYSICAL BODY'S DEAD ON THE FLOOR!
ONLY TECHNICALLY--
NO! NOT ECHNICALLY"! OU KILLED ME ND THEN YOU STOLE MY SOUL!
WHY-- WHY WOULD YOU EVEN DO THAT? WHAT SORT OF TWISTED REASONING WOULD MAKE YOU
BECAUSE WE'RE FRIENDS! OKAY?
BECAUSE YOU HAD FAITH IN ME WHEN NOBODY ELSE DID! AND I DON'T WANT TO LOSE YOU! I DON'T WANT TO WATCH YOU BLOW UP!
IS THAT GOOD ENOUGH?
...
YOU DO REMEMBER.

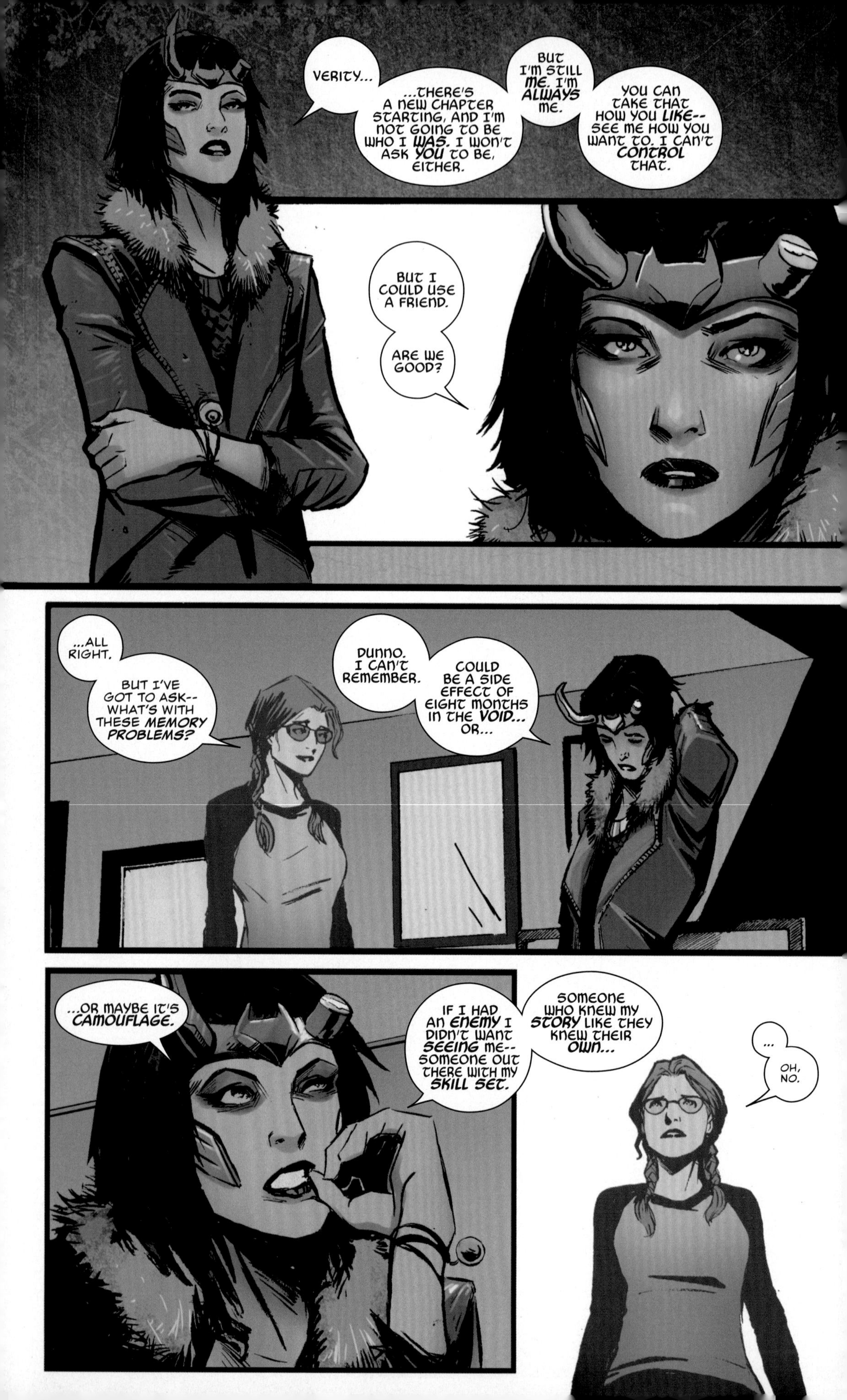
VERITY...
...THERE'S A NEW CHAPTER STARTING, AND I'M NOT GOING TO BE WHO I WAS. I WON'T ASK YOU TO BE, EITHER.
BUT I'M STILL ME. I'M ALWAYS ME.
YOU CAN TAKE THAT HOW YOU LIKE-- SEE ME HOW YOU WANT TO. I CAN'T CONTROL THAT.
BUT I COULD USE A FRIEND.
ARE WE GOOD?
...ALL RIGHT.
BUT I'VE GOT TO ASK-- WHAT'S WITH THESE MEMORY PROBLEMS?
DUNNO. I CAN'T REMEMBER.
COULD BE A SIDE EFFECT OF EIGHT MONTHS IN THE VOID... OR...
...OR MAYBE IT'S CAMOUFLAGE.
IF I HAD AN ENEMY I DIDN'T WANT SEEING ME-- SOMEONE OUT THERE WITH MY SKILL SET.
SOMEONE WHO KNEW MY STORY LIKE THEY KNEW THEIR OWN...
...
OH, NO.

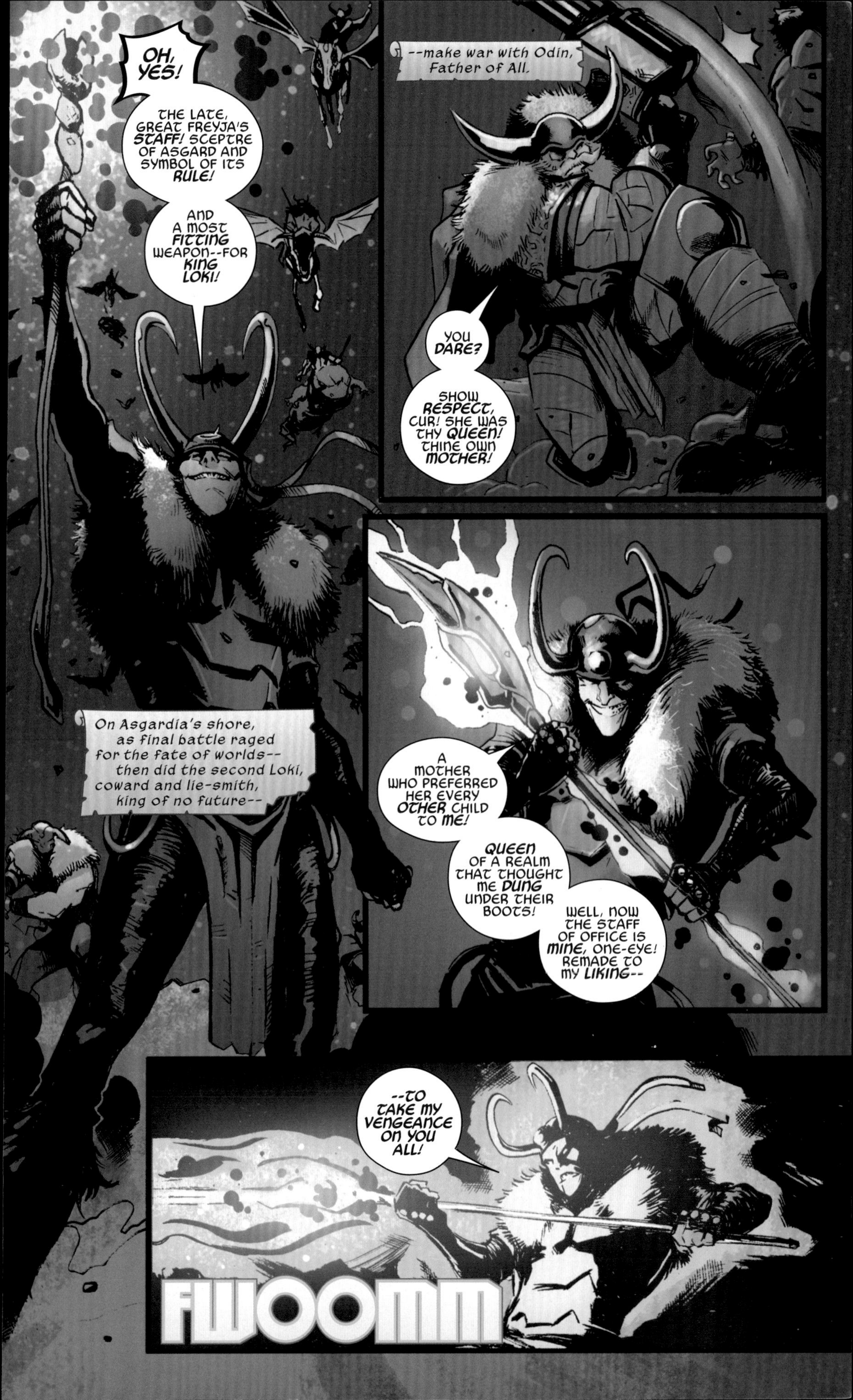
OH, YES!
THE LATE, GREAT FREYJA'S STAFF! SCEPTRE OF ASGARD AND SYMBOL OF ITS RULE!
AND A MOST FITTING WEAPON--FOR KING LOKI!
On Asgardia's shore, as final battle raged for the fate of worlds-- then did the second Loki, coward and lie-smith, king of no future--
--make war with Odin, Father of All.
YOU DARE?
SHOW RESPECT, CUR! SHE WAS THY QUEEN! THINE OWN MOTHER!
A MOTHER WHO PREFERRED HER EVERY OTHER CHILD TO ME!
QUEEN OF A REALM THAT THOUGHT ME DUNG UNDER THEIR BOOTS!
WELL, NOW THE STAFF OF OFFICE IS MINE, ONE-EYE! REMADE TO MY LIKING--
--TO TAKE MY VENGEANCE ON YOU ALL!
FWOOMM

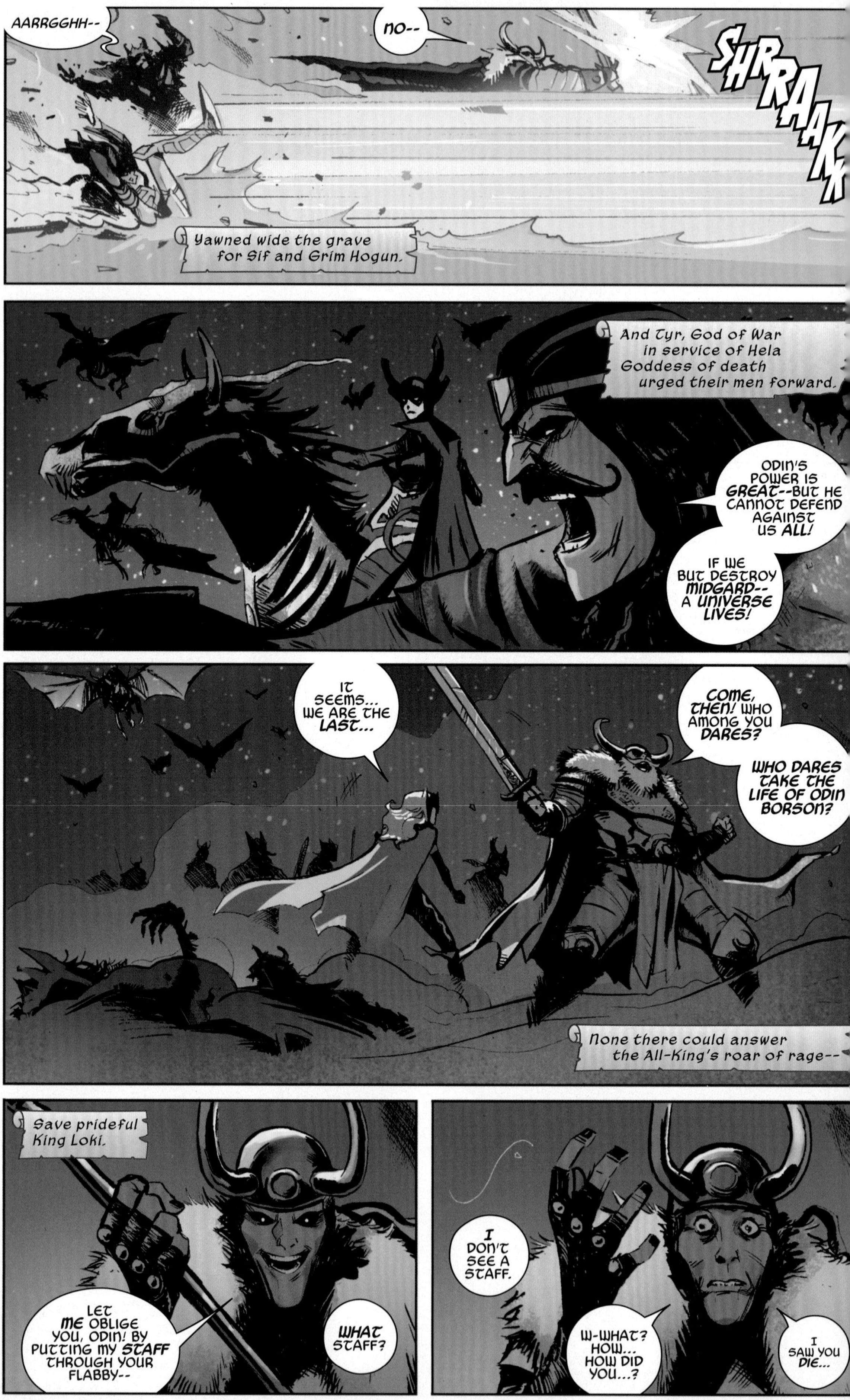

AARRGGHH--
no--
SHRRAAKK
Yawned wide the grave for Sif and Grim Hogun.
And Tyr, God of War in service of Hela Goddess of death urged their men forward.
ODIN'S POWER IS GREAT--BUT HE CANNOT DEFEND AGAINST US ALL!
IF WE BUT DESTROY MIDGARD-- A UNIVERSE LIVES!
IT SEEMS... WE ARE THE LAST...
COME, THEN! WHO AMONG YOU DARES?
WHO DARES TAKE THE LIFE OF ODIN BORSON?
None there could answer the All-King's roar of rage--
Save prideful King Loki.
LET ME OBLIGE YOU, ODIN! BY PUTTING MY STAFF THROUGH YOUR FLABBY--
WHAT STAFF?
I DON'T SEE A STAFF.
W-WHAT? HOW... HOW DID YOU...?
I SAW YOU DIE...

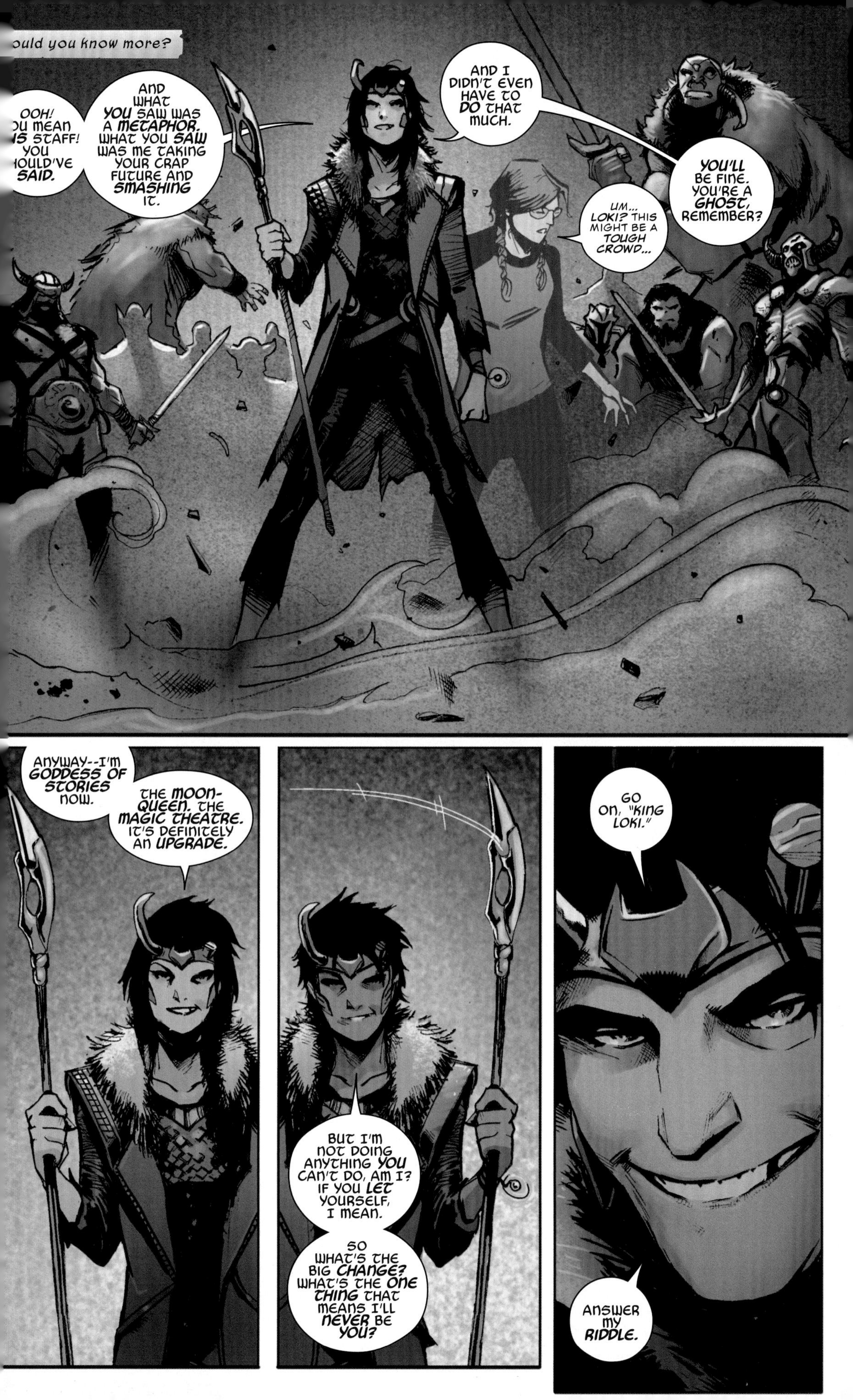
ould you know more?
OOH! OU MEAN IS STAFF! YOU HOULD'VE SAID.
AND WHAT YOU SAW WAS A METAPHOR. WHAT YOU SAW WAS ME TAKING YOUR CRAP FUTURE AND SMASHING IT.
AND I DIDN'T EVEN HAVE TO DO THAT MUCH.
UM... LOKI? THIS MIGHT BE A TOUGH CROWD...
YOU'LL BE FINE. YOU'RE A GHOST, REMEMBER?
ANYWAY--I'M GODDESS OF STORIES NOW.
THE MOON-QUEEN. THE MAGIC THEATRE. IT'S DEFINITELY AN UPGRADE.
BUT I'M NOT DOING ANYTHING YOU CAN'T DO, AM I? IF YOU LET YOURSELF, I MEAN.
SO WHAT'S THE BIG CHANGE? WHAT'S THE ONE THING THAT MEANS I'LL NEVER BE YOU?
GO ON, "KING LOKI."
ANSWER MY RIDDLE.

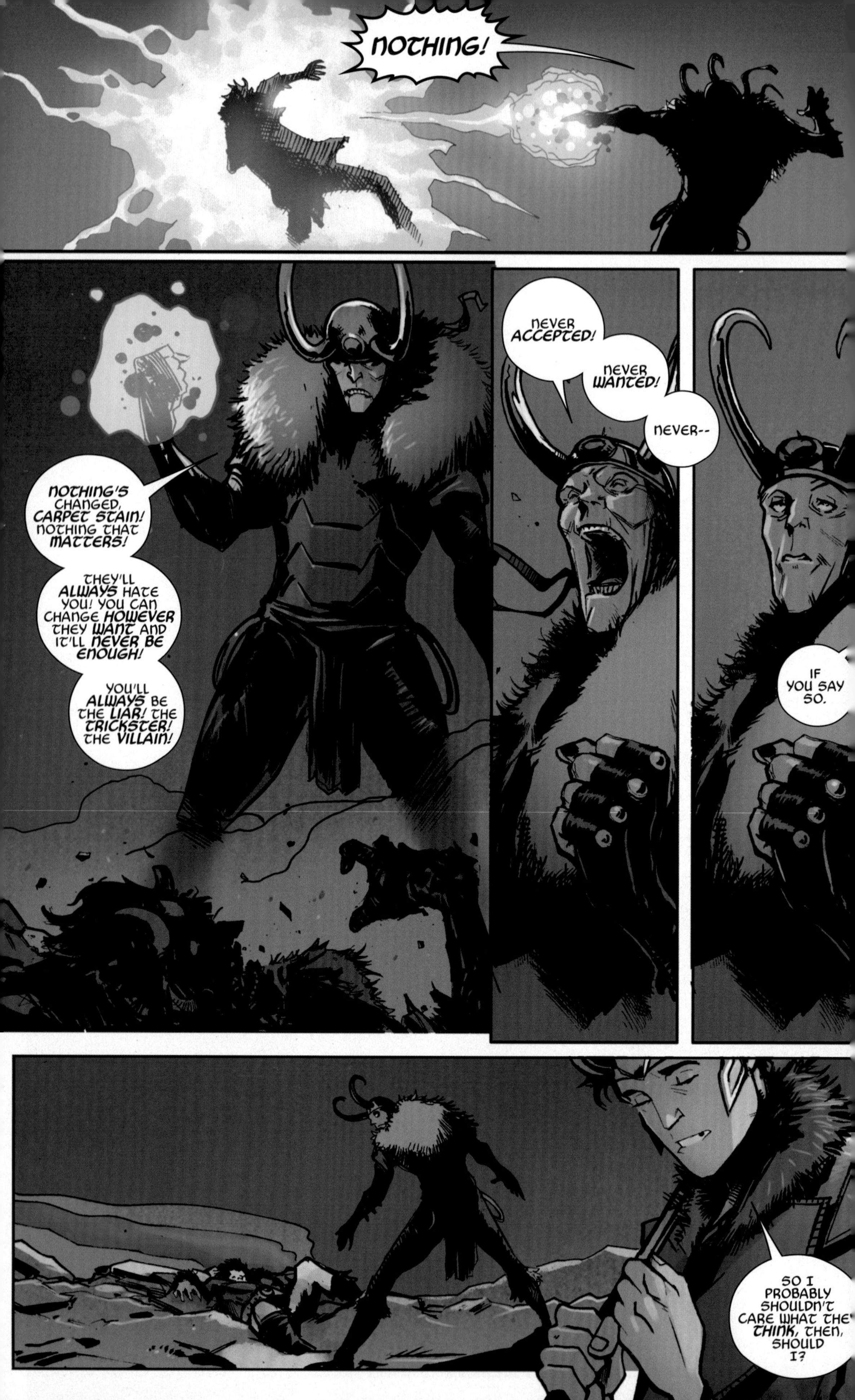
NOTHING!
NOTHING'S CHANGED, CARPET STAIN! NOTHING THAT MATTERS!
THEY'LL ALWAYS HATE YOU! YOU CAN CHANGE HOWEVER THEY WANT AND IT'LL NEVER BE ENOUGH!
YOU'LL ALWAYS BE THE LIAR! THE TRICKSTER! THE VILLAIN!
NEVER ACCEPTED!
NEVER WANTED!
NEVER--
IF YOU SAY SO.
SO I PROBABLY SHOULDN'T CARE WHAT THE THINK, THEN, SHOULD I?

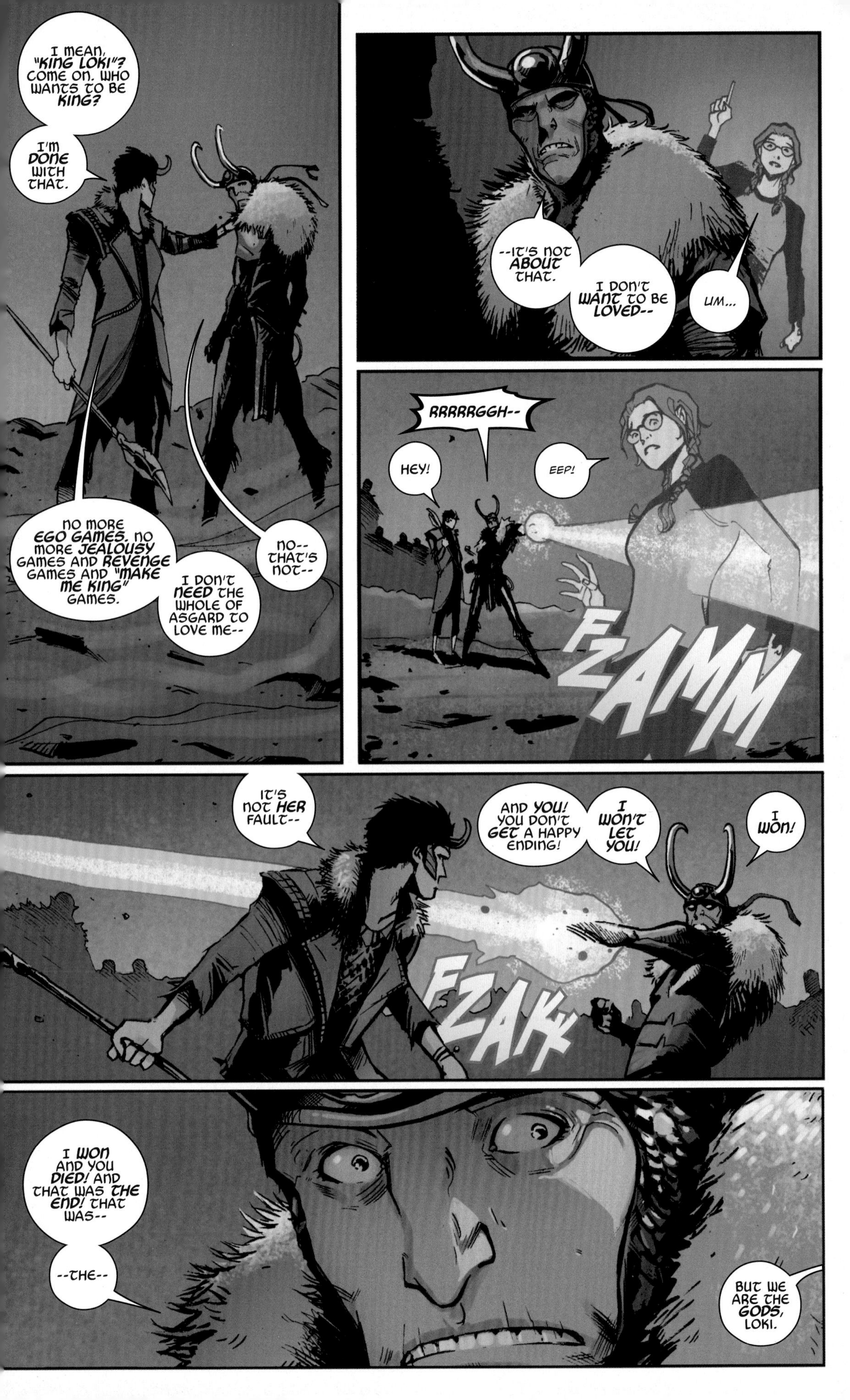
I MEAN, "KING LOKI"? COME ON. WHO WANTS TO BE KING?
I'M DONE WITH THAT.
NO MORE EGO GAMES. NO MORE JEALOUSY GAMES AND REVENGE GAMES AND "MAKE ME KING" GAMES.
NO--THAT'S NOT--
I DON'T NEED THE WHOLE OF ASGARD TO LOVE ME--
--IT'S NOT ABOUT THAT.
I DON'T WANT TO BE LOVED--
UM...
RRRRRGGH--
HEY!
EEP!
FZAMM
IT'S NOT HER FAULT--
AND YOU! YOU DON'T GET A HAPPY ENDING!
I WON'T LET YOU!
I WON!
FZAK
I WON AND YOU DIED! AND THAT WAS THE END! THAT WAS--
--THE--
BUT WE ARE THE GODS, LOKI.

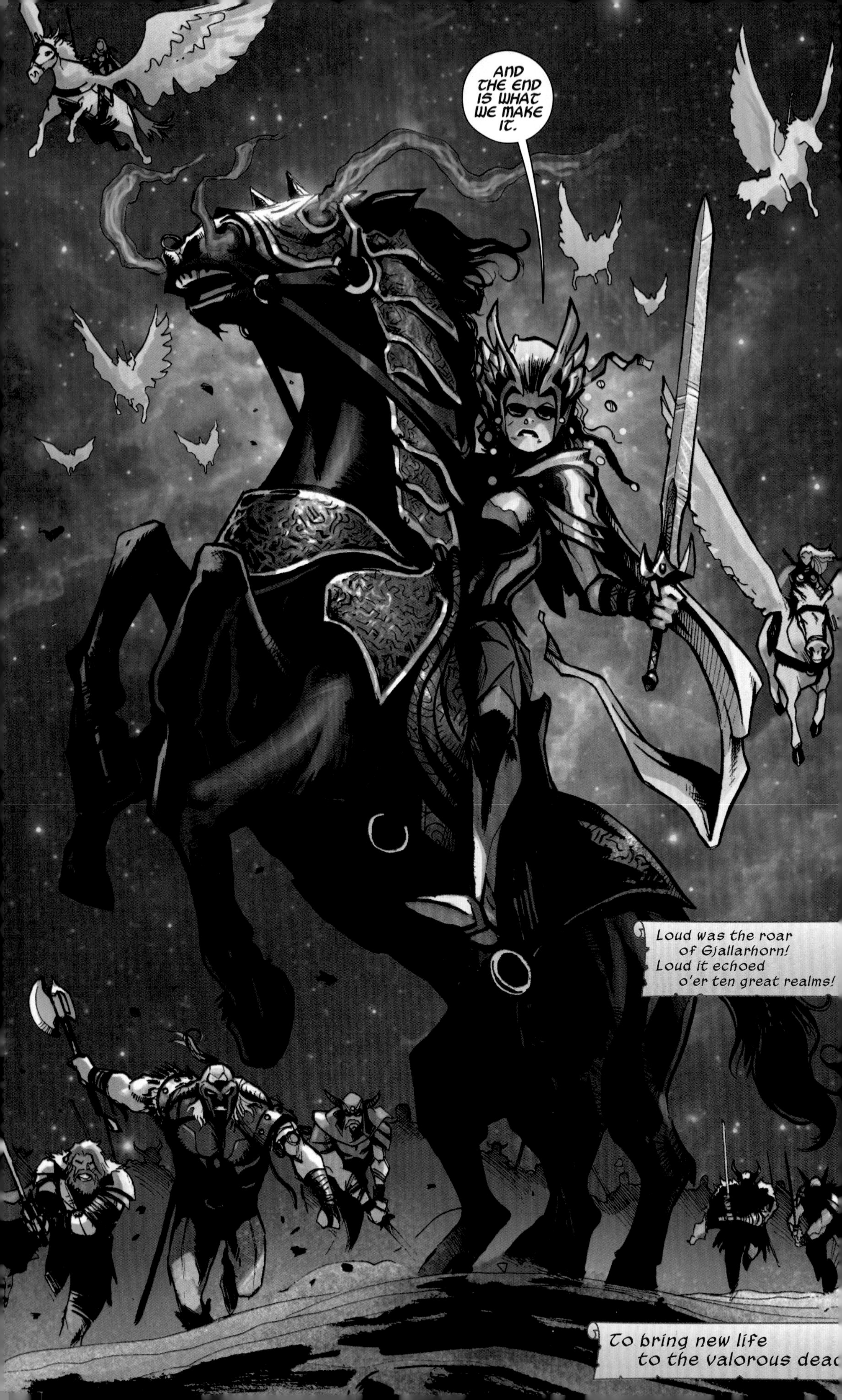
AND THE END IS WHAT WE MAKE IT.
Loud was the roar of Gjallarhorn! Loud it echoed o'er ten great realms!
To bring new life to the valorous dea

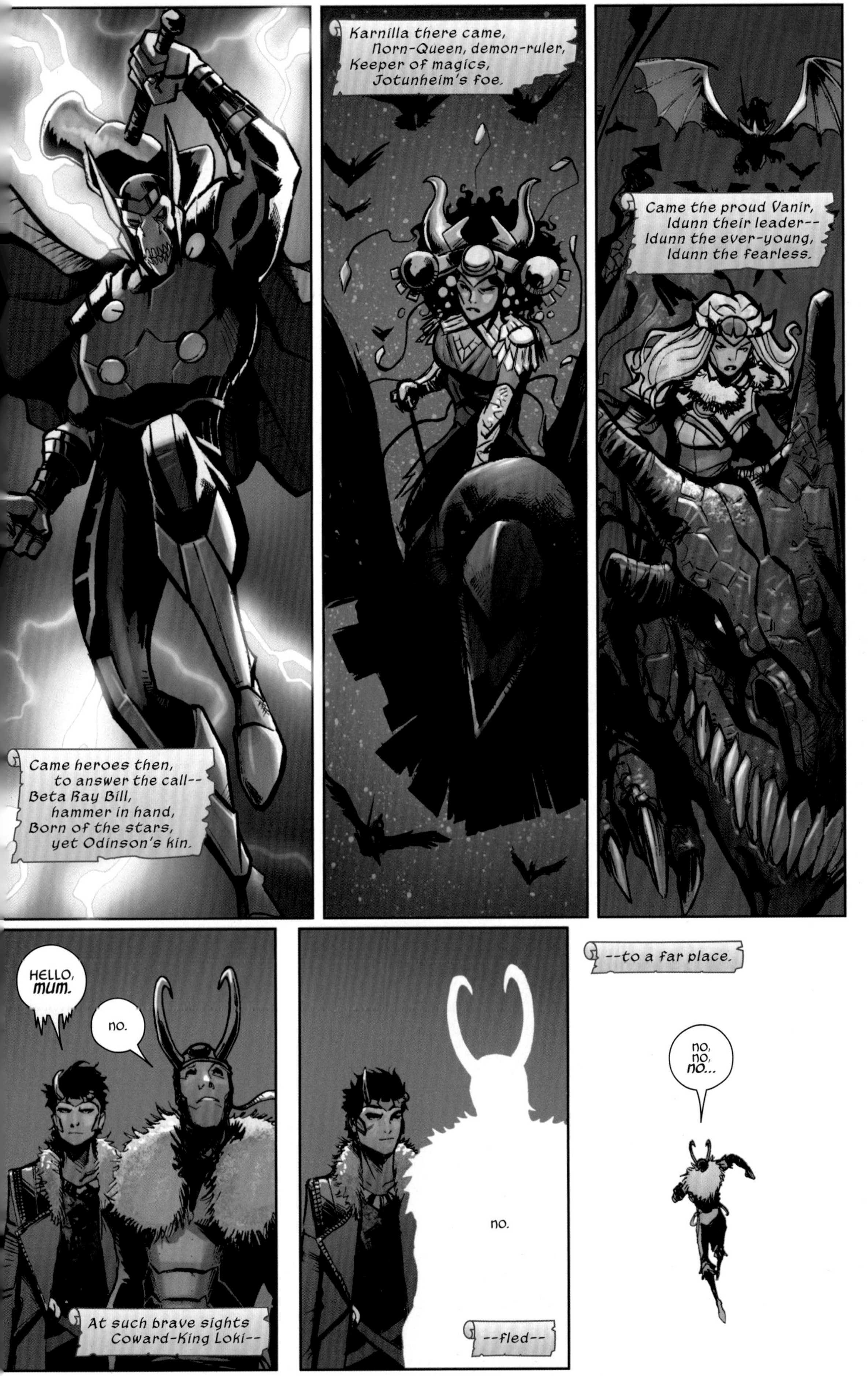
Came heroes then,
to answer the call--
Beta Ray Bill,
hammer in hand,
Born of the stars,
yet Odinson's kin.
Karnilla there came,
Norn-Queen, demon-ruler,
Keeper of magics,
Jotunheim's foe.
Came the proud Vanir,
Idunn their leader--
Idunn the ever-young,
Idunn the fearless.
HELLO, MUM.
no.
At such brave sights
Coward-King Loki--
no.
--fled--
--to a far place.
no, no, no...

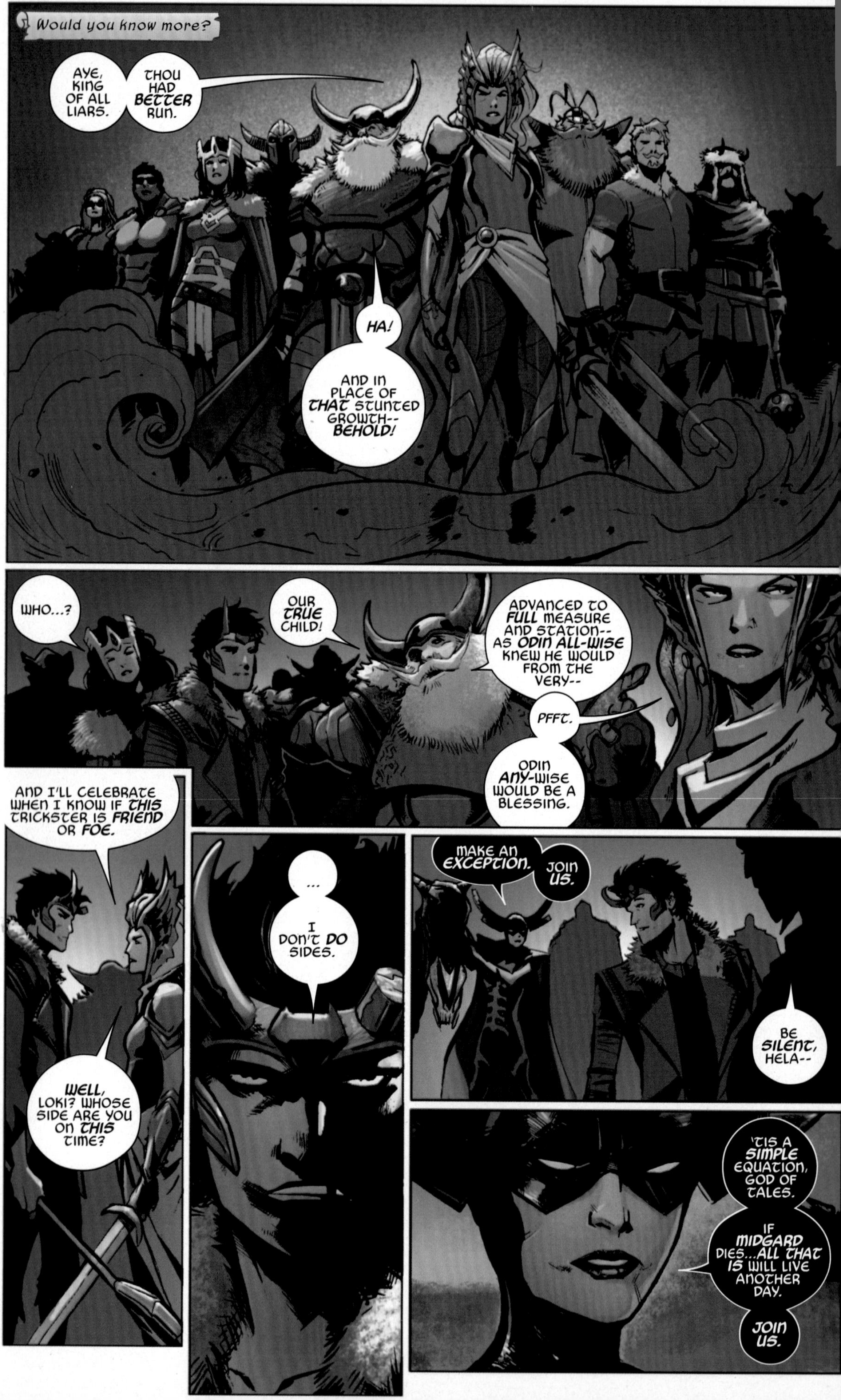
Would you know more?
AYE, KING OF ALL LIARS.
THOU HAD BETTER RUN.
HA!
AND IN PLACE OF THAT STUNTED GROWTH-- BEHOLD!
WHO...?
OUR TRUE CHILD!
ADVANCED TO FULL MEASURE AND STATION-- AS ODIN ALL-WISE KNEW HE WOULD FROM THE VERY--
PFFT.
ODIN ANY-WISE WOULD BE A BLESSING.
AND I'LL CELEBRATE WHEN I KNOW IF THIS TRICKSTER IS FRIEND OR FOE.
WELL, LOKI? WHOSE SIDE ARE YOU ON THIS TIME?
...
I DON'T DO SIDES.
MAKE AN EXCEPTION.
JOIN US.
BE SILENT, HELA--
'TIS A SIMPLE EQUATION, GOD OF TALES.
IF MIDGARD DIES...ALL THAT IS WILL LIVE ANOTHER DAY.
JOIN US.

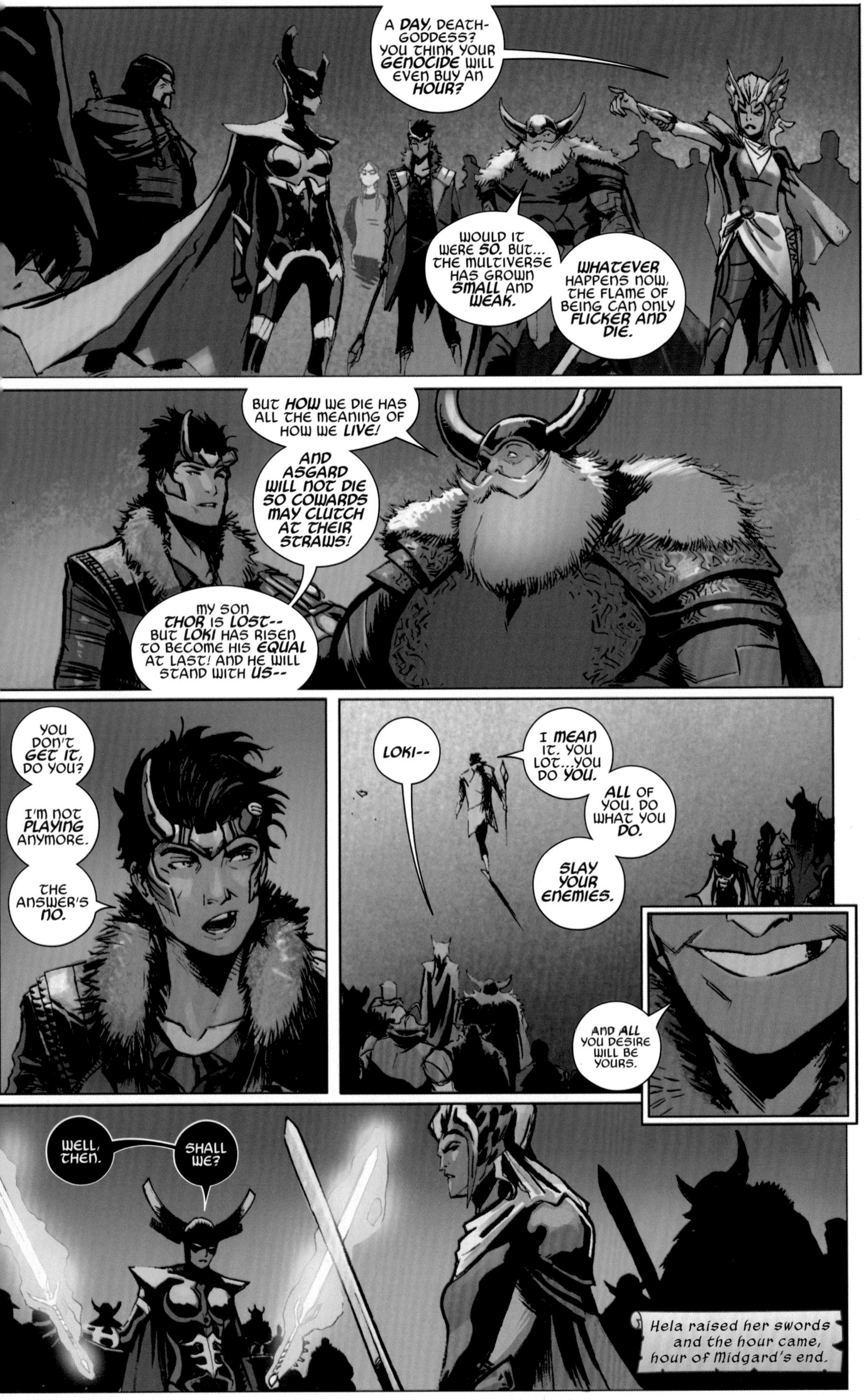
A DAY, DEATH-GODDESS? YOU THINK YOUR GENOCIDE WILL EVEN BUY AN HOUR?
WOULD IT WERE SO. BUT... THE MULTIVERSE HAS GROWN SMALL AND WEAK.
WHATEVER HAPPENS NOW, THE FLAME OF BEING CAN ONLY FLICKER AND DIE.
BUT HOW WE DIE HAS ALL THE MEANING OF HOW WE LIVE!
AND ASGARD WILL NOT DIE SO COWARDS MAY CLUTCH AT THEIR STRAWS!
MY SON THOR IS LOST-- BUT LOKI HAS RISEN TO BECOME HIS EQUAL AT LAST! AND HE WILL STAND WITH US--
YOU DON'T GET IT, DO YOU?
I'M NOT PLAYING ANYMORE.
THE ANSWER'S NO.
LOKI--
I MEAN IT. YOU LOT...YOU DO YOU.
ALL OF YOU. DO WHAT YOU DO.
SLAY YOUR ENEMIES.
AND ALL YOU DESIRE WILL BE YOURS.
WELL, THEN.
SHALL WE?
Hela raised her swords and the hour came, hour of Midgard's end.

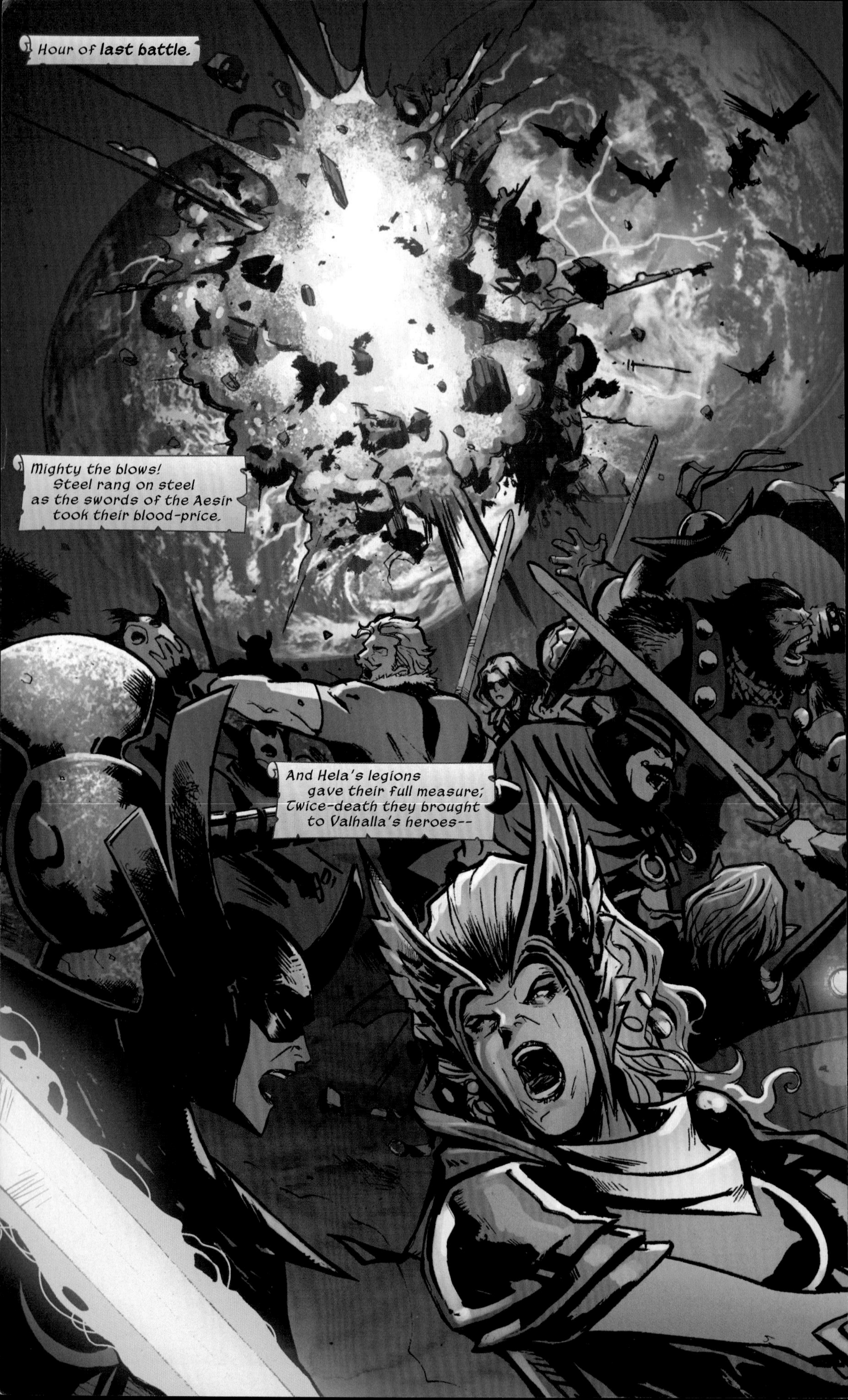
Hour of last battle.
Mighty the blows! Steel rang on steel as the swords of the Aesir took their blood-price.
And Hela's legions gave their full measure; Twice-death they brought to Valhalla's heroes--

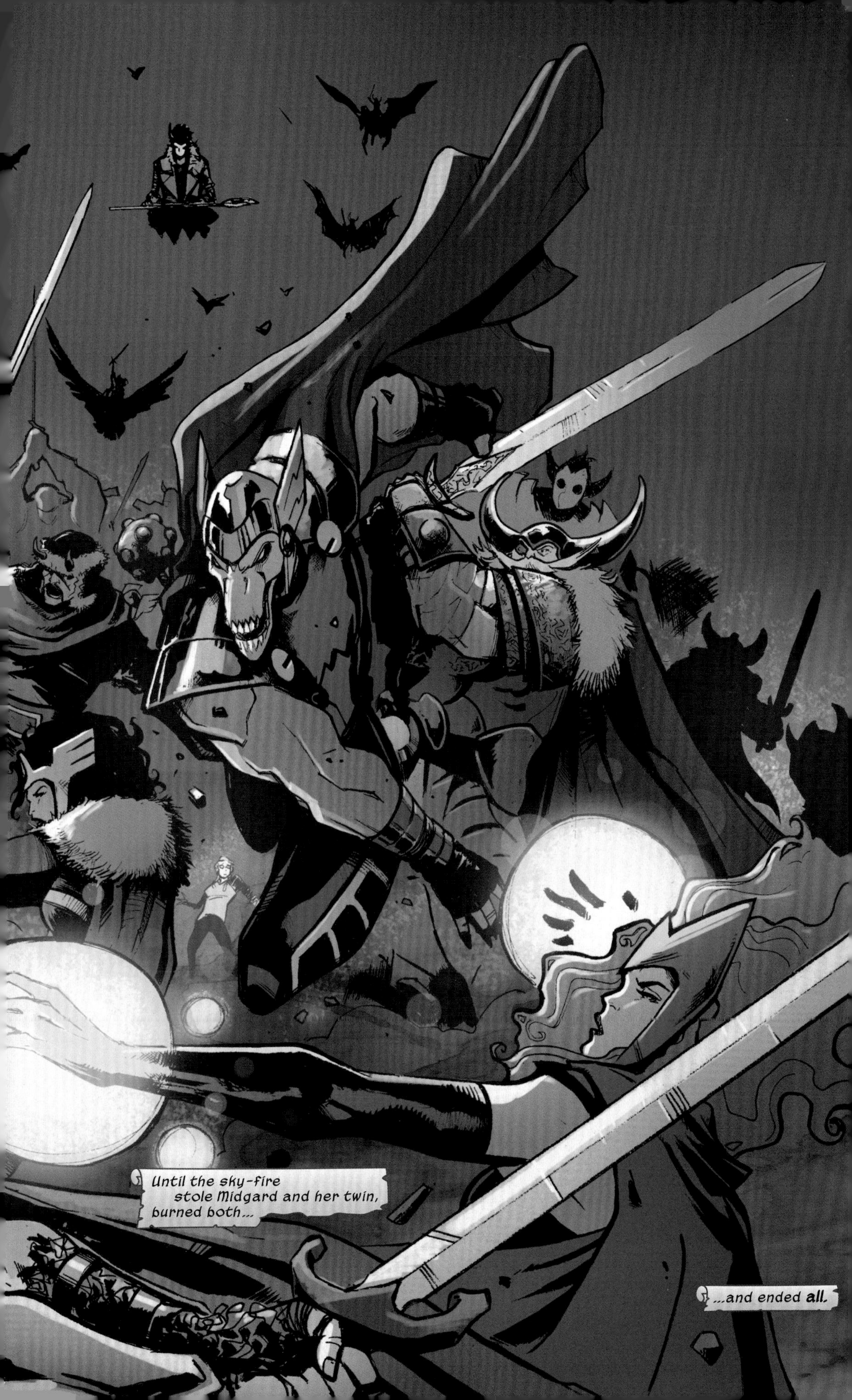
Until the sky-fire stole Midgard and her twin, burned both...
...and ended **all.**

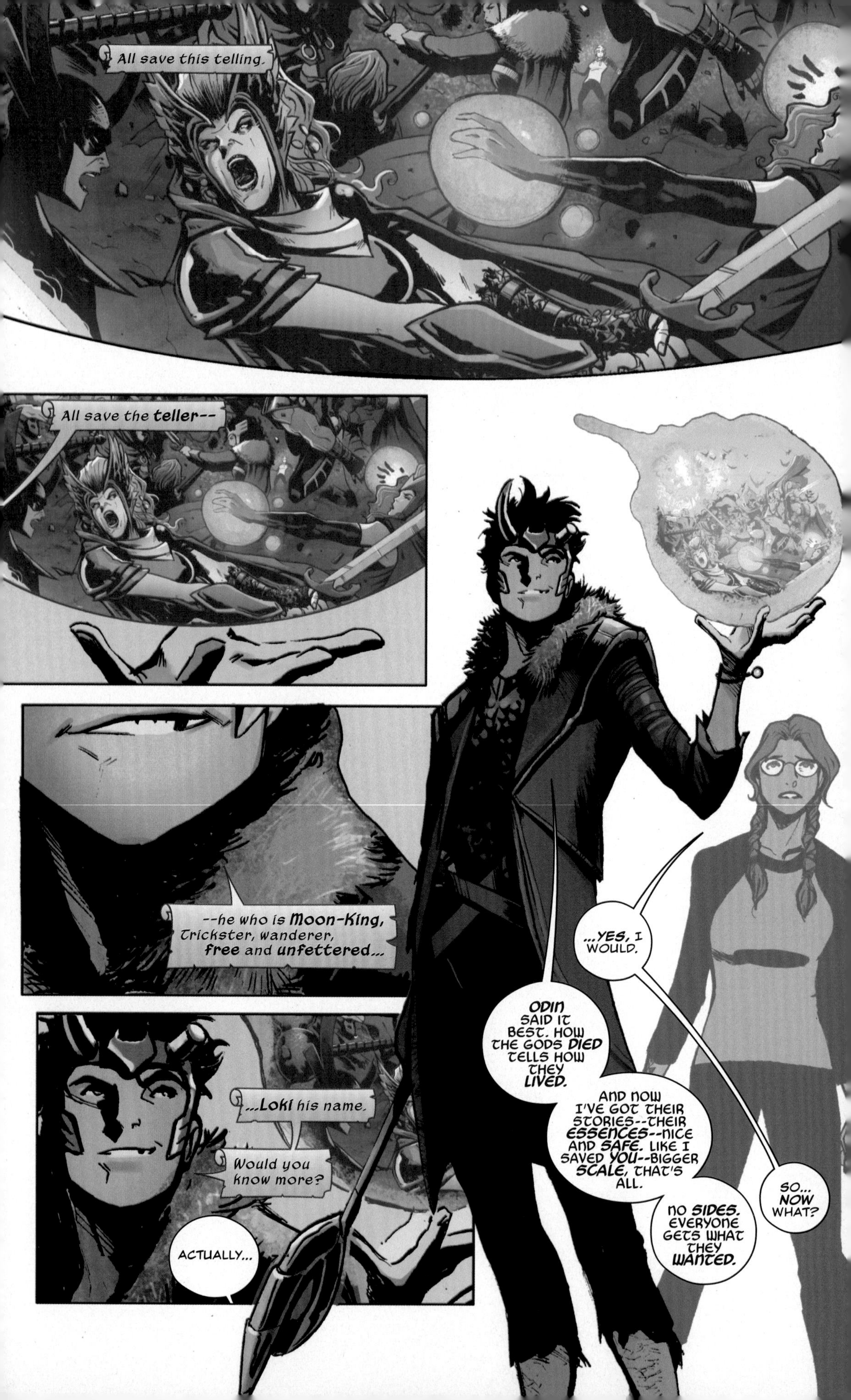
All save this telling.
All save the teller--
--he who is Moon-King, Trickster, wanderer, free and unfettered...
...Loki his name.
Would you know more?
ACTUALLY...
...YES, I WOULD.
ODIN SAID IT BEST. HOW THE GODS DIED TELLS HOW THEY LIVED.
AND NOW I'VE GOT THEIR STORIES--THEIR ESSENCES--NICE AND SAFE. LIKE I SAVED YOU--BIGGER SCALE, THAT'S ALL.
NO SIDES. EVERYONE GETS WHAT THEY WANTED.
SO... NOW WHAT?

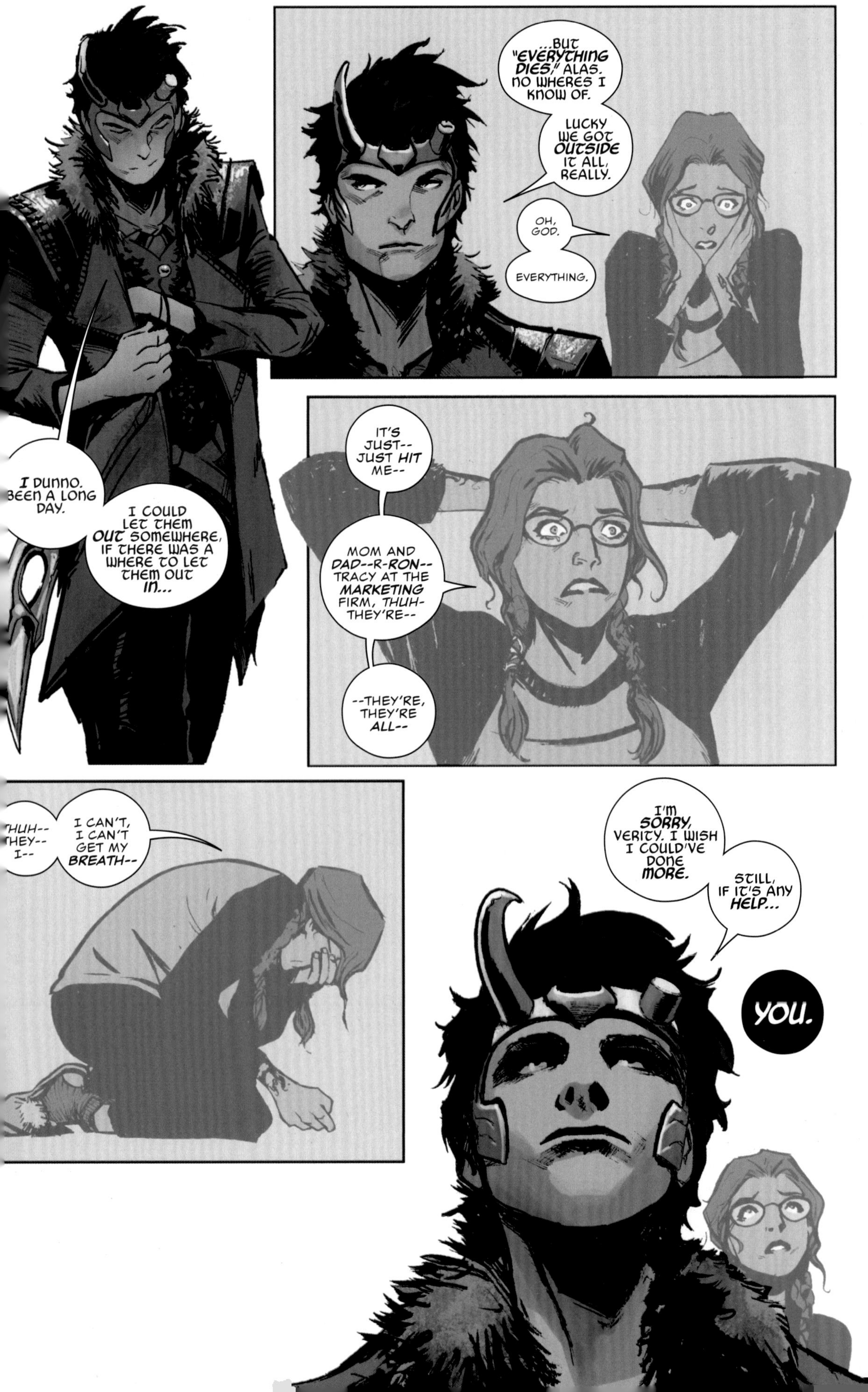
...BUT "EVERYTHING DIES," ALAS. NO WHERES I KNOW OF.
LUCKY WE GOT OUTSIDE IT ALL, REALLY.
OH, GOD.
EVERYTHING.
I DUNNO. BEEN A LONG DAY.
I COULD LET THEM OUT SOMEWHERE, IF THERE WAS A WHERE TO LET THEM OUT IN...
IT'S JUST-- JUST HIT ME--
MOM AND DAD--R-RON-- TRACY AT THE MARKETING FIRM, THUH- THEY'RE--
--THEY'RE, THEY'RE ALL--
THUH-- THEY-- I--
I CAN'T, I CAN'T GET MY BREATH--
I'M SORRY, VERITY. I WISH I COULD'VE DONE MORE.
STILL, IF IT'S ANY HELP...
YOU.

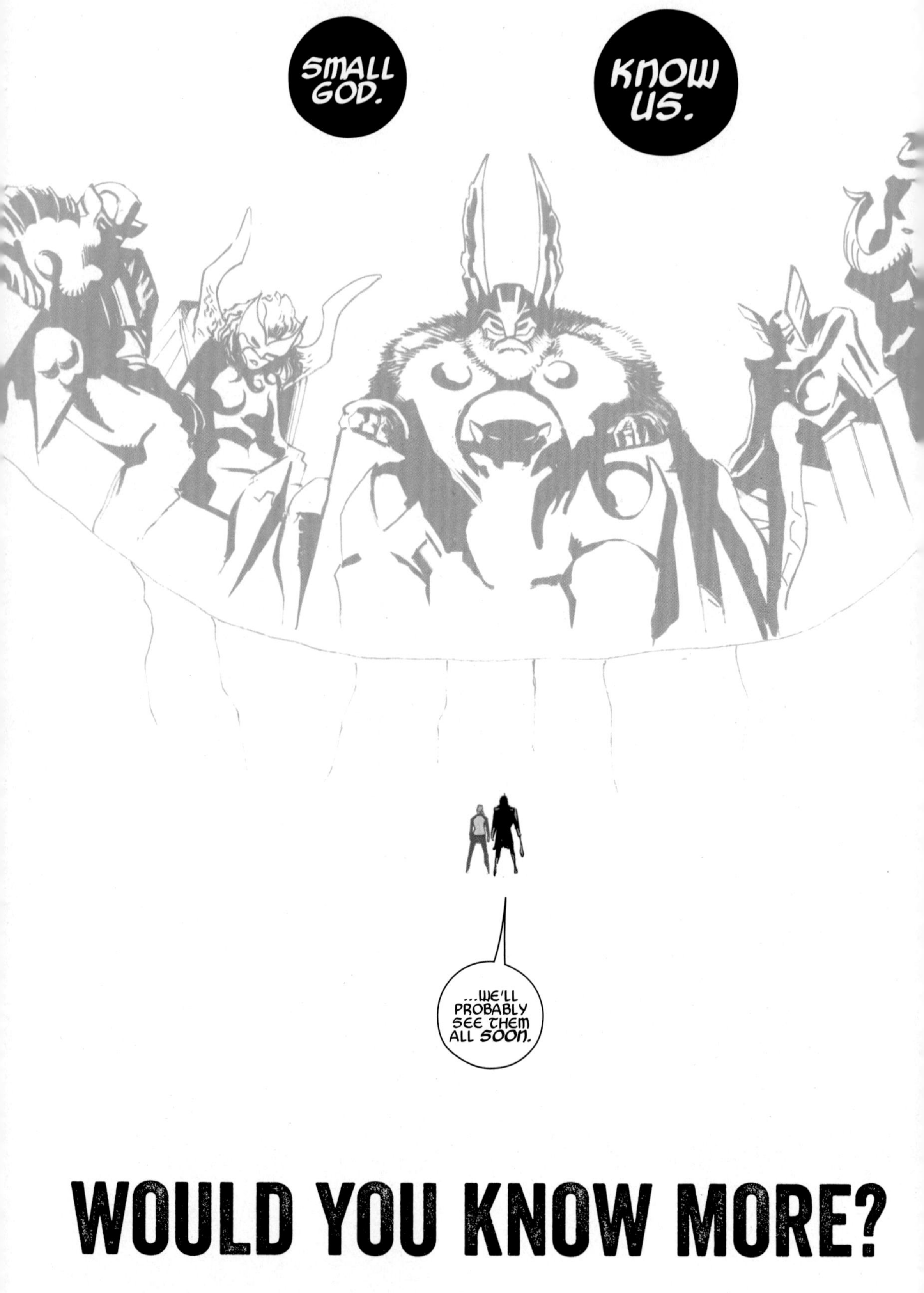
SMALL GOD.
KNOW US.
...WE'LL PROBABLY SEE THEM ALL SOON.
WOULD YOU KNOW MORE?

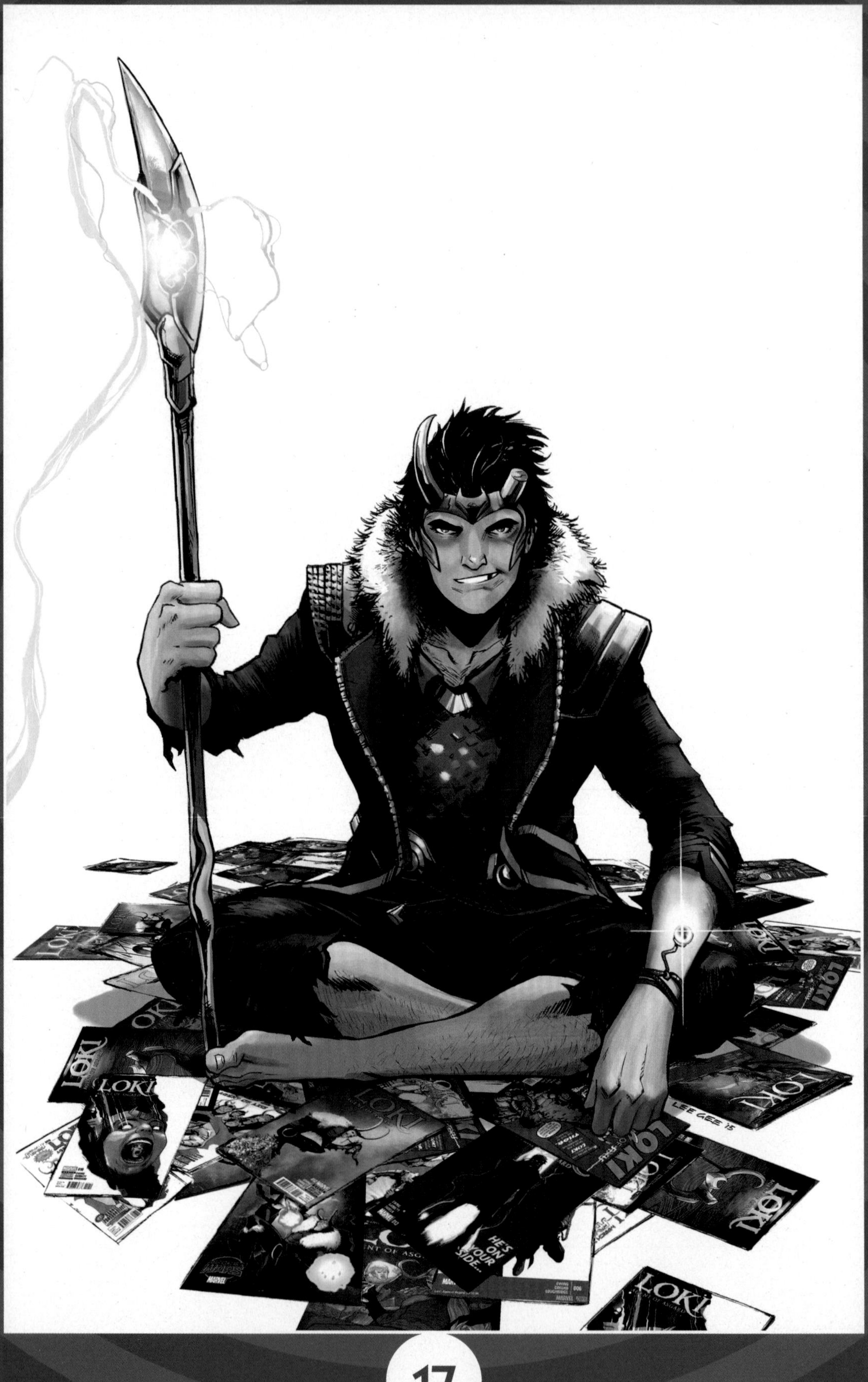
LOKI
HE'S ON YOUR SIDE...
LEE GEE '15

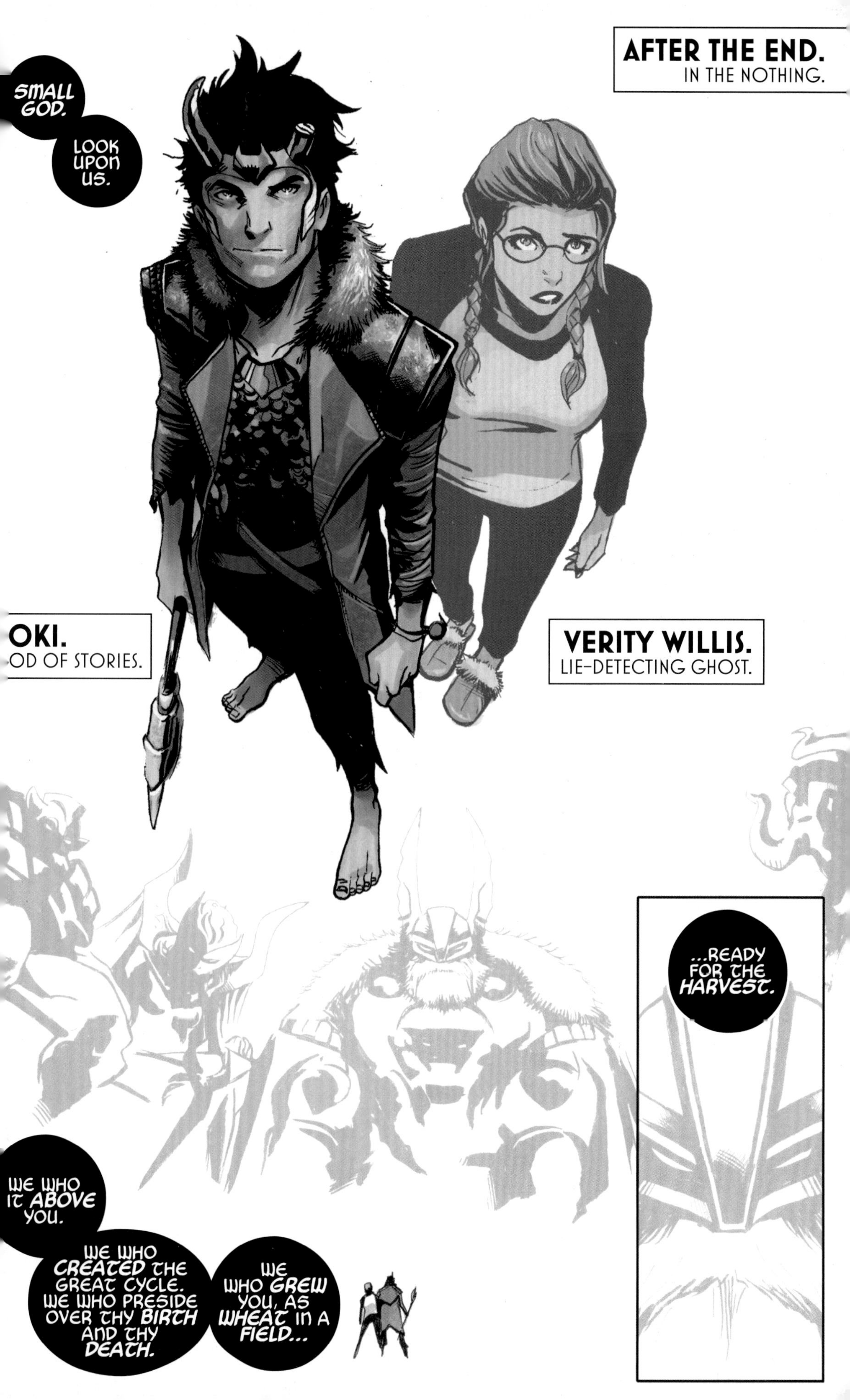
AFTER THE END.
IN THE NOTHING.
SMALL GOD.
LOOK UPON US.
OKI.
OD OF STORIES.
VERITY WILLIS.
LIE-DETECTING GHOST.
WE WHO IT ABOVE YOU.
WE WHO CREATED THE GREAT CYCLE. WE WHO PRESIDE OVER THY BIRTH AND THY DEATH.
WE WHO GREW YOU, AS WHEAT IN A FIELD...
...READY FOR THE HARVEST.

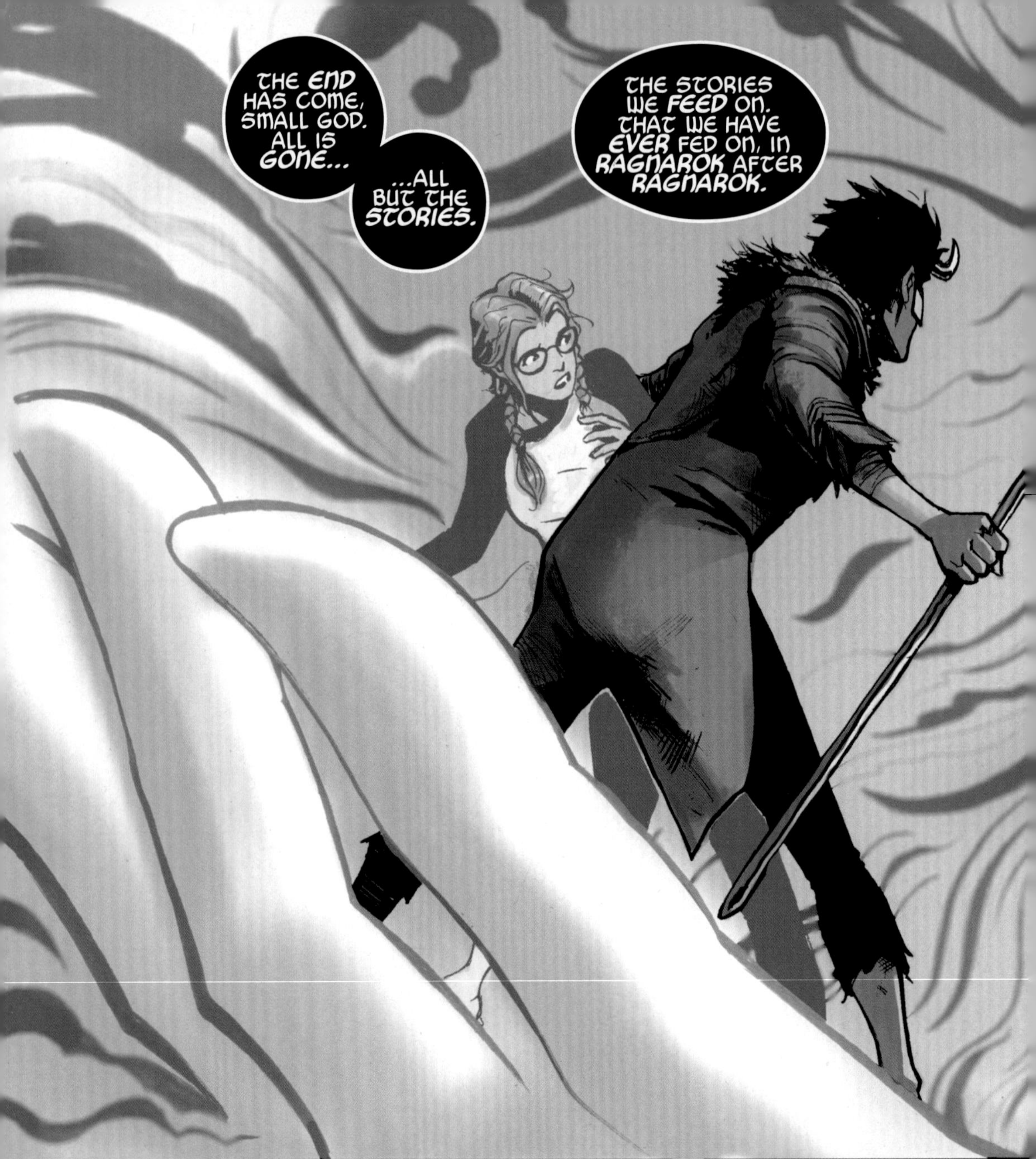
THE END HAS COME, SMALL GOD. ALL IS GONE...
...ALL BUT THE STORIES.
THE STORIES WE FEED ON. THAT WE HAVE EVER FED ON, IN RAGNAROK AFTER RAGNAROK.

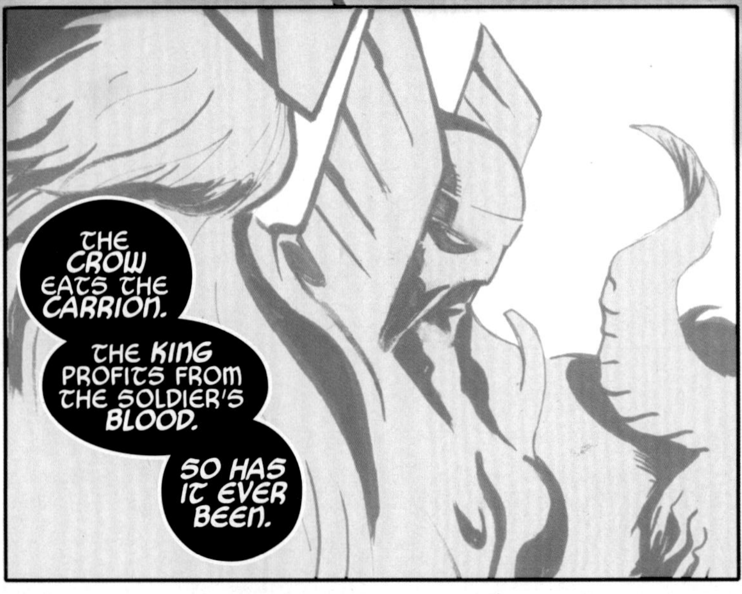
THE CROW EATS THE CARRION.
THE KING PROFITS FROM THE SOLDIER'S BLOOD.
SO HAS IT EVER BEEN.

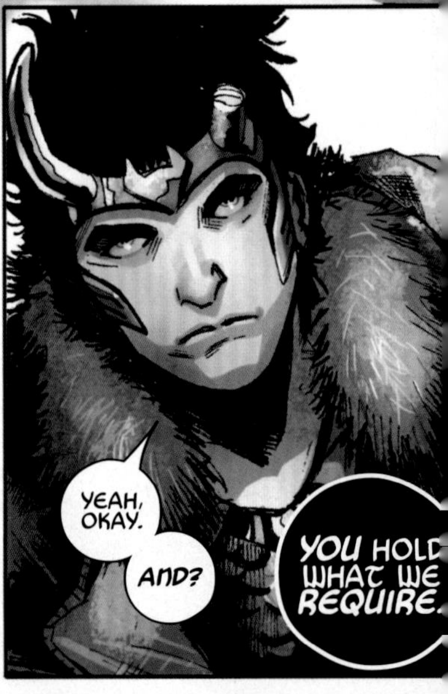
YEAH, OKAY.
AND?
YOU HOLD WHAT WE REQUIRE.

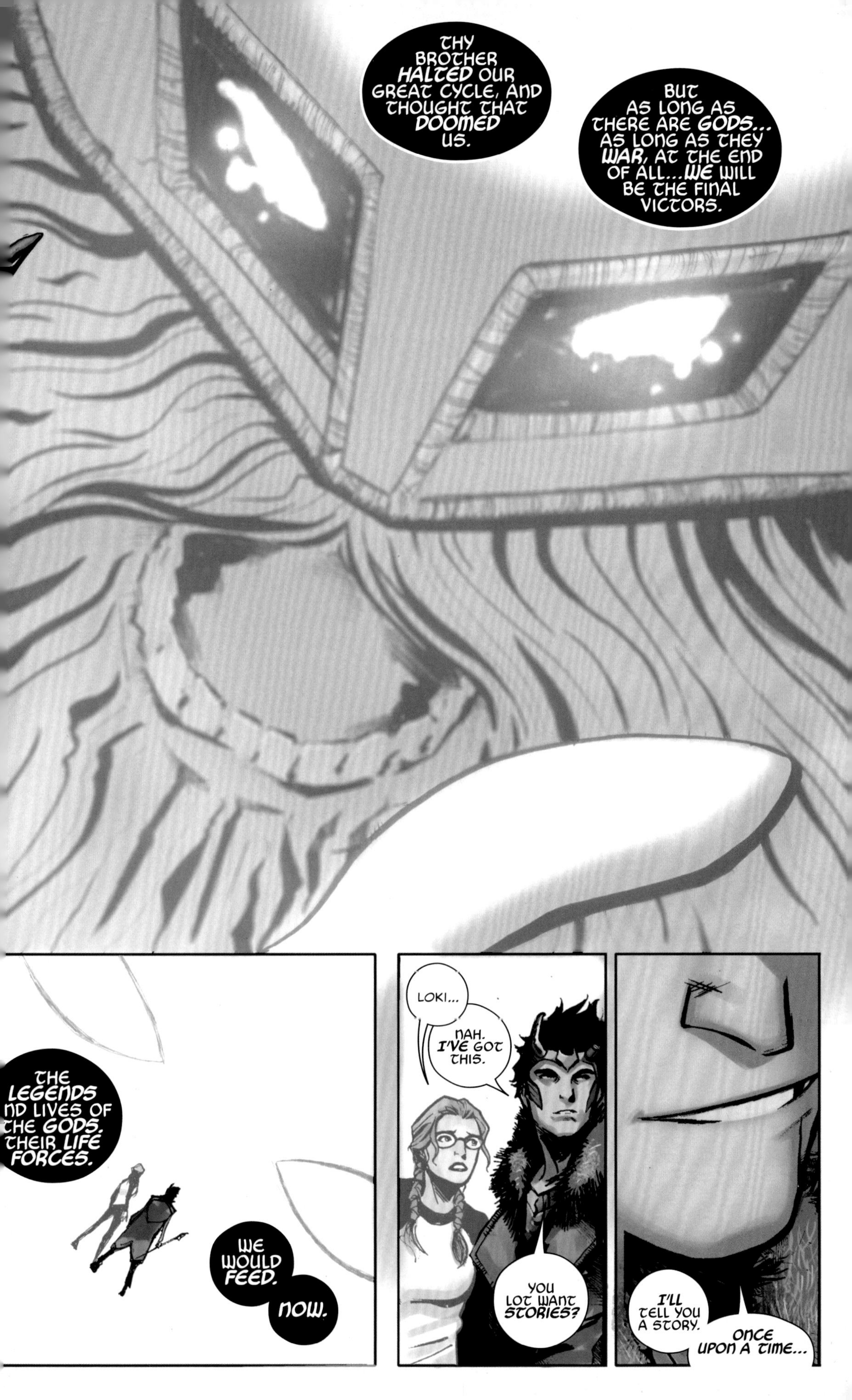
THY BROTHER HALTED OUR GREAT CYCLE, AND THOUGHT THAT DOOMED US.
BUT AS LONG AS THERE ARE GODS... AS LONG AS THEY WAR, AT THE END OF ALL...WE WILL BE THE FINAL VICTORS.
THE LEGENDS ND LIVES OF HE GODS. THEIR LIFE FORCES.
WE WOULD FEED.
NOW.
LOKI...
NAH. I'VE GOT THIS.
YOU LOT WANT STORIES?
I'LL TELL YOU A STORY.
ONCE UPON A TIME...

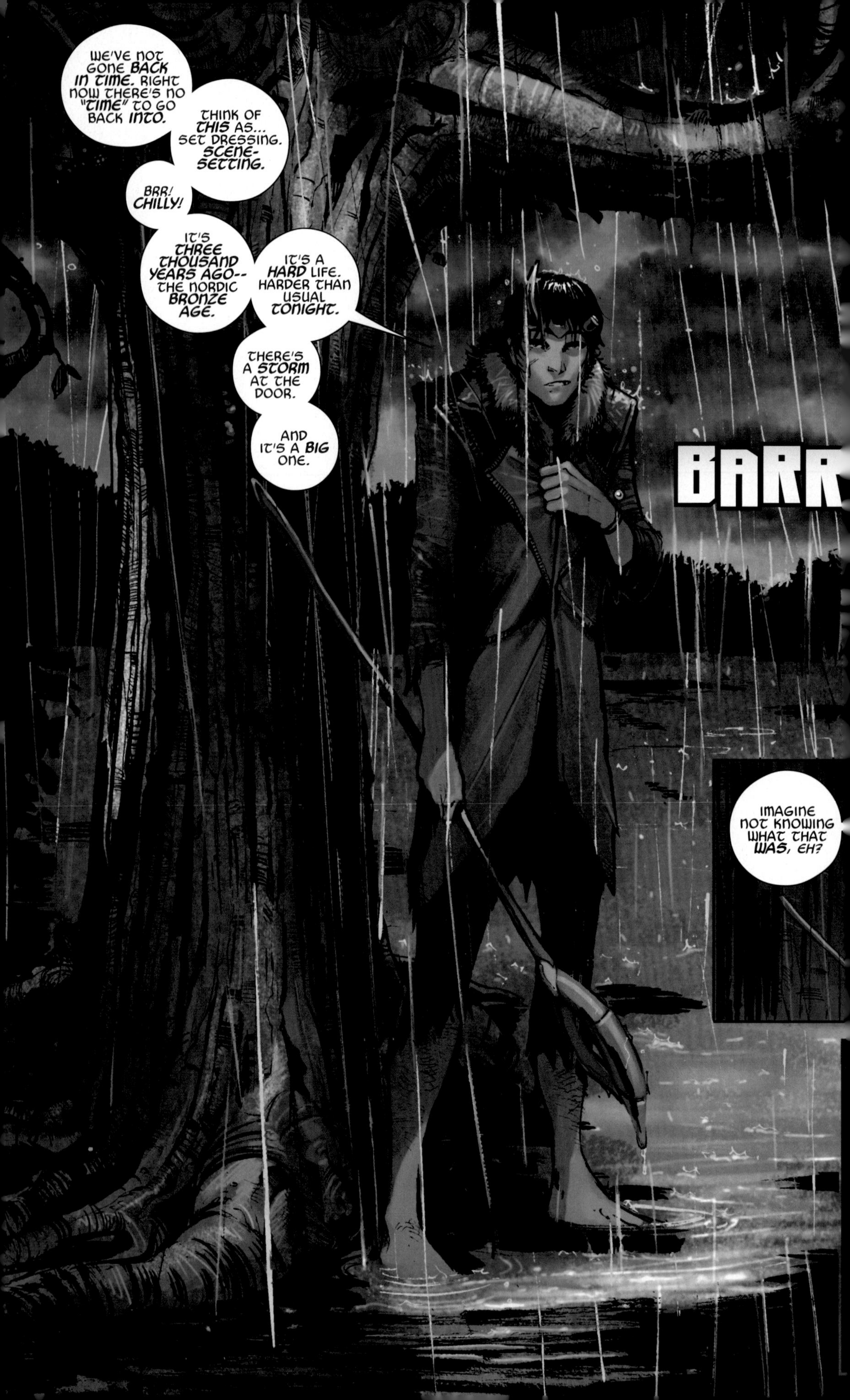
WE'VE NOT GONE BACK IN TIME. RIGHT NOW THERE'S NO "TIME" TO GO BACK INTO.
THINK OF THIS AS... SET DRESSING. SCENE-SETTING.
BRR! CHILLY!
IT'S THREE THOUSAND YEARS AGO-- THE NORDIC BRONZE AGE.
IT'S A HARD LIFE. HARDER THAN USUAL TONIGHT.
THERE'S A STORM AT THE DOOR.
AND IT'S A BIG ONE.
BARR
IMAGINE NOT KNOWING WHAT THAT WAS, EH?

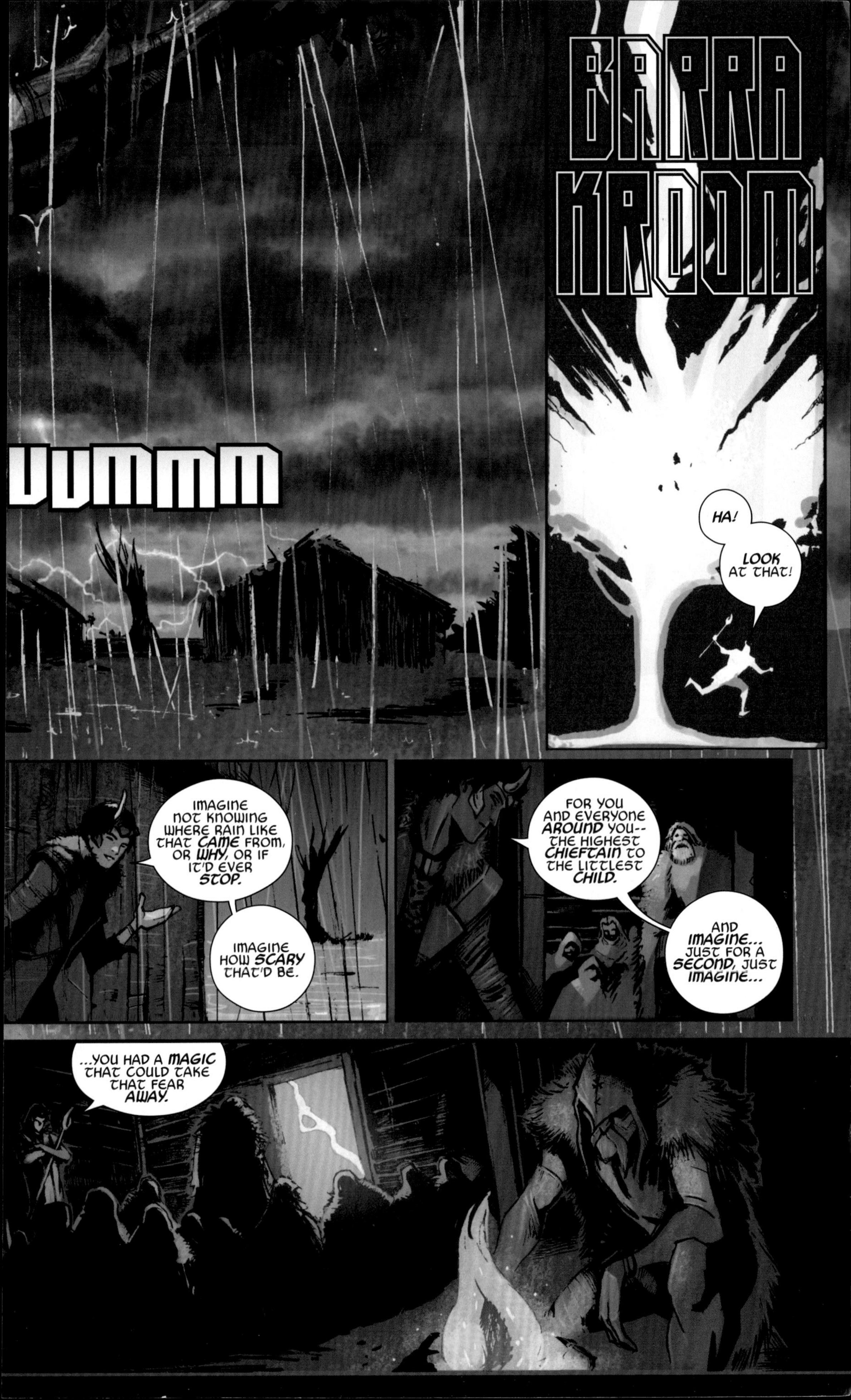
BARRA
KROOM
VVMMM
HA!
LOOK AT THAT!
IMAGINE NOT KNOWING WHERE RAIN LIKE THAT CAME FROM, OR WHY, OR IF IT'D EVER STOP.
IMAGINE HOW SCARY THAT'D BE.
FOR YOU AND EVERYONE AROUND YOU-- THE HIGHEST CHIEFTAIN TO THE LITTLEST CHILD.
AND IMAGINE... JUST FOR A SECOND, JUST IMAGINE...
...YOU HAD A MAGIC THAT COULD TAKE THAT FEAR AWAY.

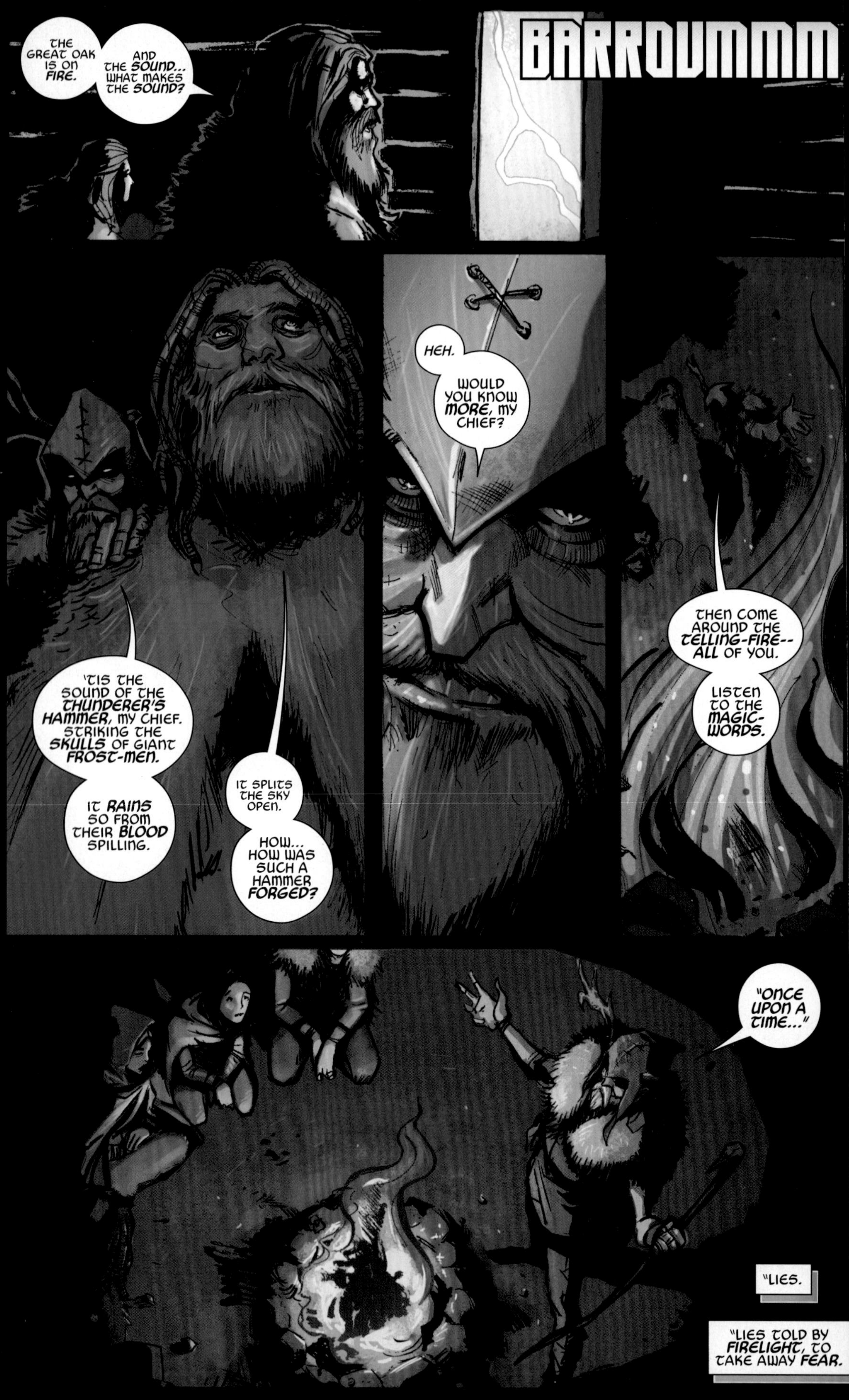

THE GREAT OAK IS ON FIRE.
AND THE SOUND... WHAT MAKES THE SOUND?
BARROUMMMM
'TIS THE SOUND OF THE THUNDERER'S HAMMER, MY CHIEF. STRIKING THE SKULLS OF GIANT FROST-MEN.
IT RAINS SO FROM THEIR BLOOD SPILLING.
IT SPLITS THE SKY OPEN.
HOW... HOW WAS SUCH A HAMMER FORGED?
HEH.
WOULD YOU KNOW MORE, MY CHIEF?
THEN COME AROUND THE TELLING-FIRE-- ALL OF YOU.
LISTEN TO THE MAGIC-WORDS.
"ONCE UPON A TIME..."
"LIES.
"LIES TOLD BY FIRELIGHT, TO TAKE AWAY FEAR.

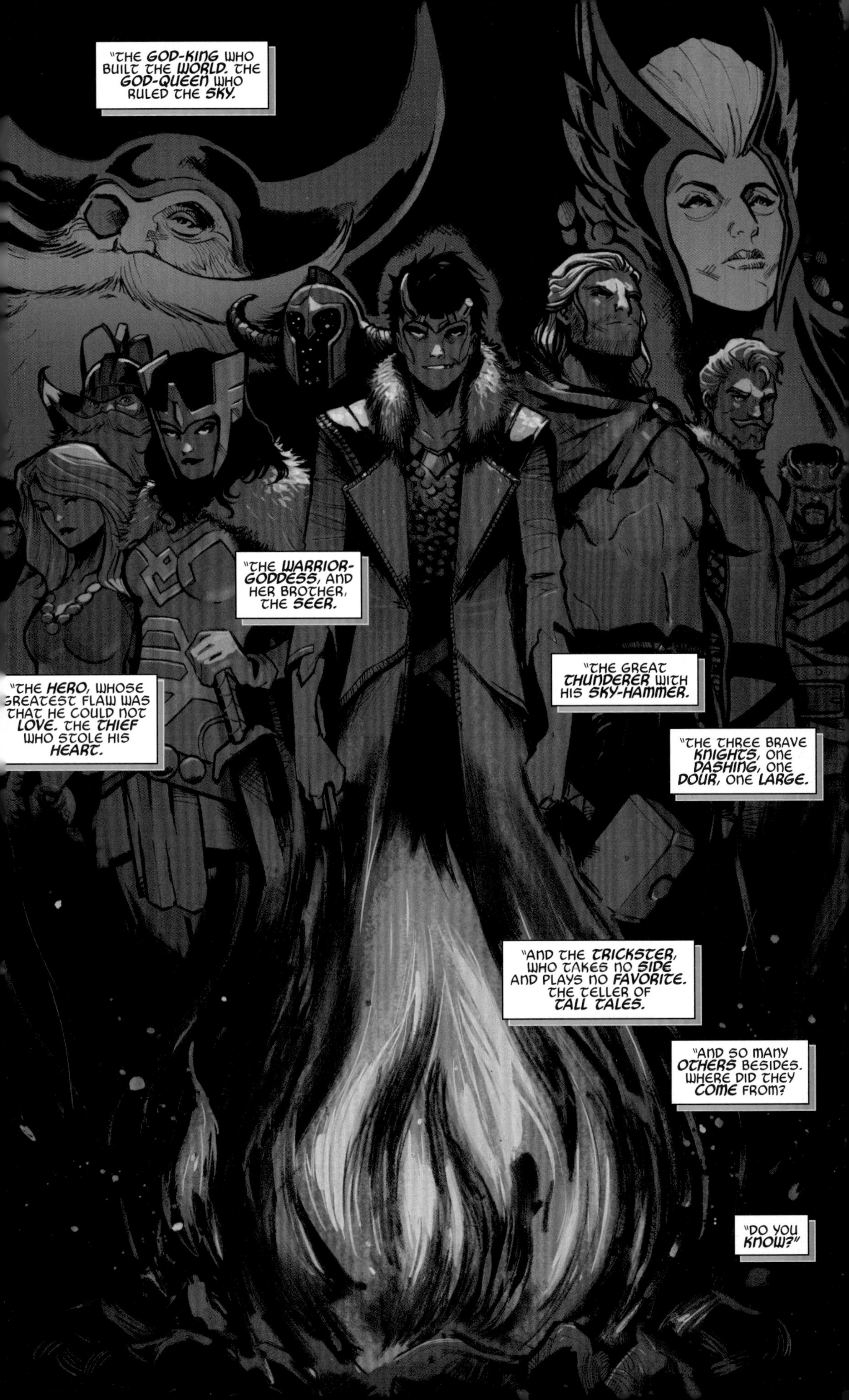
"THE GOD-KING WHO BUILT THE WORLD. THE GOD-QUEEN WHO RULED THE SKY.
"THE WARRIOR-GODDESS, AND HER BROTHER, THE SEER.
"THE HERO, WHOSE GREATEST FLAW WAS THAT HE COULD NOT LOVE. THE THIEF WHO STOLE HIS HEART.
"THE GREAT THUNDERER WITH HIS SKY-HAMMER.
"THE THREE BRAVE KNIGHTS, ONE DASHING, ONE DOUR, ONE LARGE.
"AND THE TRICKSTER, WHO TAKES NO SIDE AND PLAYS NO FAVORITE. THE TELLER OF TALL TALES.
"AND SO MANY OTHERS BESIDES. WHERE DID THEY COME FROM?
"DO YOU KNOW?"

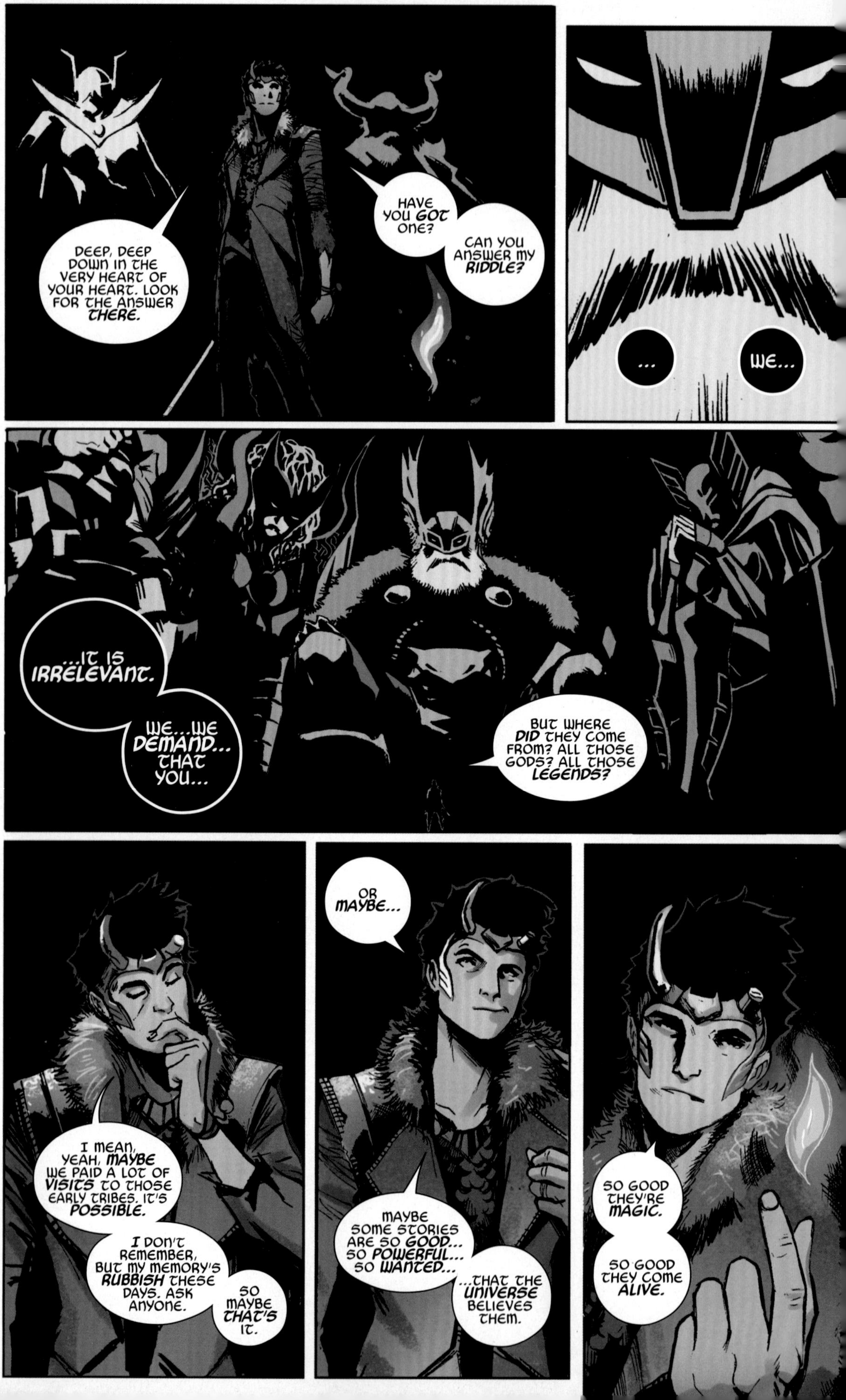
DEEP, DEEP DOWN IN THE VERY HEART OF YOUR HEART. LOOK FOR THE ANSWER THERE.
HAVE YOU GOT ONE?
CAN YOU ANSWER MY RIDDLE?
...
WE...
...IT IS IRRELEVANT.
WE...WE DEMAND... THAT YOU...
BUT WHERE DID THEY COME FROM? ALL THOSE GODS? ALL THOSE LEGENDS?
I MEAN, YEAH, MAYBE WE PAID A LOT OF VISITS TO THOSE EARLY TRIBES. IT'S POSSIBLE.
I DON'T REMEMBER, BUT MY MEMORY'S RUBBISH THESE DAYS. ASK ANYONE.
SO MAYBE THAT'S IT.
OR MAYBE...
MAYBE SOME STORIES ARE SO GOOD... SO POWERFUL... SO WANTED...
...THAT THE UNIVERSE BELIEVES THEM.
SO GOOD THEY'RE MAGIC.
SO GOOD THEY COME ALIVE.

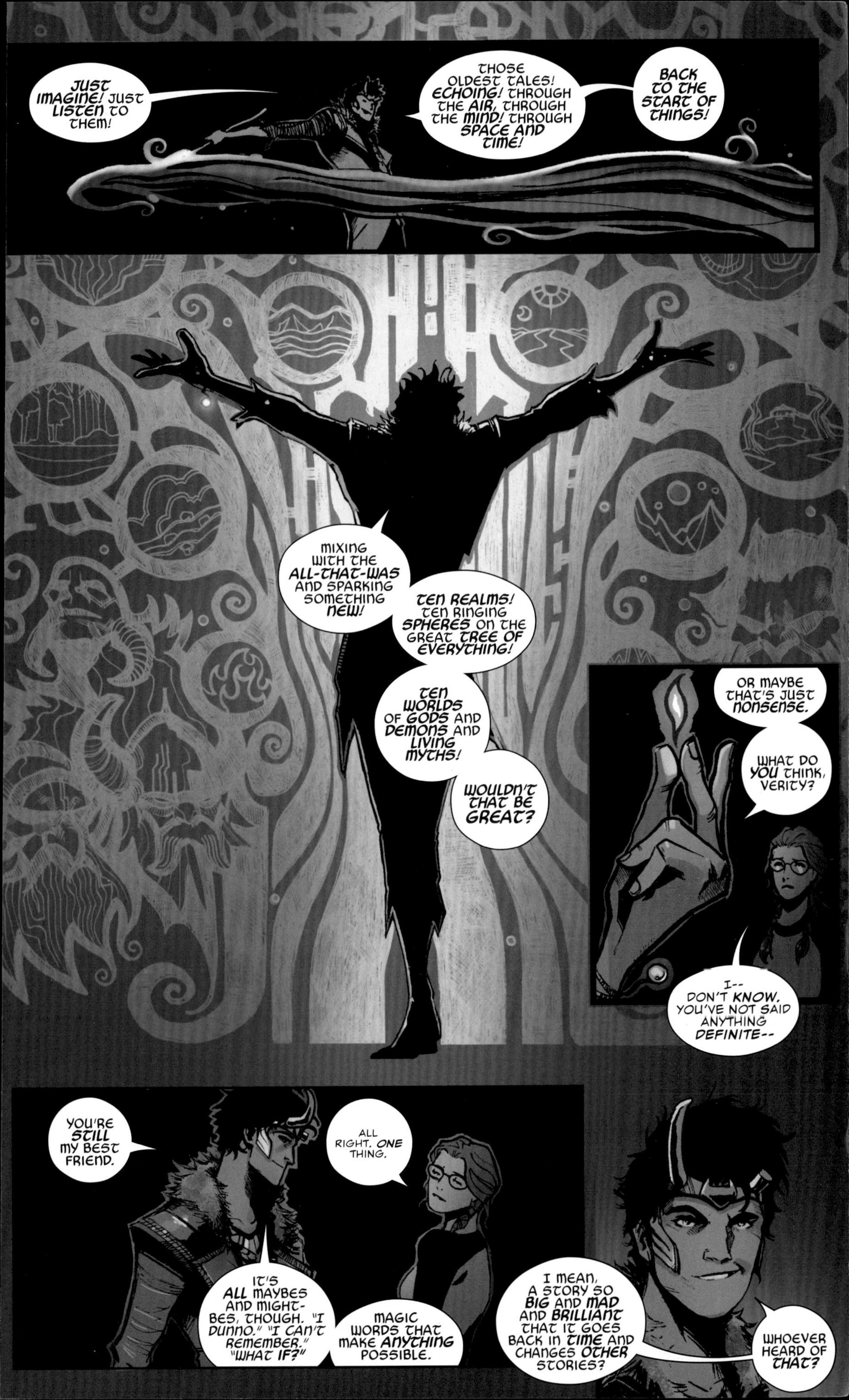
JUST IMAGINE! JUST LISTEN TO THEM!
THOSE OLDEST TALES! ECHOING! THROUGH THE AIR, THROUGH THE MIND! THROUGH SPACE AND TIME!
BACK TO THE START OF THINGS!
MIXING WITH THE ALL-THAT-WAS AND SPARKING SOMETHING NEW!
TEN REALMS! TEN RINGING SPHERES ON THE GREAT TREE OF EVERYTHING!
TEN WORLDS OF GODS AND DEMONS AND LIVING MYTHS!
WOULDN'T THAT BE GREAT?
OR MAYBE THAT'S JUST NONSENSE.
WHAT DO YOU THINK, VERITY?
I-- DON'T KNOW. YOU'VE NOT SAID ANYTHING DEFINITE--
YOU'RE STILL MY BEST FRIEND.
ALL RIGHT. ONE THING.
IT'S ALL MAYBES AND MIGHT-BES, THOUGH. "I DUNNO." "I CAN'T REMEMBER." "WHAT IF?"
MAGIC WORDS THAT MAKE ANYTHING POSSIBLE.
I MEAN, A STORY SO BIG AND MAD AND BRILLIANT THAT IT GOES BACK IN TIME AND CHANGES OTHER STORIES?
WHOEVER HEARD OF THAT?

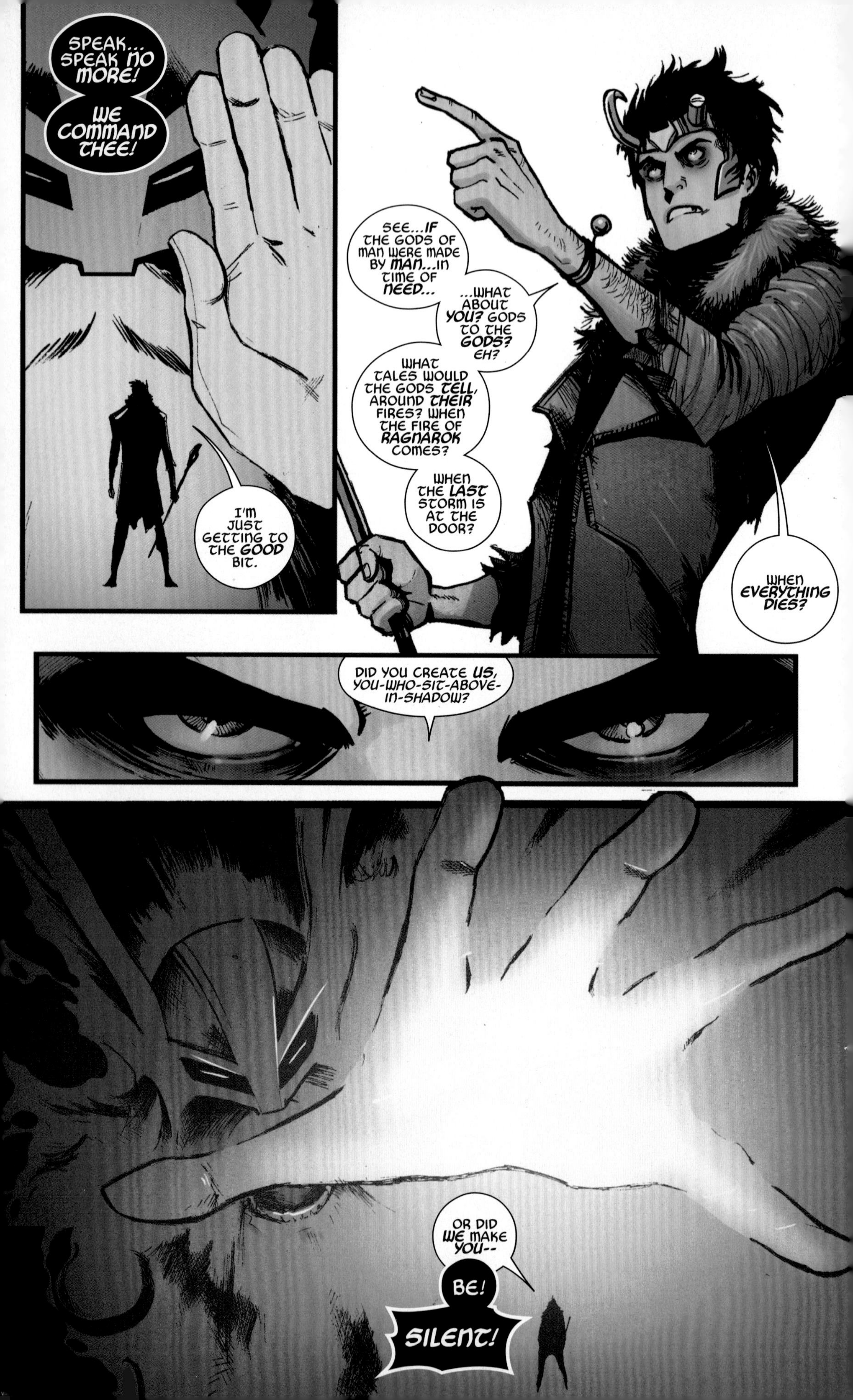
SPEAK... SPEAK NO MORE!
WE COMMAND THEE!
I'M JUST GETTING TO THE GOOD BIT.
SEE...IF THE GODS OF MAN WERE MADE BY MAN...IN TIME OF NEED...
...WHAT ABOUT YOU? GODS TO THE GODS? EH?
WHAT TALES WOULD THE GODS TELL, AROUND THEIR FIRES? WHEN THE FIRE OF RAGNAROK COMES?
WHEN THE LAST STORM IS AT THE DOOR?
WHEN EVERYTHING DIES?
DID YOU CREATE US, YOU-WHO-SIT-ABOVE-IN-SHADOW?
OR DID WE MAKE YOU--
BE!
SILENT!

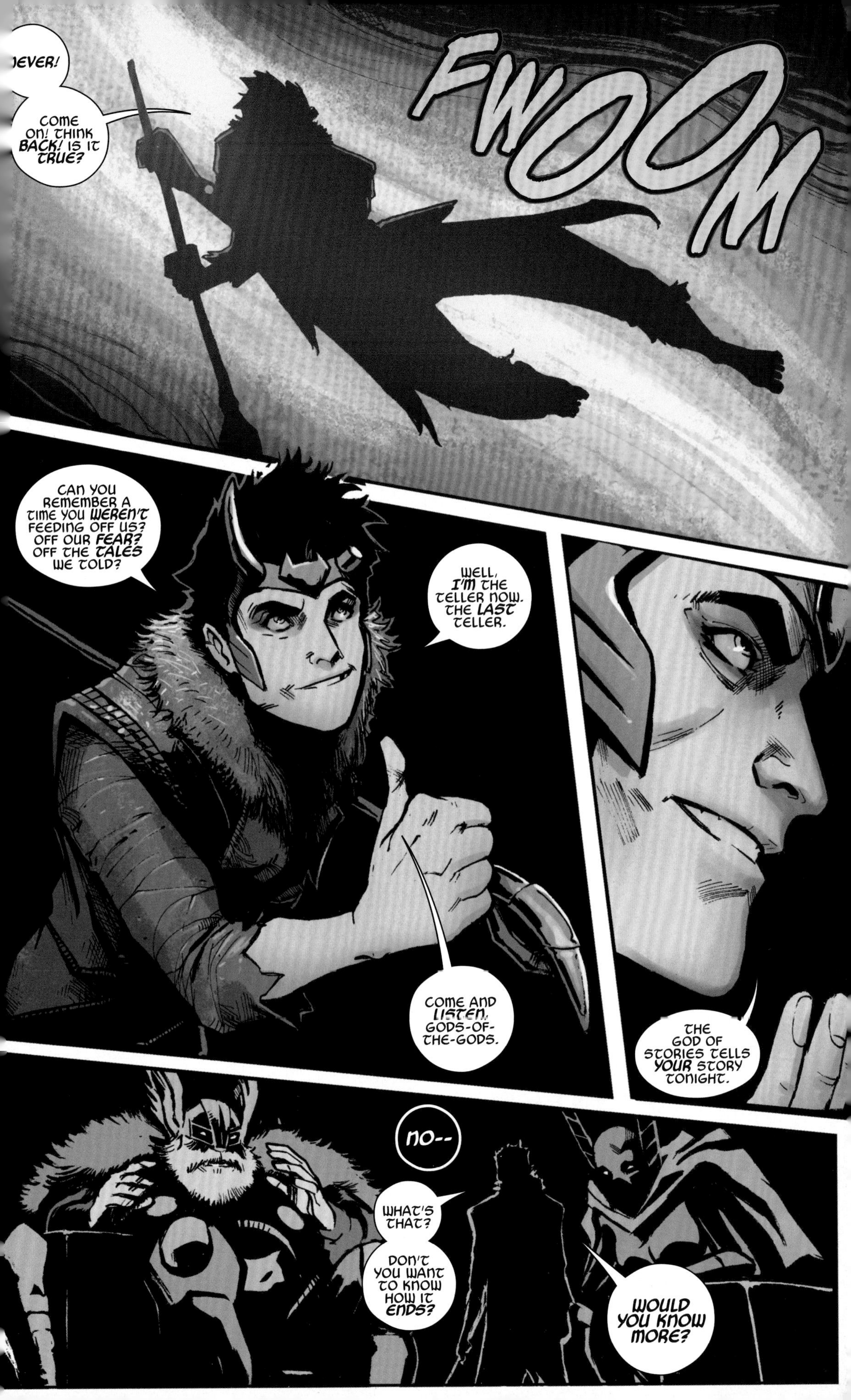

NEVER!
COME ON! THINK BACK! IS IT TRUE?
FWOOM
CAN YOU REMEMBER A TIME YOU WEREN'T FEEDING OFF US? OFF OUR FEAR? OFF THE TALES WE TOLD?
WELL, I'M THE TELLER NOW. THE LAST TELLER.
COME AND LISTEN, GODS-OF-THE-GODS.
THE GOD OF STORIES TELLS YOUR STORY TONIGHT.
NO--
WHAT'S THAT?
DON'T YOU WANT TO KNOW HOW IT ENDS?
WOULD YOU KNOW MORE?

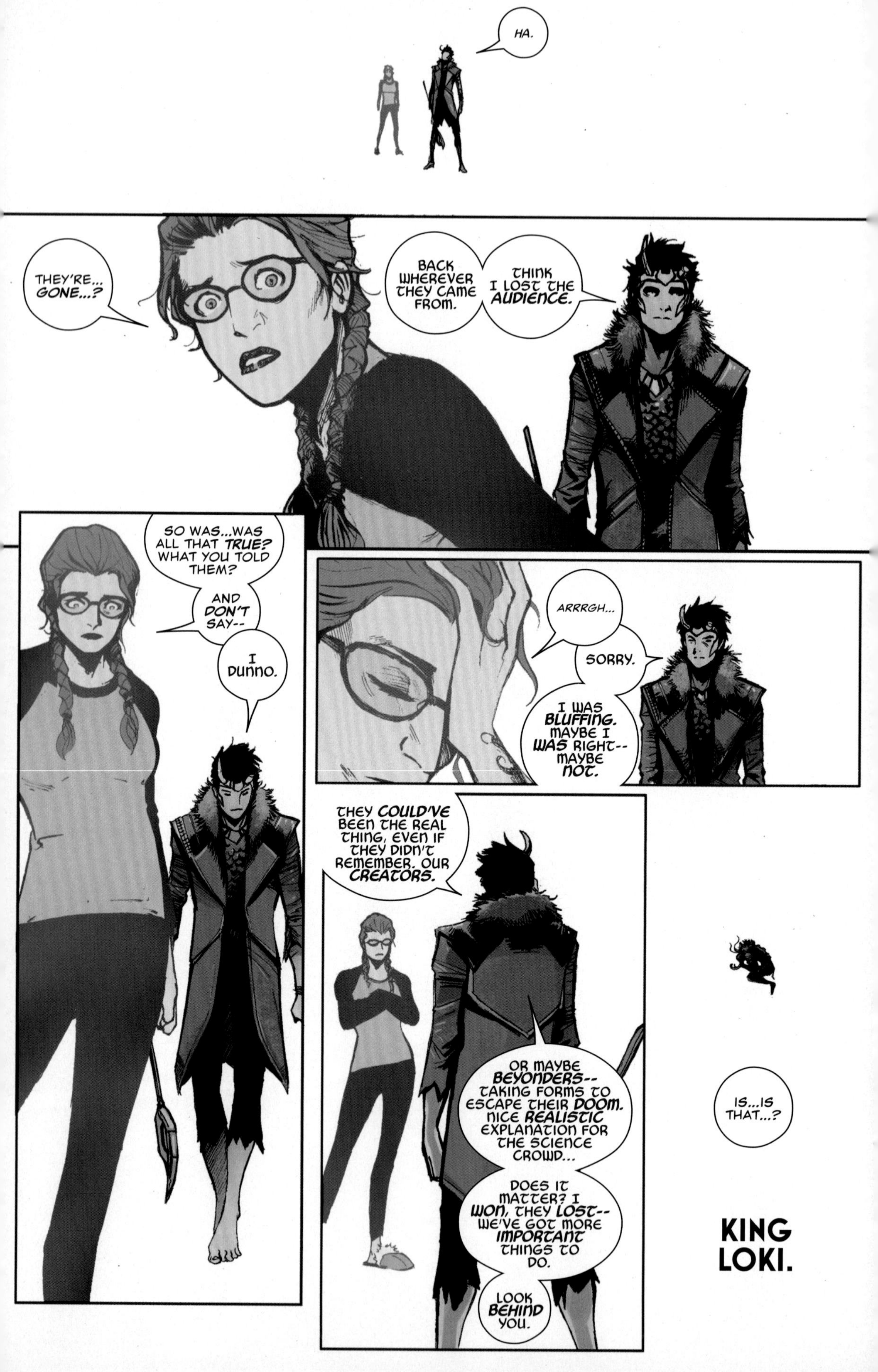

HA.
THEY'RE... GONE...?
BACK WHEREVER THEY CAME FROM.
THINK I LOST THE AUDIENCE.
SO WAS...WAS ALL THAT TRUE? WHAT YOU TOLD THEM?
AND DON'T SAY--
I DUNNO.
ARRRGH...
SORRY.
I WAS BLUFFING. MAYBE I WAS RIGHT-- MAYBE NOT.
THEY COULD'VE BEEN THE REAL THING, EVEN IF THEY DIDN'T REMEMBER. OUR CREATORS.
OR MAYBE BEYONDERS-- TAKING FORMS TO ESCAPE THEIR DOOM. NICE REALISTIC EXPLANATION FOR THE SCIENCE CROWD...
DOES IT MATTER? I WON, THEY LOST-- WE'VE GOT MORE IMPORTANT THINGS TO DO.
LOOK BEHIND YOU.
IS...IS THAT...?
KING LOKI.

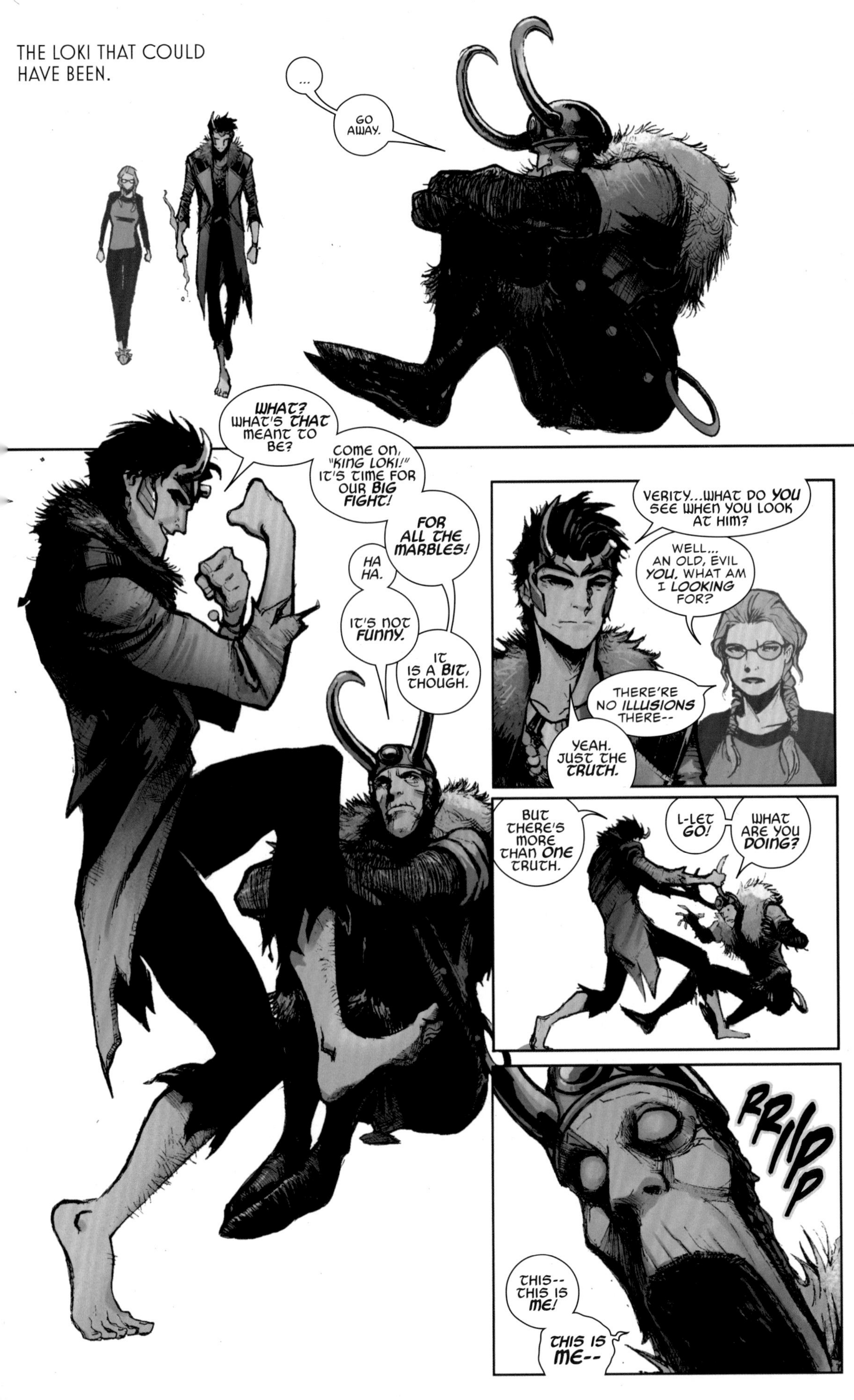
THE LOKI THAT COULD HAVE BEEN.
...
GO AWAY.
WHAT? WHAT'S THAT MEANT TO BE?
COME ON, "KING LOKI!" IT'S TIME FOR OUR BIG FIGHT!
FOR ALL THE MARBLES!
HA HA.
IT'S NOT FUNNY.
IT IS A BIT, THOUGH.
VERITY...WHAT DO YOU SEE WHEN YOU LOOK AT HIM?
WELL... AN OLD, EVIL YOU. WHAT AM I LOOKING FOR?
THERE'RE NO ILLUSIONS THERE--
YEAH. JUST THE TRUTH.
BUT THERE'S MORE THAN ONE TRUTH.
L-LET GO!
WHAT ARE YOU DOING?
RRIPP
THIS-- THIS IS ME!
THIS IS ME--

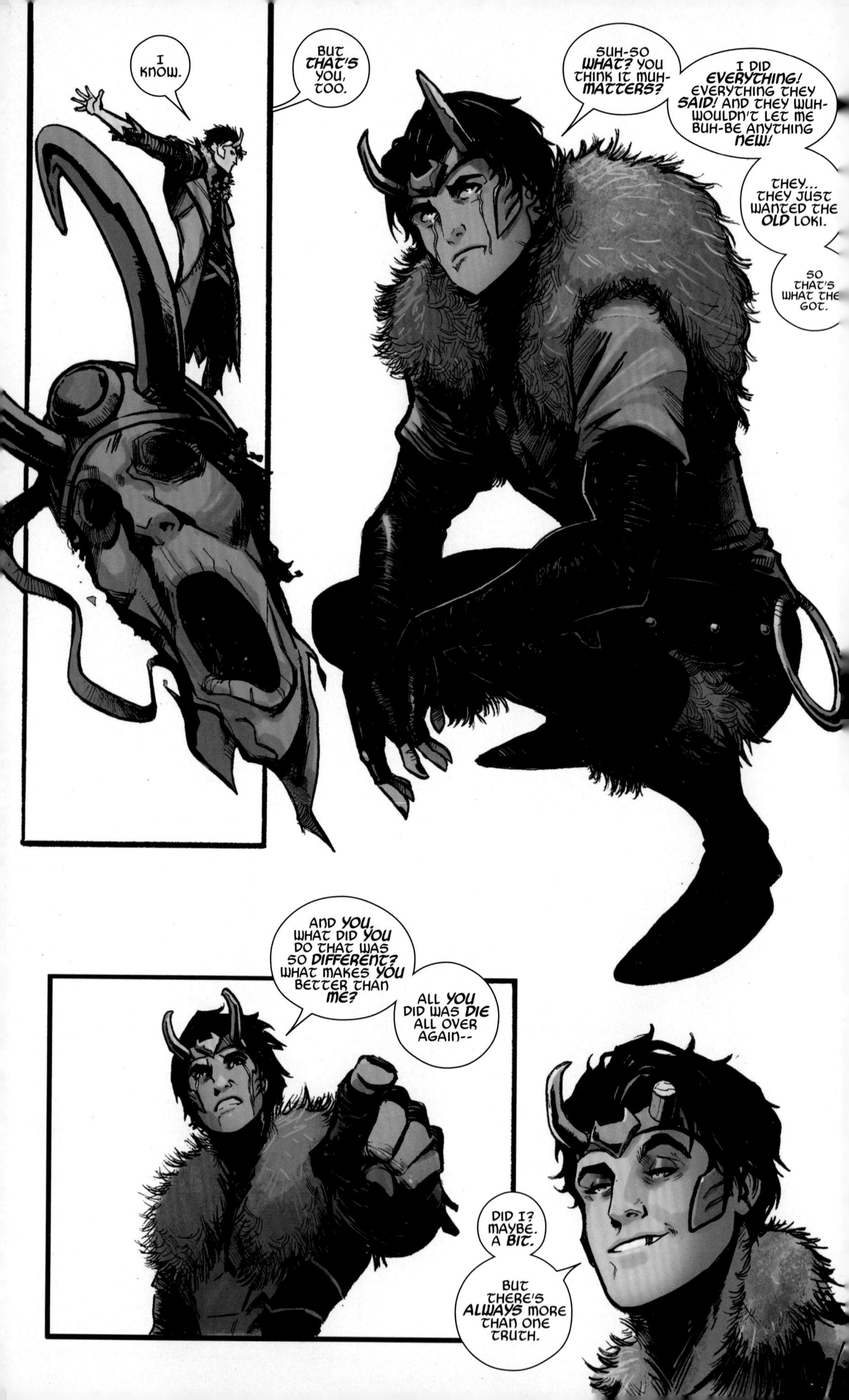
I KNOW.
BUT THAT'S YOU, TOO.
SUH-SO WHAT? YOU THINK IT MUH-MATTERS?
I DID EVERYTHING! EVERYTHING THEY SAID! AND THEY WUH-WOULDN'T LET ME BUH-BE ANYTHING NEW!
THEY... THEY JUST WANTED THE OLD LOKI.
SO THAT'S WHAT THE GOT.
AND YOU. WHAT DID YOU DO THAT WAS SO DIFFERENT? WHAT MAKES YOU BETTER THAN ME?
ALL YOU DID WAS DIE ALL OVER AGAIN--
DID I? MAYBE. A BIT.
BUT THERE'S ALWAYS MORE THAN ONE TRUTH.

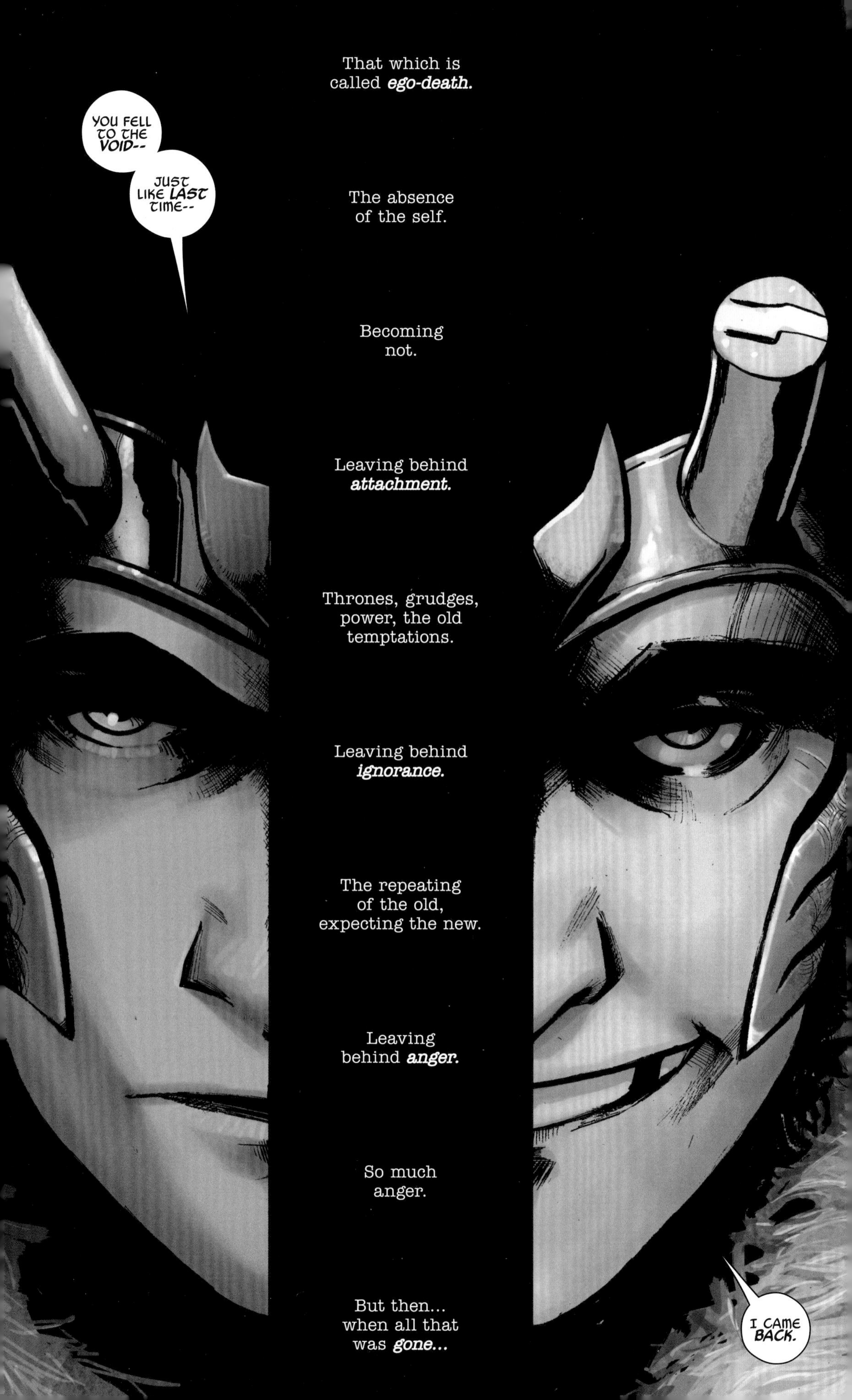
That which is called *ego-death.*
YOU FELL TO THE **VOID**--
JUST LIKE **LAST** TIME--
The absence of the self.
Becoming not.
Leaving behind ***attachment.***
Thrones, grudges, power, the old temptations.
Leaving behind ***ignorance.***
The repeating of the old, expecting the new.
Leaving behind ***anger.***
So much anger.
But then... when all that was ***gone...***
I CAME **BACK.**

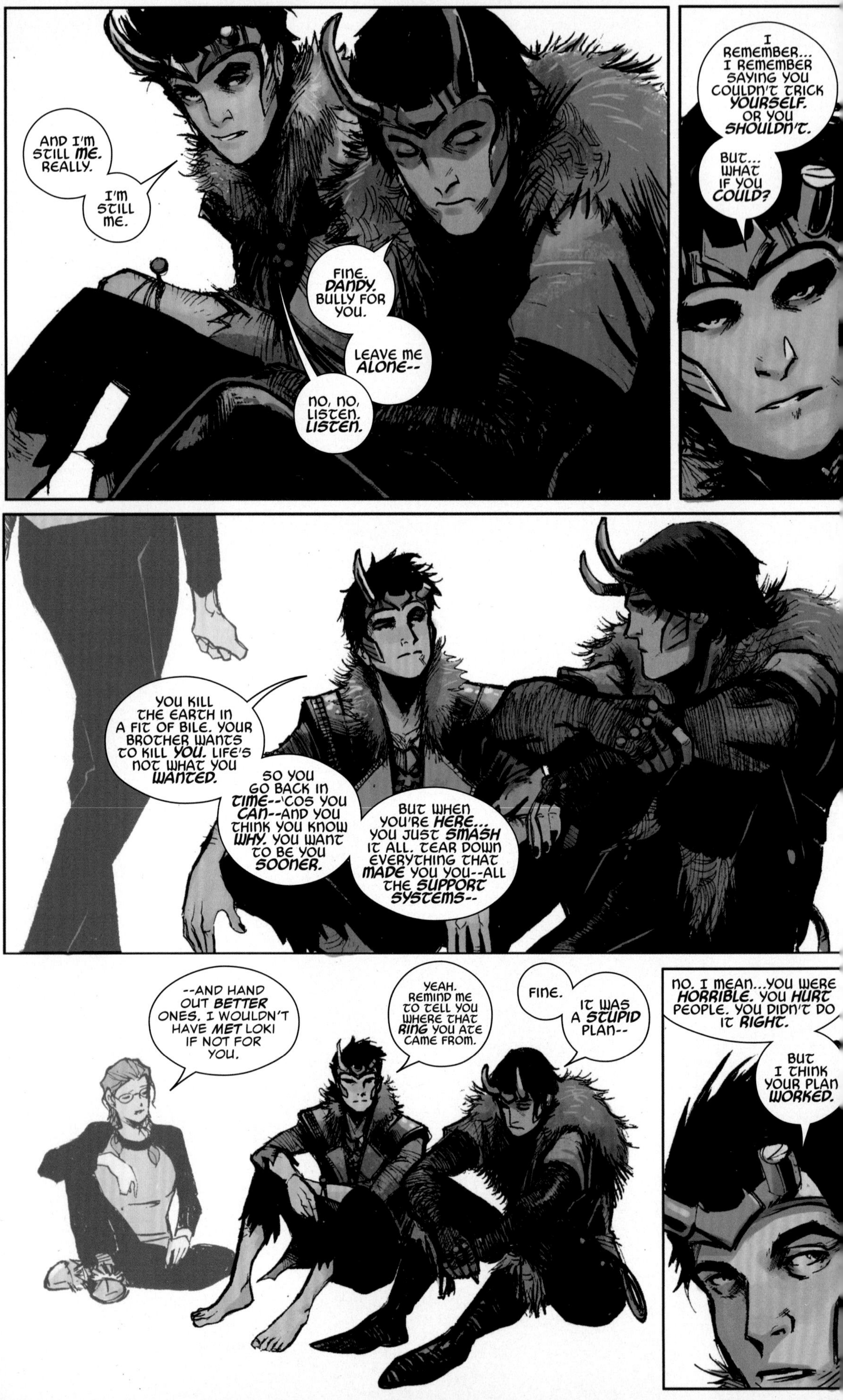

AND I'M STILL ME. REALLY.
I'M STILL ME.
FINE. DANDY. BULLY FOR YOU.
LEAVE ME ALONE--
NO, NO, LISTEN. LISTEN.
I REMEMBER... I REMEMBER SAYING YOU COULDN'T TRICK YOURSELF. OR YOU SHOULDN'T.
BUT... WHAT IF YOU COULD?
YOU KILL THE EARTH IN A FIT OF BILE. YOUR BROTHER WANTS TO KILL YOU. LIFE'S NOT WHAT YOU WANTED.
SO YOU GO BACK IN TIME--'COS YOU CAN--AND YOU THINK YOU KNOW WHY. YOU WANT TO BE YOU SOONER.
BUT WHEN YOU'RE HERE... YOU JUST SMASH IT ALL. TEAR DOWN EVERYTHING THAT MADE YOU YOU--ALL THE SUPPORT SYSTEMS--
--AND HAND OUT BETTER ONES. I WOULDN'T HAVE MET LOKI IF NOT FOR YOU.
YEAH. REMIND ME TO TELL YOU WHERE THAT RING YOU ATE CAME FROM.
FINE.
IT WAS A STUPID PLAN--
NO. I MEAN...YOU WERE HORRIBLE. YOU HURT PEOPLE. YOU DIDN'T DO IT RIGHT.
BUT I THINK YOUR PLAN WORKED.

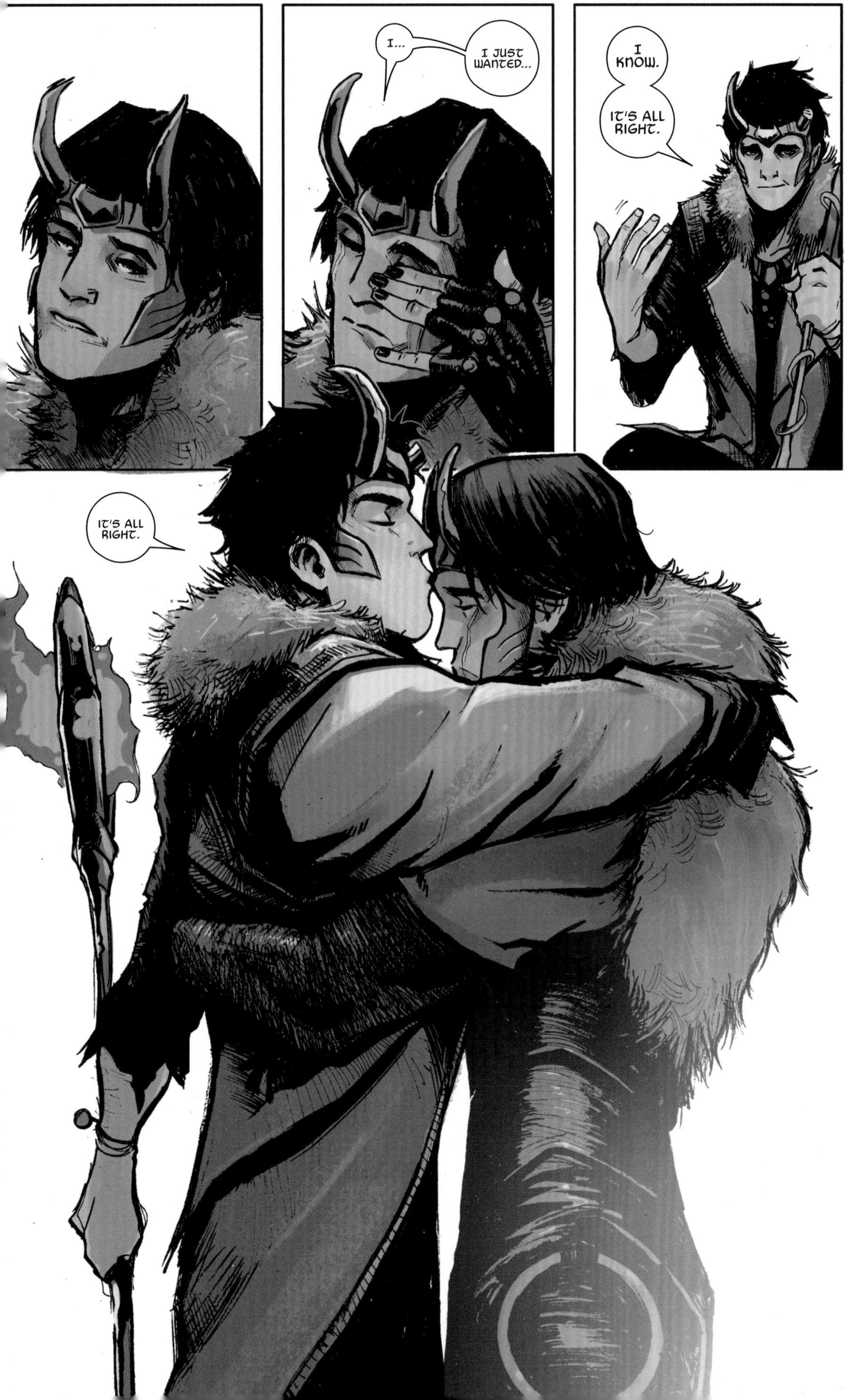
I...
I JUST WANTED...
I KNOW.
IT'S ALL RIGHT.
IT'S ALL RIGHT.

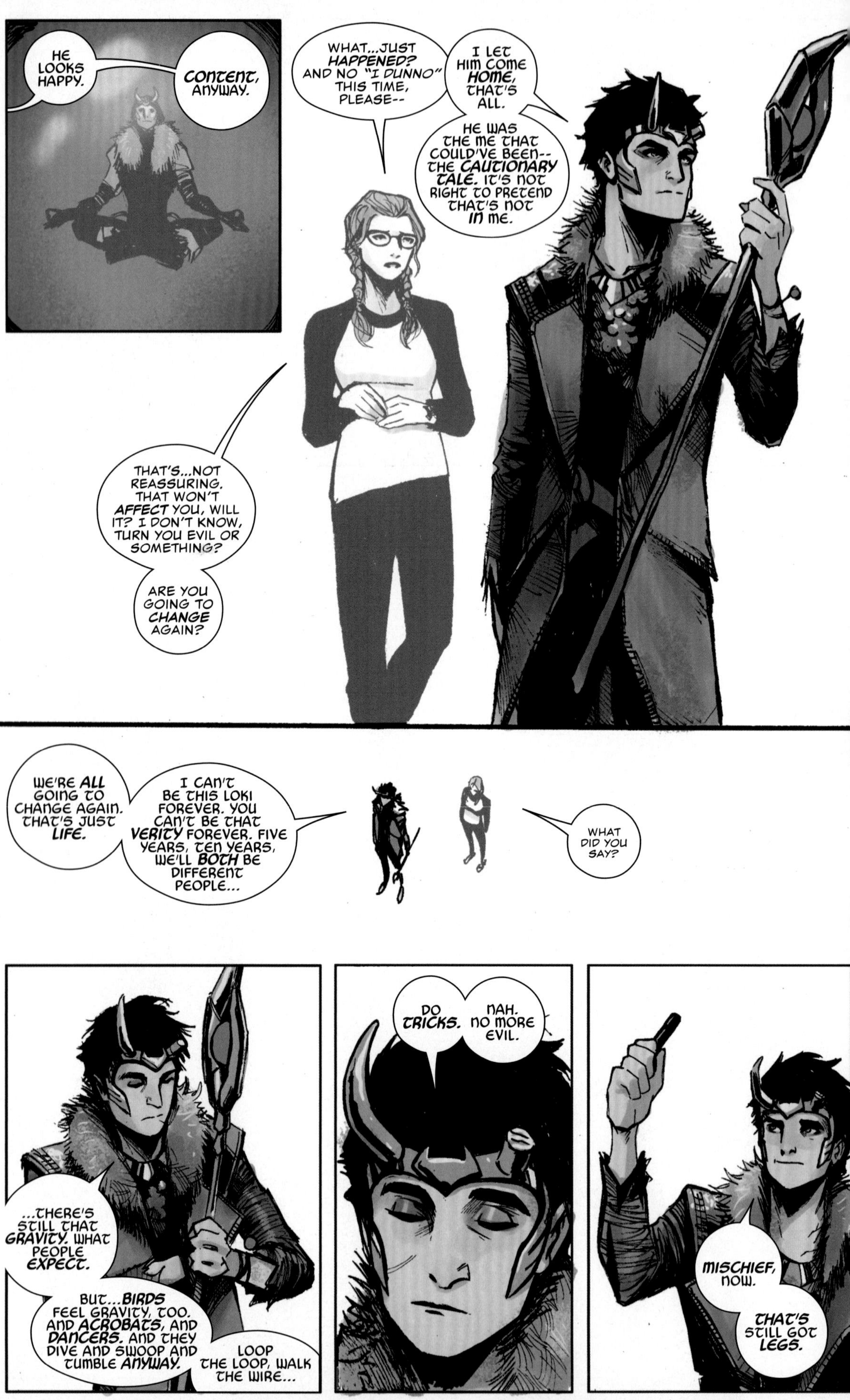
HE LOOKS HAPPY.
CONTENT, ANYWAY.
WHAT...JUST HAPPENED? AND NO "I DUNNO" THIS TIME, PLEASE--
I LET HIM COME HOME, THAT'S ALL.
HE WAS THE ME THAT COULD'VE BEEN--THE CAUTIONARY TALE. IT'S NOT RIGHT TO PRETEND THAT'S NOT IN ME.
THAT'S...NOT REASSURING. THAT WON'T AFFECT YOU, WILL IT? I DON'T KNOW, TURN YOU EVIL OR SOMETHING?
ARE YOU GOING TO CHANGE AGAIN?
WE'RE ALL GOING TO CHANGE AGAIN. THAT'S JUST LIFE.
I CAN'T BE THIS LOKI FOREVER. YOU CAN'T BE THAT VERITY FOREVER. FIVE YEARS, TEN YEARS, WE'LL BOTH BE DIFFERENT PEOPLE...
WHAT DID YOU SAY?
...THERE'S STILL THAT GRAVITY. WHAT PEOPLE EXPECT.
BUT...BIRDS FEEL GRAVITY, TOO. AND ACROBATS, AND DANCERS. AND THEY DIVE AND SWOOP AND TUMBLE ANYWAY.
LOOP THE LOOP, WALK THE WIRE...
DO TRICKS.
NAH. NO MORE EVIL.
MISCHIEF, NOW.
THAT'S STILL GOT LEGS.

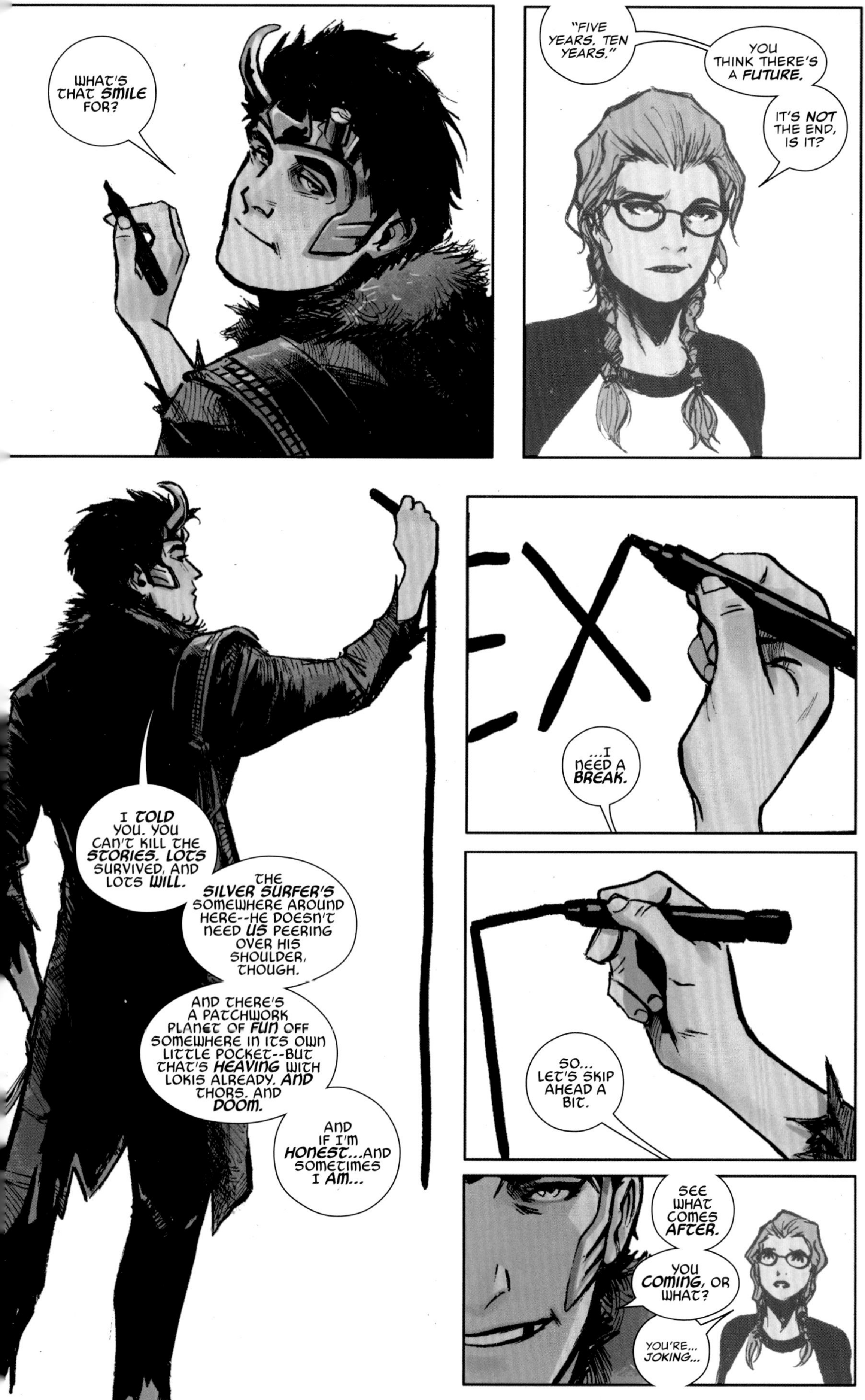
WHAT'S THAT SMILE FOR?
"FIVE YEARS. TEN YEARS."
YOU THINK THERE'S A FUTURE.
IT'S NOT THE END, IS IT?
I TOLD YOU. YOU CAN'T KILL THE STORIES. LOTS SURVIVED, AND LOTS WILL.
THE SILVER SURFER'S SOMEWHERE AROUND HERE--HE DOESN'T NEED US PEERING OVER HIS SHOULDER, THOUGH.
AND THERE'S A PATCHWORK PLANET OF FUN OFF SOMEWHERE IN ITS OWN LITTLE POCKET--BUT THAT'S HEAVING WITH LOKIS ALREADY. AND THORS. AND DOOM.
AND IF I'M HONEST...AND SOMETIMES I AM...
...I NEED A BREAK.
SO... LET'S SKIP AHEAD A BIT.
SEE WHAT COMES AFTER.
YOU COMING, OR WHAT?
YOU'RE... JOKING...

NEXT:

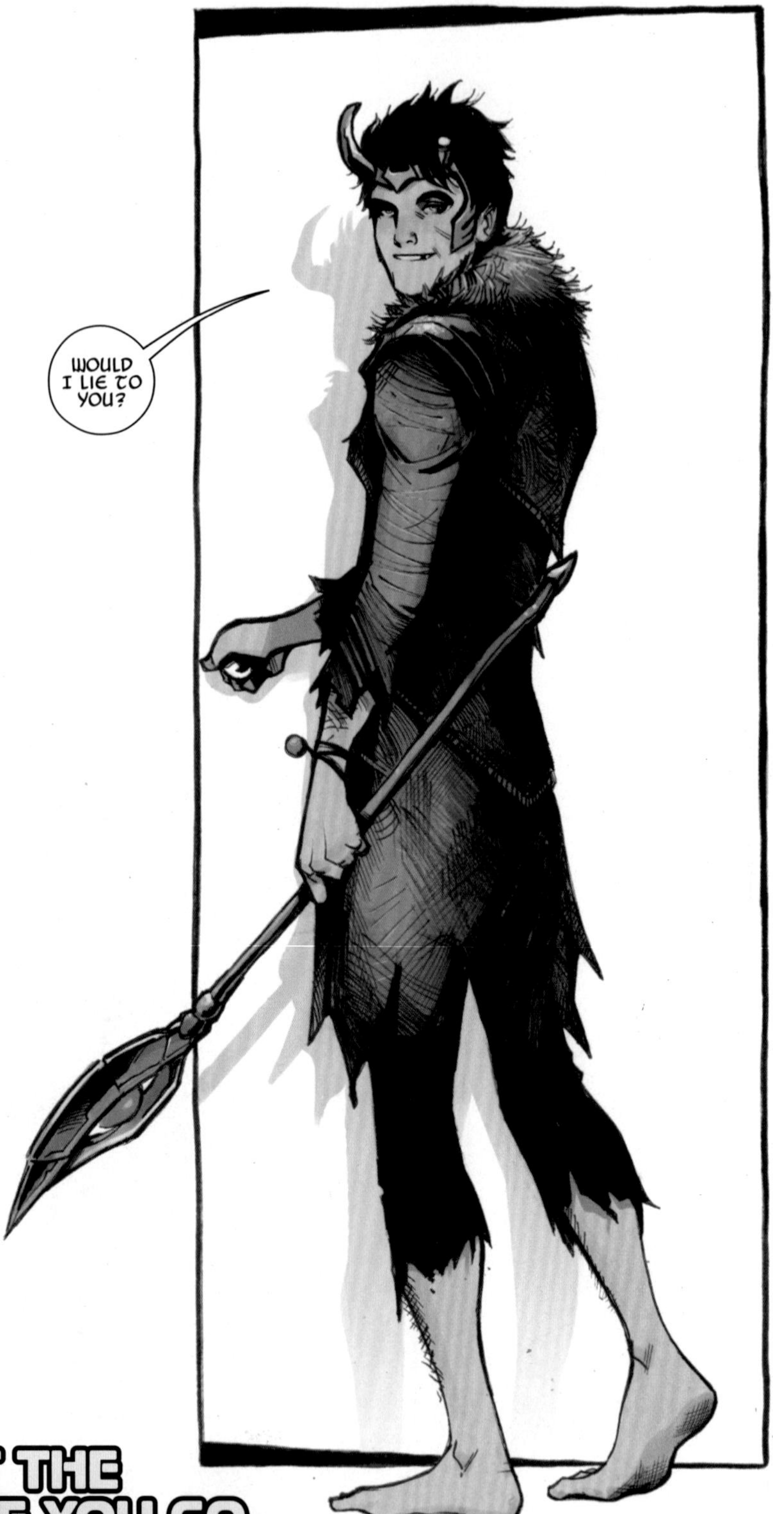
WOULD I LIE TO YOU?

OUT THE GATE YOU GO AND NEVER STOP

CHARACTER SKETCHES
by Lee Garbett

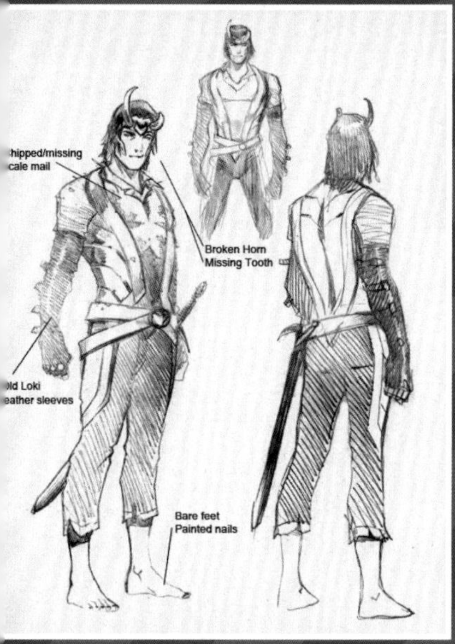
hipped/missing
cale mail
Broken Horn
Missing Tooth
ld Loki
eather sleeves
Bare feet
Painted nails

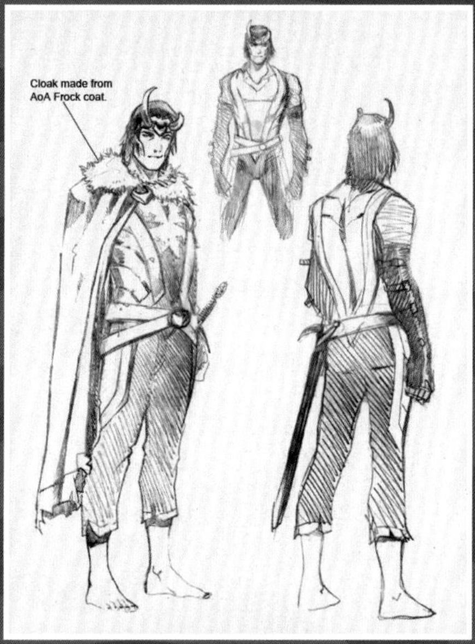
Cloak made from
AoA Frock coat.

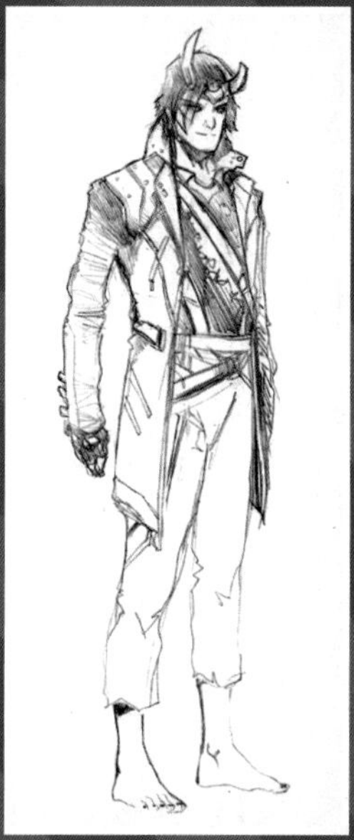

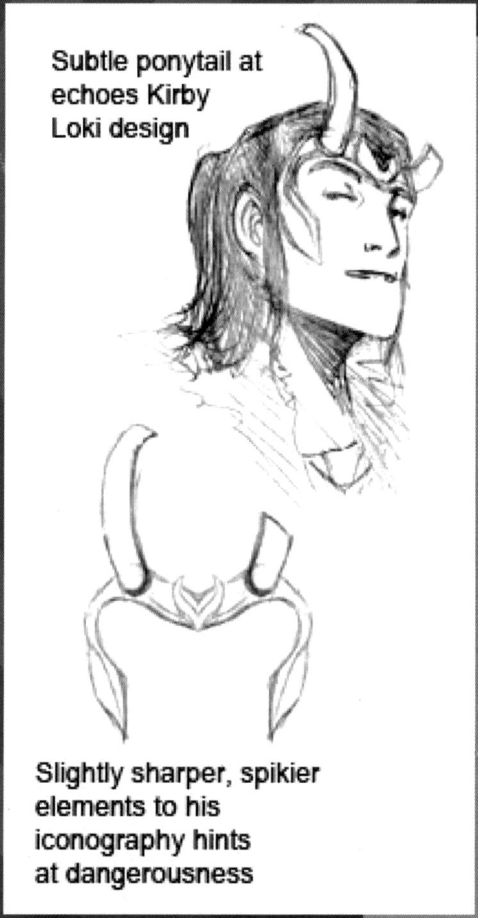
Subtle ponytail at
echoes Kirby
Loki design
Slightly sharper, spikier
elements to his
iconography hints
at dangerousness

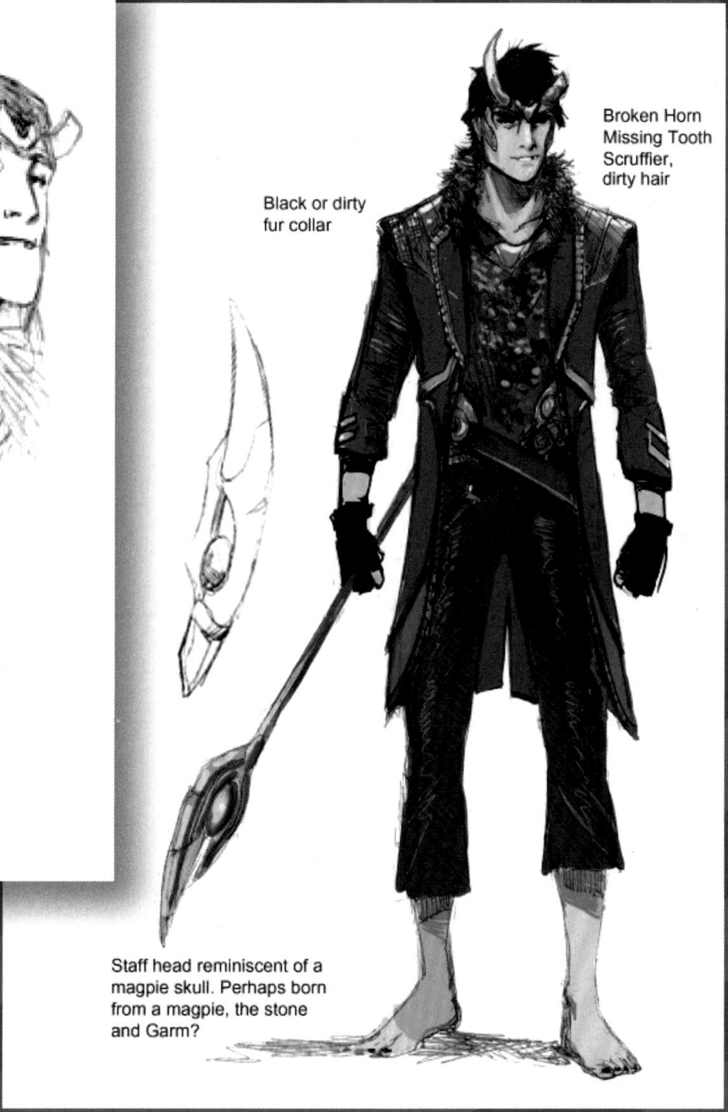
Broken Horn
Missing Tooth
Scruffier,
dirty hair
Black or dirty
fur collar
Staff head reminiscent of a
magpie skull. Perhaps born
from a magpie, the stone
and Garm?

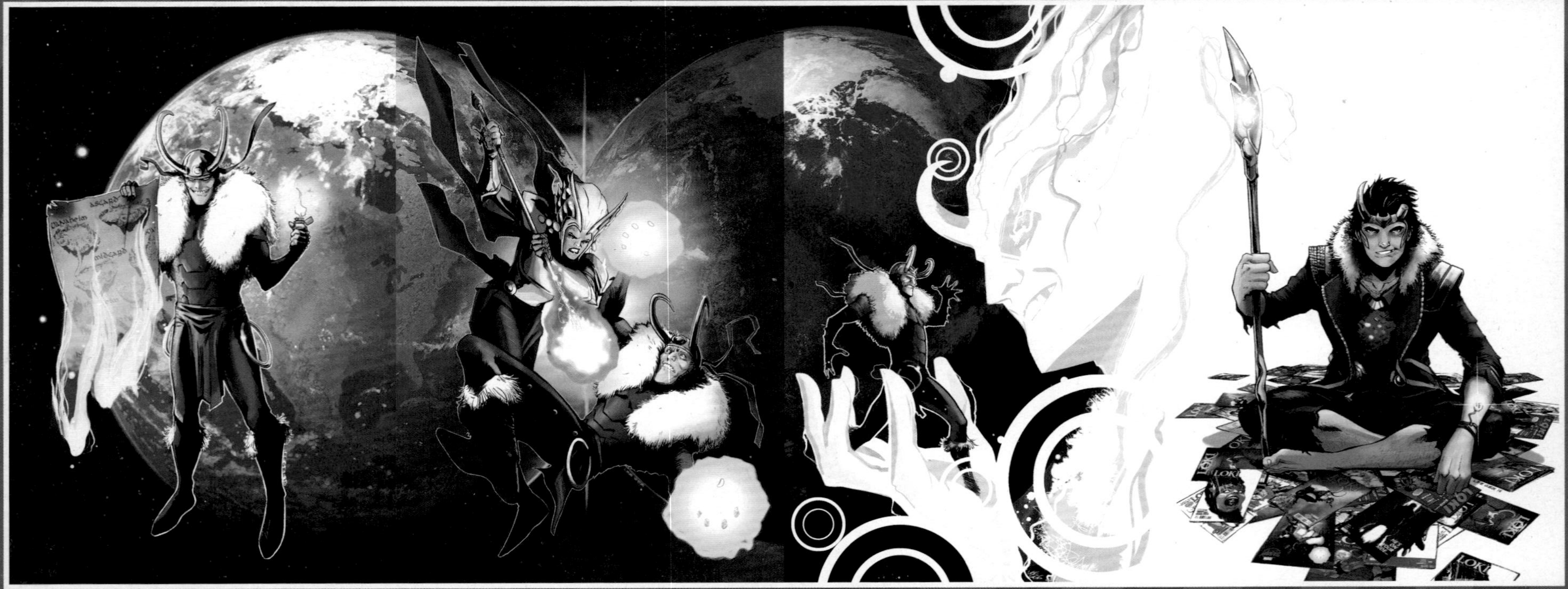

#14-17 COMBINED COVERS
by Lee Garbett